Purgatory
Luodovico Caracci

ALL SOULS'
"FORGET-ME-NOT"

A PRAYER AND MEDITATION BOOK
for
The Solace of the Poor Souls in Purgatory

BY THE
REV. LOUIS GEMMINGER
Translated and Edited by CANON MOSER
1889

Reprinted from the Original by:

MEDIATRIX PRESS

MMXVII

ISBN: 978-1-953746-05-4

Nihil Obstat:
✠ VICTOR J. SCHOBEL, S.T.D.,
 Censor Deputatus.

Imprimatur.
✠ HENRICUS EDUARDUS,
Card. Archiep. Westmonast.
Die 12 Sept., 1889.

Mediatrix Press
607 6th St.
Post Falls, ID 83854
http://www.mediatrixpress.com

TABLE OF CONTENTS

DEDICATION

IN LOVING MEMORY OF

CICELY PATRICIA HARDEN

DEDICATION FOR ALL THE FAITHFUL DEPARTED

Some souls, alas! in darkness lie,
Afar from God and light—sad lot I
For them this little book must cry,
"Forget-me-not! forget-me-not!"

Oh, read its pages o'er and o'er!
It urges thee to plead—to pray
For those dear friends thou seest no more
On earth. Alas! where now are they?

And wheresoever thou dost find
One prayerful soul that loves the dead,
Then call this little book to mind,
And recommend it to be read.

All ye with loving hearts possess'd,
Remember them in every prayer.
To plead for their eternal rest
Be it your first, your constant care.

Oh, may your love each day increase
For these poor souls, and brightly shine
That all their sufferings soon may cease,
Assisted by this book of mine!

With loving fervour, therefore, take
This book, and keep it near at hand;
That its devotion may thee make
Worthy thy holy Fatherland!

For blest are they who help the dead
By their unceasing prayers and love;
For all these prayers in pity said,
Flow back as blessings from above!

PREFACE TO THE ENGLISH TRANSLATION

THIS BOOK of prayers and spiritual reading has been translated into English from the German, by a kind and devout friend of the Holy Souls. The Editor was moved to present it to the English Catholic public mainly by the desire to promote as much as possible, in this Protestant country, the Catholic practice of helping the poor souls in Purgatory. The original has run through five editions in the space of a few years. This shows how very popular the devotion to the Holy Souls is in Catholic countries. The Church sets the example. She invariably ends her public prayers, or the Divine Office, as becomes a mother of many children, with that sweet and tender desire: "May the souls of the faithful departed, through the mercy of God, rest in peace. Amen." She moreover ordains, besides the rite of Christian burial, that the Sacrifice for the living and the dead—the Holy Mass—should be offered on the day of decease or burial, and again on the 3rd, 5th, 7th, and 30th days after death, as also on the anniversary day. Hence, in Catholic countries, confraternities have been at all times established, in order to obtain these benefits for the poor who die without friends and means.

We know also that many a noble institution, such as All Souls' College, Oxford, founded by Archbishop Chichele, and many a charity and church of old, when England was Catholic, owed its origin to the piety of the faithful towards the dead. Alas! it is different in the present day. How many Catholics die, not only among the poor but also among the better classes, to whom these blessings are never granted by their friends and relatives! Are they not simply buried and forgotten? The wealthy have an expensive funeral, and spend vast sums of money on flowers, which are placed where the rubrics strictly forbid them to be placed. This evil example is followed to some extent by the poor. The flowers speedily fade: so do the dead from the memory of the living. The Office for the Dead is seldom recited; often the Holy Sacrifice is not offered, and the poor souls are abandoned and forgotten.

These thoughts have haunted me for many years, and have inspired me with the desire of erecting a church under the name of All Souls, in order to bring home to the minds of the people, as much as possible, the Catholic piety of former times towards the poor souls in Purgatory, and also to make some reparation to them for the Masses and charities, of which they were deprived at the Reformation.

From the many contributions and edifying letters I have received, from all parts of the world, during the last ten years, I find that this pious practice is alive and cherished by many, and requires only to be fanned into an universal flame. To further this object I have thought it well to edit the present little book. In it all the prayers and devotions are specially prepared with reference to the souls in Purgatory. The Office for the Dead is given at the end of the book (page 261), together with the English version, so as to enable the laity to follow and understand better, what the Church wishes us to do for the dead in her public liturgy.

Though the English garb in which the book appears might be better, still the Editor has reason to hope that the grain of gold will be perceived even under the rough surface, and that the 'Forget-me-not' will find a place in every Catholic household.

WILLIAM, CANON MOSER
All Souls' Day, 1889.
Queen Street, Peterborough.

PREFACE

WHY DOES this little prayer-book take its name from the simple flower, Forget-me-not? What resemblance have these little flowers to the poor suffering souls in Purgatory? Why do they remind one of those poor, forgotten, and often neglected souls? The forget-me-not grows in marshy places, by the banks of rivers and streams. And is not Purgatory a dismal swamp wherein the tears of sorrow and desire are ever flowing? These sweet flowers grow and wither by thousands, unseen in their lonely haunts; and who can count the myriads of souls lingering and suffering in Purgatory, since nothing with the smallest spot of impurity can enter Heaven? The forget-me-nots are blue, and blue are the heavens toward which they are ever gazing. And are not the poor souls, also, forever looking up toward their heavenly home, sighing, languishing, and incessantly calling to us "Forget-me-not, Forget-me-not?"

Our Faith tells us we can help these poor souls; the Church permits us to pray for them; our own heart tells us that we should and must contribute to their aid in every way that we can. On these grounds, therefore, we venture to publish this little prayer-book which, under the title of "The Forget-me-not of the Souls in Purgatory," admonishes the living not to forget the dead. And as that sweet little flower gladdens the eye that rests upon it, so may this book also rejoice many a Christian heart, and awaken in them an ardent love for the poor souls, a love, a devotion that will live and bloom forever!

THE AUTHOR

Morning Prayers

N the Name of the Father, ✠ who has created me, in the Name of the Son, ✠ who has redeemed me, and in the Name of the Holy Ghost, ✠ who has sanctified me, I arise this day. O most Holy Trinity, to Thee I offer up the first thoughts of my heart. Thee I most humbly adore, and fervently thank for the repose of the past night. To Thee I devote and consecrate this day with all my thoughts, words, and actions.

O most sweet Jesus, I offer to Thee my body and soul. In Thy most holy Name I desire to begin this day's work, and I ask Thy blessing that I may perform it perfectly. Protect me this day from every sin, but particularly from that into which I am most likely to fall. With Thy grace I will begin and finish this day.

O my dearest Mother Mary, lead me along by thy holy hand and keep thy child from stumbling or falling. I cast myself into thy motherly arms. To thee and thy Divine Son I offer up all the actions and sufferings of this day, in expiation for the sins of the poor souls in Purgatory.

Night Prayers

UR FATHER, who art in Heaven, I thank Thee for having by Thy paternal care brought me through this day.

Praised and blessed be Thy Name for all the graces

and benefits bestowed on me to-day!

If it should happen to be my last on earth, my cry will be, Thy kingdom come.

If it be Thy Divine Will that I die tonight, death will be welcome. Thy Will be done on earth as it is in Heaven.

For one thing only I ask: Give us this day our daily bread, not for the body alone, but especially for the soul; viz., the grace to confess the sins of this day and to repent of them. [Examination of conscience.]

O Father, how badly I have spent this day, yet what mercy Thou hast shown me! Sinner that I am, have mercy on me, Thou who art all-merciful. Forgive me my trespass, as I forgive those that have offended me this day, particularly N. N. Lead us not into temptation, O Father, and watch over me this night, that I may awake in Thy sight pure and holy in body and soul. Deliver us from evil, the evil of sin, from all visible and invisible enemies, from all injuries of soul and body, but particularly from the misfortune of dying in a state of mortal sin. Amen.

Hail, Mary, full of grace! To thy maternal protection I recommend myself this night. The Lord is with thee. Grant that He may also dwell with me, and never be separated from me. Blessed art thou amongst women, and among all the saints and angels in Heaven, and blessed is the fruit of thy womb, Jesus, unto whose loving Heart I commend my poor soul!

Holy Mary, Mother of God, pray for me, that I may fall asleep with some pious thought; and if I die this night, pray for me, poor sinner, now and at the hour of my death. Amen.

O holy angel-guardian, defend me! O my holy patron saint, pray for me! O my Lord, give eternal rest to the poor suffering souls in Purgatory. For their repose I offer to Thee in brotherly love all the indulgences and graces I have gained to-day. Amen.

PRAYERS AT MASS

FIRST METHOD

Prayer before Mass

Father of mercy and Giver of all consolation, with deepest humility I approach Thine Altar, to appeal to Thy divine tenderness for the release of the poor souls who are still suffering and lamenting amidst the purifying flames of Purgatory. As gold in the crucible, so are faithful souls purified in the fire of Thine infinite holiness. Their burning tears, their ardent desires for eternal life, are all they have to sustain and soothe them in their sufferings. Have pity on them, O Lord! Show Thyself unto them! Bestow on them the kiss of peace, for which they long in the midst of their inexpressible woe. They know that Thou alone canst shorten, canst put an end to, their sufferings; therefore, they cry with all the strength of their soul and from the very depths of their heart: 'Forget me not, O Father of mercy! Forget me not! O sweetest Jesus, have pity on me! Forget me not! Forget me not!'

I who am still living in this valley of tears join my cries to theirs, and from the depths of my heart I cry to Thee: 'Remember them, Lord, for the sake of the precious Blood of Thy Divine Son, which was shed for them! Look down on them! Have mercy on the souls of my poor suffering fellow Christians, particularly my parents, sisters, brothers, and those bound to me by the ties of blood or friendship. Grant them the happy release they long for, and let Thy Light shine upon them! O Lord, hear my prayer, and let my cry come to Thee!'

At the Kyrie

In the spirit of deepest humility and most hearty sorrow for all my sins, I prostrate myself in Thy presence, O my God, confessing and deploring my numerous sins and offences. I openly acknowledge them. Yes, see plainly that my evil inclinations would have led me into greater sins and even more dreadful errors, were it not for Thy saving grace, which upheld me under temptation. O my God, pardon me all my sins! I bow my head and descend in spirit even to the very flames of Purgatory, those flames that I have so often deserved by my transgressions. Prom the depths of Purgatory I hear resounding this cry of woe, 'Forget me not! forget me not!' Heart and hands I raise to Thee in supplication, O my God! I unite my prayers with those of the priest at the altar, saying, '*Kyrie eleison!*' Lord, have mercy on the poor souls! Christ, have mercy on the poor souls! Lord, have mercy on the poor abandoned suffering souls!

At the Epistle

From the holy writings of Thy prophets and Apostles, O Lord, it is given us to understand that the earthly dwellings, which we at present inhabit, will one day fall to pieces, and that Thou hast prepared for Thy faithful servants a stately mansion, built by no mortal hands, but which shall stand for ever.

But before we attain this unspeakable happiness we must all stand before the judgment-seat of Christ, in order to receive the eternal reward or punishment of our good or bad actions on earth.

This judgment has already been passed on numberless Christians, and many have been cast into the flames of Purgatory because they were not found sufficiently pure for Heaven. Perhaps, amongst those suffering souls, there may be many of my friends and relations now crying out to me, 'Forget me not! forget me not!' Oh, how could I ever forget them? Oh no! I will offer up for them the holy Sacrifice of the Mass, and will beg of Thee, O most merciful God, to grant that the merits of Thy precious Blood may fall on their poor souls, and that they may soon exchange their present sad abode for the everlasting joys of Heaven!

At the Gospel

O Jesus Christ, Thou art the Resurrection and the Life! He that believeth in Thee, even if he be dead, shall live; he shall not die for ever! From temporal death he shall pass to life everlasting!

Relying on these Thy promises, I beg of Thee to release those poor suffering souls still held in fiery bondage! They were created after Thine image, and marked with the seal of Thine adoption. In Thee did they hope. To Thee have they prayed. Thou didst place them in the bosom of Thy holy Church. Therefore, O sweetest Jesus, forget them not, even though their sins have justly incurred the Divine wrath. For the sake of their faith grant them a speedy deliverance from the pains of Purgatory.

At the Offertory

O Almighty and Eternal God, graciously look down on this altar, upon which Thine only-begotten Son, our Lord Jesus Christ, is being offered up in sacrifice by the hands of Thy priest. It is the holiest sacrifice that can be presented Thee. Behold the priest uncovers the chalice, and the holy Sacrifice begins! He raises the bread and wine, which are to conceal the adorable Body and Blood of Thy Divine Son. Oh, look down, most adorable Lord! and graciously accept the holy Offering. The happy moment is fast approaching in which the only Mediator between God and man will intercede for us. How my heart rejoices to know that our poor pleadings will soon ascend together with the unfailing appeals of Thine only-begotten Son! Oh, for His sake, have pity on us, and forget them not! In Thy mercy forget not those poor suffering souls in Purgatory! Grant that they may partake of the merits of the most holy Sacrifice of the altar; and may they rest in peace!

At the Preface

To Thee, O most blessed Trinity, be all honour, praise, and glory! As the priest, with hands uplifted, stands before the altar and raises his voice, blessing and extolling Thine infinite goodness, I join my feeble voice with his, and cry, Holy! Holy! Holy! is the Lord God of Sabaoth! The heavens and the earth are full of Thy glory! To Thee hosts of blessed Angels in heaven, standing in Thy sight, give praise. To Thee do men on earth, upon whom Thou lookest graciously, give glory. To Thee the souls in Purgatory who, by the merits of this holy Sacrifice, are delivered and admitted unto Thine everlasting beatific

Vision, give praise, and thanks, and glory!

Bless our pastors and all the Bishops of the whole world. Be merciful to our superiors, and to those who are participating in this holy Sacrifice. Be merciful to all our friends and enemies, and to all Christians throughout the Universal Church.

Jesus Christ, Thine only-begotten Son, is about to descend from Heaven to earth; He is about to make this altar His throne of grace and compassion. He comes in order to offer to Thee His Body and Blood as a sacrifice of atonement for our sins.

Relying on His infinite merits, I venture to approach Thee confidently, and to beg Thee to bestow upon me the gift of His love, and the grace of holy perseverance. Oh, pour into my barren soul the dew of Thy sanctifying grace, and grant that it may produce there the gifts and the virtues of the Holy Ghost.

At the Consecration

Now the solemn moment approaches. Heaven opens, and hosts of Angels surround the altar! The priest prostrates himself, opens his lips, and pronounces those sacred words, and, behold, Jesus Christ cometh, the Son of God is present! Jesus, the Strength of my life; Jesus, my Consolation in death!

Jesus, my All in eternity! O Jesus, for Thee I live! O Jesus, for Thee I die! I give myself to Thee in life and death. Be Thou a thousand times welcome, O sweetest Saviour. Cast one look on me, so that, like Peter, I may obtain grace to bewail and do penance for my many sins. Speak but one word to my soul—but one word—so that I may fall down at Thy feet like holy Magdalena. Oh, I beseech Thee, pass me not by, but come to me as Thou didst to Thy disciples at Emmaus. Let my soul shine in the splendour of Thy countenance, and enrich it with the treasures of Thy love and grace. Send the rays of Thy divine love into my cold heart; fill it and inflame it with some of Thy divine charity. This I humbly beg and implore; O sweetest Jesus, forget me not! forget me not!

After the Consecration

I can scarcely realize or comprehend that my Lord and God is so nigh to me, that He offers Himself anew for me to His Heavenly Father. For so great an act of love is this, that no human language is able to describe, or human heart to grasp and fully feel it. But the very greatness of this love gives courage to me—poor sinner!—to come and plead, not only for myself, but also for others. Notwithstanding my numerous faults and transgressions, I venture to come into Thy holy presence, O my God; with the lowliest reverence I supplicate Thee, O Light of the world, to enlighten me, and guide my steps, as Thou didst guide the Israelites of old. Take possession of my heart, and so rule over it, that all my thoughts, desires, and inclinations, may become spiritualized by Thy grace. I also plead and appeal to Thy mercy for my deceased friends. Oh, what golden benefits Thou canst bestow on them, O my God! See the rich flood of the most precious Blood of Thy Divine Son, which is flowing for us sinners! Oh, let it penetrate to the depths of Purgatory, where there are so many poor souls suffering imprisonment! Oh, hear His voice pleading for them: Accept this Offering in atonement for their sins! O Father, forget them not! Oh, may they become pure and unspotted by the merits of our Saviour's Blood, so that they may be worthy of the glory of Heaven, where nothing impure may enter. I beseech Thee, O Lord, particularly to look on those friends of mine nearest and dearest to my heart, to whom I owe most love and gratitude. Let them also share in the merits of this most holy Sacrifice, and gain some of the fruits of its sanctity.

At the Pater Noster

O most merciful God, as Thou art our Father, so also art Thou Father of our sisters and brothers who are suffering in Purgatory, and who deserve better than myself to be numbered with Thy children. I unite with them in honouring and glorifying Thy most holy Name. Oh, let them speedily enter into the possession of Thy heavenly kingdom, and forget not the patience with which they have borne their punishment, but give them the reward of their long-suffering. Oh, forgive them and me all the sins which we have committed, and give me the grace to avoid the danger of falling into mortal sin, that I may hope to enjoy with them the glories of the life to come. Amen.

At the Agnus Dei

O Lamb of God, who alone art able to turn aside the Divine wrath, break down the barrier which has been made by sin between Almighty God and the poor suffering souls in Purgatory.

O Lamb of God, who camest down on earth to save sinners, let those poor souls who are still suffering in Purgatory feel the wonderful effects of Thy Passion and Death.

O Lamb of God, Thou who hast offered Thyself on the Cross for the salvation of the world, through the merits of Thy precious Blood, which is the price of our redemption, shorten the pains of the suffering souls; give them relief from their torments, and free them from their imprisonment.

At the Communion

O Lord, I am not worthy to receive Thee. I deeply feel my unworthiness when I glance back at my sins of the past, and see the wickedness of my heart. And yet my soul is drawn to Thee as if by force, for how can I hope to live without Thee! how raise myself from the torpor of sin, without Thy help and protection! Alas! I know I cannot walk straight in the path of virtue for one day without the help of Thy saving grace. Therefore I turn longingly to Thee, and cry out, O my Lord, look not on my wicked deeds; forget my offences, and look only on my poverty, my utter weakness, and my good intentions. Turn not away from Thy poor erring child at this holy moment, but come spiritually into my heart, and forget me not, O Jesus, my Love, forget me not!

As Thou dost now enter into the heart of the priest, and fill it with blessings and graces, so also descend, I beseech Thee, into the flames of Purgatory, in order to extinguish them, and succour the poor souls there by Thy divine presence. Vouchsafe to bring out many from that place of torment, and to shorten for others the time of their suffering. And, O my God, if my prayers at this holy Sacrifice have been acceptable in Thy sight, and my goodwill and intention pleasing to Thy Heart, then hear my supplication, and grant me the deliverance of that soul for whom I am most obliged to pray, and whose eternal happiness I desire above all.

At the Last Prayers

The holy Sacrifice of the Mass has come to an end, and is completed. A thousand thanks to Thee, O my Lord, who hast strengthened my faith and increased my charity during its holy celebration. Thou hast also increased my love and sympathy for those poor souls for whom I have been praying. But when faith and charity increase, hope is strengthened likewise; for they are sister-virtues. Therefore also is my heart now filled with hope and confidence, that as God in His infinite mercy has permitted me to assist at the holy Sacrifice of the Mass, He will also grant me the fruits and salutary effects of that saving sacrifice. Both I and those for whom I have prayed will feel and experience the wonderful blessings of this holy Mass. Filled with the hope of having obtained grace and help for my poor soul, as well as for those poor souls in Purgatory for whom I prayed, I conclude with the priest at the altar, returning thanks to God for His great mercy, and now begin my daily work, saying with the royal prophet: Unto Thee, O Lord, have I hoped; let me not be confounded for ever! Amen.

SECOND METHOD OF HEARING MASS

Before Mass

 Divine Saviour, in Thy infinite mercy Thou hast appointed the most holy Sacrifice of the Mass, not alone for the good of the living, but also for those who have died in the grace of God. Therefore I offer up this holy Mass and all my prayers for the souls of N. N., and all the other poor souls who are still suffering in Purgatory, in order to soothe their pains, to atone for their sins, to shorten their term of suffering, to procure their speedy deliverance, and obtain their prayers for me in Heaven, that before my death I may do penance and make satisfaction for all my sins. I beseech Thee, O kindest Jesus, that Thou wouldst graciously accept my poor prayers, and those of the saints in intercession, and unite them with the present holy Sacrifice of the Altar, and with Thine own most painful sufferings and death on the Cross. Offer them up to Thy Heavenly Father, so that through them the poor souls for whom I particularly pray may find solace in their sufferings, or be delivered entirely from the fire of Purgatory.

At the Introit

O Almighty and Eternal God, show Thyself merciful to the poor suffering souls in Purgatory! Are they not created after Thine own image? and hast Thou not destined them to the eternal happiness of heaven? I know, indeed, that they are not yet pure enough in Thy sight, and therefore not yet worthy to behold Thy Face in beatific vision. I know that Thine awful justice must be satisfied, and that in their lowly prison they must abide, until they have paid the last farthing. But I know also that Thou art as merciful as Thou art just, and that, as the Psalmist says, Thy mercy is without end. Thy Divine Heart is overflowing with love and compassion for the children of men. It is Thy wish and desire that we should ever appeal to it, so as to give Thee occasion for showing forth Thy mercy in the most striking manner, and thus to give joy to the living, and relief and deliverance to the dead.

O Jesus Christ, Son of the living God, show unto Thy Father the wounds of Thy Body, the instruments of Thy torture, the Cross on which Thou hast died! Remind Him that Thou hast died also for the salvation of those poor souls, who are now enduring such torments in atonement for their sins. O sweetest Saviour, look down with loving compassion on them, who so often invoked Thy holy Name on earth, who so often knelt and prayed at the foot of Thy Cross, who found such consolation in meditating on Thy sufferings, and who placed all their hope in Thy bitter Passion and Death. Oh, forget them not, sweetest Jesus!

O Holy Ghost and Divine Spirit of love and consolation, show Thy love and compassion to the poor abandoned souls in Purgatory, and comfort them in their pains. Thou, who art love itself, knowest best the painful yearnings of love. These are the souls upon whom Thou hast descended in holy Confirmation, and given strength to their faith. To them Thou gavest Thyself as often as they received the holy Sacraments. They are the children of that Church which Thou rulest, and with which Thou hast promised to remain even to the end of the world. Is it possible that Thou couldst forget, and no longer remember them, Thou of comforters the best, Thou the soul's delightful Guest! No! Thou wilt surely hearken to my prayers, and comfort those poor souls by pouring down the dew of Thy heavenly grace upon the burning flames and saving them from all the pains of fire.

From the Kyrie eleison to the Offertory

O Mary, who art justly called the Mother of the poor souls, listen to the cries and sighs of thy poor afflicted children, who have been redeemed by the precious Blood of thy Divine Son. Oh, plead for them at the throne of God. We know that thy maternal love is as great as thy intercession is powerful. For it is a pious opinion that especially on thy festivals, and days consecrated to thy honour, God is pleased to release innumerable souls from the pains and torments of Purgatory. Therefore, O most merciful Mother, I beseech thee to have pity especially on the souls for whom I am most concerned. At thy request water was changed into wine. At thy prayer, also, the burning heat will be changed into refreshing shade, pain and sorrow into joy and happiness, punishment into reward, and the woe of Purgatory into the eternal bliss of Paradise.

O all you holy guardian-angels, to whom the care of the salvation of mankind is committed by God, look down into the flames of Purgatory and see the poor souls that love you and suffer so hopelessly. Behold the many sighs they send up to you in Heaven! How ardently they desire to be with you! Oh, let your hearts be moved to compassion by their piteous cries. Pray to God graciously to condone the remainder of their punishment. Come down from Heaven and visit them. Comfort, strengthen, and refresh them, and, if it be the Divine Will, lead them out of their imprisonment to the everlasting joy of Heaven.

O all you Saints and chosen friends of God, look with compassion on all your suffering sisters and brothers in Jesus Christ. They belong to you, and are destined to be

your companions in the heavenly realms. For a time,
appointed by God's justice, they must still linger and pine
in the dark prison of Purgatory. Help us by your prayers
to shorten their term of expiation and purification. Your
prayers are of more avail with God than ours, for you are
so near to God. Oh, pray, then, without ceasing to the
God of all mercy to grant eternal rest and peace to the
poor suffering souls in Purgatory.

From the Offertory to the Consecration

O God, Almighty and Eternal, give me now the grace
of fully entering into the spirit of this most adorable
Sacrifice, at which Thou hast deigned to let me be present
and participate in, that, together with the priest, I may
offer a most acceptable oblation to Thy Divine Majesty.
Accept it, O Heavenly Father, for Thine honour and for
the salvation of the living and the dead; I offer it up to
Thee especially for the soul of N. N., and for all the other
souls who are still detained in Purgatory. All the torments
they endure, all the sighs they send forth, all the tears
which they shed, I put them spiritually into the chalice,
that so united with the present holy Sacrifice and the
merits of Jesus Christ they may be a sacrifice of expiation
to Thee on their behalf. Look down, O God, with
compassion on Thine only-begotten and well-beloved
Son, who for me and all mankind has shed His Blood
upon the Cross, and deliver the poor soul for whom this
Mass is offered, as also all the poor souls that suffer still
in Purgatory, and especially those who are nearest the
gates of Heaven.

Look down, O most benign Father, on that Head
crowned with thorns, on those Eyes red with tears, that

Face streaming with blood, pale and ghastly, those Lips purple and livid, and have mercy on those poor sufferers of whose sins and sufferings I may have been the cause.

Look down, O most gracious Father, upon His outstretched Arms, His Hands and Feet all pierced with nails, His transfixed Heart, and have pity on that poor soul in Purgatory whose pain is greatest.

Look down, O most compassionate Father on this sacred body, all mangled and bleeding from head to foot, His veins all swollen, His limbs distorted and out of joint, and have mercy on that poor soul whose pain is longest.

Look down, O most merciful Father, on Thine innocent Son, Jesus Christ, who, in His death agony, was not only derided and insulted, but was also abandoned by Heaven and earth, Angels and men, and even by Thee, and have mercy on that poor soul who is most abandoned and neglected.

Look down also, O most Heavenly Father, upon their own martyrdom, pains, and torments, and let Thy mercy overcome Thy wrath; let Thy Heart be touched unto pity; give to all the souls departed eternal rest, and let perpetual light shine upon them. Amen.

During and after the Elevation

I firmly believe, O my Lord Jesus, that Thou art really present upon this Altar; and that Thy adorable Body is concealed under the form of bread. I adore Thee, O Jesus, in this most sacred Host. Oh, deign to turn Thine eyes from this altar into the depths of Purgatory, and gladden the poor souls suffering there, with one glance of pity and consolation. O Jesus, I adore Thy most precious Blood in this holy chalice. Oh, let but one drop of this sanctifying

Blood flow into Purgatory, and it will be all-powerful to extinguish the flames and soothe the sufferings of those poor souls!

It is the same precious Blood which Thou didst so plentifully shed for us sinners in the Garden of Olives, during that dreadful night when Thy Body was bathed with a bloody sweat, which ran trickling down in great drops to the ground. O Jesus, all dripping with Blood for love of us, cleanse and purify in that holy stream the souls of the faithful departed from all the stains that still may cleave to them.

It is the same precious Blood which flowed from Thy whole Body in the courtyard of the house of Pilate, when Thou wert most cruelly scourged at a pillar. O sweet Jesus, so cruelly scourged, offer but one little drop of that most precious Blood to Thy Heavenly Father, and it will be sufficient to satisfy for all the sins of the souls in Purgatory.

It is the same precious Blood which the crown of thorns pressed from the adorable Head of my sweetest Jesus. O my thorn-crowned King, and Lord Jesus Christ, grant but the smallest drop of this precious Blood to the poor souls, and it will be enough for them to purchase with it the joys of eternal life.

It is the same most precious Blood which has flowed from the wounded Hands, and Feet, and sacred Heart of my crucified Saviour. O my crucified Love, let the Blood of Thy loving Heart flow down into Purgatory, so that it may soothe and comfort the suffering souls of my poor departed sisters and brothers, and may bring them eternal rest and peace.

At the Agnus Dei and Communion

O my crucified Love, Jesus Christ, I humbly salute and adore the sacred wound of Thy right Hand, and commend unto it the poor suffering souls of my parents, friends, and relations. I beseech Thee, for the sake of the Blood which has flowed from it, and the pains which Thou hast suffered in it, have pity on them; deliver them from their place of banishment.

O most benign Jesus, I humbly salute and adore the holy wound of Thy left Hand, and recommend it to the poor suffering souls who have most claim on my prayers, and are now, perhaps, calling on me for intercession. Through the Blood that was shed from it, and the great pain Thou didst suffer in it, I pray Thee stretch forth that gentle Hand and beckon them to come to Thee in Heaven.

O most gracious Jesus, I devoutly salute and adore the holy wound of Thy right Foot, and commend unto it those poor souls for whom Thou most desirest that I should pray. I beg of Thee, for the sake of the Blood which it has shed, and the pain which it has caused Thee, to come to their relief with those blessed words of consolation: 'This day thou shalt be with Me in Paradise.'

O gentlest Jesus, I humbly salute and venerate the holy wound of Thy left Foot, and earnestly commend unto it those poor souls that had a special devotion to Thy bitter Passion, and to the dolours of Thy sorrowful Mother, Mary, I beg of Thee, through the Blood which flowed from it, and all the torture Thou didst endure in it, send to them Thy Angel of deliverance, and condone the remainder of their punishment.

O most merciful Jesus, I humbly salute and venerate the wound of Thy sacred Heart, and recommend unto it the soul for which I undertook to hear this Mass. In memory of the Blood and Water which flowed from it, and of all the internal and external sufferings of that sacred Heart, I beseech Thee call them to Thee, and let them enter into Thine open and merciful Heart.

At the End of the Mass

From the depths of my heart I give Thee thanks, O my God, for the grace of having been allowed to assist at this most adorable Sacrifice, which Thy Divine Son has offered up anew to Thee for the salvation of the living and the relief of the dead. I feel how the bond of love that unites my soul with my Creator, Redeemer, and Sanctifier, has now been strengthened. I feel this holy Mass has increased my faith, confirmed my hope, and kindled anew my charity. I return richer in grace and stronger in spirit to overcome the rebellious inclinations of the flesh. The enemy will find it difficult to ensnare me in his pitfalls, and the charms and distractions of this world will have less power over me. I feel new courage within me to follow with joyful resignation in the sorrowful path of the Cross, where Christ Himself has walked before me, and to bear with patience all the sufferings of this life. This holy Mass has also been a solace for the poor suffering souls in Purgatory. For it is never offered up for them in vain. Each time its saving effects are experienced and felt in Purgatory. We can always and everywhere pray for the dead; but nowhere so effectively, or with such happy results as during the Holy Sacrifice of the Mass. For here Jesus pleads with us; here His Cross, His Blood, His holy Wounds, His bitter Agony and Death, call out to His Heavenly Father for mercy on these poor sufferers. And who could doubt of the success of such holy and all-powerful intercession! Therefore, O my Lord and my God, I heartily thank Thee for the happiness of having been vouchsafed to assist at this holy Mass, which I fervently hope has given grace to my soul, as well as solace to the poor suffering souls in Purgatory. In return I pray Thee accept the sacred promise that I will co-operate to the best of my power with Thy divine grace received. O you holy souls who have obtained peace and rest through the merits of this holy Sacrifice, pray for me that I may keep the good resolutions I have formed, and faithfully carry them out. Amen.

THIRD METHOD OF HEARING MASS

O Almighty God and Heavenly Father, Thy Divine Son, Jesus Christ, has united, in the bond of love, His people, whom He has acquired by His words of doctrine and His death on the Cross. This love can never die, nor its bond be severed. It lives beyond death and the tomb, uniting all the faithful of Christ into one living communion of Saints.

Animated by the spirit of this holy love, we now come to make commemoration, in this most solemn Sacrifice of the Mass, of the departed, and to beseech Thee to give grace and pardon to our suffering brethren in Purgatory, who have still to expiate some offences in the purifying flames before they become worthy of Thy divine presence.

O God most High, nothing impure can enter into Thy kingdom. Therefore has Thy wisdom and love appointed an intermediate place, wherein those who die unworthy of Thy divine presence may be tried like gold in the crucible, and cleansed from all their stains and imperfections. We humbly adore Thine unsearchable judgments. Thou art their Father, and lovest them more than we. Thou knowest best what is for their advantage. Thy holy will be done. But the intensity of our love for them urges us to appeal again and again to Thee for mercy. Thou Thyself hast inspired us with this love for them. Thou hast placed it in our hearts, and it is Thy divine will that we should pray for them. Father, most merciful Father, have mercy on them. They have died believing in Thee and Thy Son Jesus Christ. Ah! let them speedily enjoy the fruit of their faith, and make them partakers of the blessed fruits of Thy Redemption. Oh, forgive them their sins, and satisfy their ardent desires for Thy holy presence, and the joys of eternal life.

O Heavenly Father, graciously vouchsafe to accept this unbloody Sacrifice of the new Covenant, which is now being offered for the solace of the poor suffering souls, and hearken to the fervent petitions of Thy holy Church!

As to myself, grant that the memory of my departed fellow Christians may prove a wholesome lesson to me. My earthly course will soon come to an end; for short are the days of this life. How often, alas! does death surprise and carry off those who least expect it. Alas! O God of holiness, who is pure in Thy sight! And as nothing sinful or imperfect can come into Thy presence, how shall it be with me, careless and miserable sinner—I, who have hitherto been so careless of the things of eternity, and so anxious and solicitous of those of the world? How many and great are the sins that burden my conscience! How different will then appear to me those faults and failings which hitherto I considered mere trifles!

O my God, give me grace that for the future I may count my days, and become wiser and better before it is too late. Enlighten me, and give me strength henceforth to live in such a manner as I shall one day wish to have lived. Place me, O merciful Father, under Thy discipline. Purify me now from all stains of sin which, should death surprise at this moment, would debar me from the happiness of Thy divine presence. Enable me to do penance for my sins now, that then I may be spared. Let me be cleansed in the Blood of the Lamb, so that I may appear pure and innocent in Thy sight.

I readily submit myself to all Thy visitations and chastisements, by means of which it may please Thee to prepare me for Heaven.

I humbly kiss Thy Fatherly Hand, which, even in chastisement, shows love and goodness.

O my God, have pity on me, and have mercy on the souls of the faithful departed, and let eternal light shine upon them in the communion of Thy saints.

Let us Pray

O most merciful Lord and God, hear our prayers for the souls of Thy servants N. N., for whom we offer up this holy Sacrifice of the Mass. Perhaps they are still in the place of torments, making expiation for their sins to Thy divine justice. We therefore beseech Thee to compensate by Thy grace for whatever faults and consequences of human weakness may still cleave to them. Oh, call them to their blissful rest, and gladden them with Thy heavenly light, through Jesus Christ, Thy Son, our Lord, who, with Thee and the Holy Ghost, liveth and reigneth one God, world without end. Amen.

The Epistle

Brethren, we will not have you ignorant concerning them that are asleep, that you be not sorrowful, even as others who have no hope. For if we believe that Jesus died, and rose again, even so them who have slept through Jesus, will God bring with Him. For this we say unto you in the word of the Lord, that we who are alive, who remain unto the coming of the Lord, shall not prevent them who have slept. For the Lord Himself shall come down from Heaven with commandment; and with the voice of an Archangel, and with the trumpet of God; and the dead who are in Christ shall rise first. Then we who are alive, who are left, shall be taken up together with them in the clouds, to meet Christ, into the air, and so shall we be always with the Lord. Wherefore, comfort ye one another with these words (1 Thess. iv. 12-17).

The Sequence for the Dead
(Dies Irae)

The day of wrath, that dreadful day,
Shall the whole world in ashes lay,
As David and the Sybil say.

What horror must invade the mind,
When the approaching Judge shall find
Few venial faults in all mankind.

The last loud trumpet's wondrous sound
Shall through the rending tombs rebound,
And wake the nations underground.

Nature and death shall with surprise
Behold the trembling sinner rise,
To view his Judge with conscious eyes

Then shall, with universal fear,
The seven-sealed judgment book appear,
To scan the whole of life's career.

The Judge ascends His awful throne,
Each secret sin shall here be known.
All must with shame confess their own.

Ah, wretched! what shall I then say,
What patron find, my fears t' allay,
When even the just shall dread that day?

Thou mighty, formidable King!
Of mercy unexhausted spring!
Save me! O save! and comfort bring.

Remember what my ransom cost;
Let not my dear-bought soul be lost,
In storms of guilty terrors lost.

In search of me, why feel such pain
Why on Thy Cross such pangs sustain,
If now those sufferings must be vain?

Avenging Judge, whom all obey,
Cancel my debt, too great to pay,
Before the sad accounting day.

O'erwlelmed, oppressed with doubts and fears,
Their load my soul in anguish bears:
I sigh, I weep—accept my tears.

Thou, who wert moved at Mary's grief.
Who didst absolve the dying thief,
Dost bid me hope: O grant relief.

Reject not my unworthy prayer,
Preserve me from the dangerous snare,
Which death and gaping hell prepare.

Give my immortal soul a place
Among Thy chosen right-hand race,
The sons of God and heirs of grace.

From that insatiate abyss,
Where flames devour and serpents hiss,
Deliver me and raise to bliss.

Prostrate, my contrite heart I rend,
My God, My Father, and my Friend,
Do not forsake me in the end.

Well may they curse their second birth,
Who rise to a surviving death.
Thou great Creator of mankind,
Let all Thy faithful mercy find. Amen.

The Gospel

At that time: Jesus said to the multitude of the Jews: All that the Father giveth Me, shall come to Me; and him that cometh to Me, I will not cast out. Because I came down from Heaven, not to do Mine own will, but the will of Him that sent Me. Now this is the will of the Father that sent Me: that of all that He hath given Me, I should lose nothing, but should raise it up again in the last day. And this is the will of My Father who sent Me; that every one who seeth the Son, and believeth in Him, may have life everlasting, and I will raise him up in the last day. (John vi. 37-49.)

The Offertory

O Almighty and Eternal God, ✠ graciously accept this oblation, which I, unworthy as I am, offer up to Thee, through the hands of Thy priest, in atonement for my numerous sins and offences, in intercession for all here present, for all the faithful living and dead, that it may be for mine and their salvation unto life eternal. Together with this offering of Bread and Wine, which is about to be changed into the Body and Blood of Jesus Christ, I also offer myself and all I possess to Thee. As Jesus is One with Thee, so let me in holy love be one with Him. Let the Blood of Jesus, Thy Son, purify me from my sins. May the fire of Thy divine love destroy in me all that is evil and displeasing in Thy sight. May Thy Holy Spirit lead me in the way of truth and justice, so as to make my whole life a sacrifice of thanks and praise most pleasing in Thy sight, through Jesus Christ our Lord. Amen.

O most Holy Trinity, graciously vouchsafe to accept

in Thine infinite goodness this oblation, which we offer
to Thee in memory of the passion, resurrection, and
ascension of Jesus Christ our Lord, in honour of the
Blessed Virgin Mary, St. John the Baptist, SS. Peter and
Paul, and all the Saints, that it may be unto their honour
and unto our salvation, and that they may intercede for us
in Heaven whose memory we venerate on earth, through
the same Jesus Christ our Lord. Amen.

The Preface

Penetrated with the most reverential love, I lift my
heart and hands to Heaven, and worship Thine infinite
goodness, O Eternal Father. In truth it is meet and just
that we should everywhere and always thank Thee and
praise Thee, O Almighty and Eternal God, through our
divine Lord Jesus Christ. Through Him the angels praise
Thy Majesty, the dominations adore Thee, and the powers
in holy awe tremble before Thee. Through Him the
heavens, and the powers of the heavens, the Cherubim
and Seraphim in united choir bless Thee. Grant us, we
suppliantly pray, to join our voices with their transports
of joy, singing Holy, Holy, Holy, is the Lord God of
Sabaoth! The heavens and earth are full of His glory!
Hosannah in the highest! Blessed is He who cometh in
the Name of the Lord! Hosannah in the highest! Glory,
honour and praise be to Him for ever and ever in all
eternity. Amen.

The Canon

The nearer the most holy moment of this Sacrifice
approaches, the more fervently we recommend to Thee,
O God, whatever we have most at heart. Bless Thy holy

Church upon earth, purify and preserve it in the unity of love and peace all over the world. Bless with the fulness of Thy blessing Thy servant and representative Pope N., our bishop N., and all confessors of the true Catholic and Apostolic faith. Give peace, union, and wisdom to kings, princes, and rulers, that they may govern the people according to Thy will, and Thy kingdom be ever more extended on earth.

Remember also, O Lord, Thy priest, standing at the Altar and offering up the holy Sacrifice, and all here present, whose faith and devotion are known to Thee. I most especially recommend to Thee those souls who have a claim on my gratitude and love—my parents, brothers and sisters, as well as all benefactors and friends.

Comfort all the afflicted and distressed; convert the sinners, strengthen the righteous, have mercy on the dying, and let them depart in peace. Turn away from us all dangers of body and soul. All ye holy angels and saints and elect of God in Heaven, whose memory we venerate upon earth, unite your prayers with my most earnest supplications. Through Christ our Lord. Amen.

O Jesus, Son of the living God! I firmly believe that Thou art here really present under the appearances of bread and wine; I adore Thee! O let not the merits of Thy bitter Passion and Death be lost upon me! Jesus have mercy on me! O Jesus take pity on me! O Jesus forgive me my sins!

O most precious Blood, once flowing from the Cross in streams for my salvation! I adore and worship Thee, in union with all the angels and saints. Cleanse me from all my sins and strengthen my soul, so that Thy life and charity and virtue be and grow also in me, and unite me finally and inseparably with Thee in eternal life. Jesus, for Thee I will live! Jesus, for Thee will I die! Jesus, I am Thine whether in life or in death.

After Consecration

O my crucified Saviour! it was Thy command that until the end of time—until Thy second coming—Thy Church should renew the memory of Thy unspeakable love and Thy salutary death. Therefore hast Thou instituted the most holy Sacrament of the Altar, which is offered up to God at Mass as the great Sacrifice of expiation of the New Testament, and is prepared as a spiritual food for the faithful, and distributed as a pledge of their future resurrection and eternal life.

We should be one with Thee in ardent charity, and our spirit should be most intimately united with Thine. Come, then, O Jesus, and nourish my heart and soul. Let me be of one mind and will with Thee, so that I may be able to say with the Apostle:

"I live, now not I, but Christ liveth in me. And that I live now in the flesh; I live in the faith of the Son of God, who loved me and delivered Himself for me" (Gal. ii. 20).

Let Thy faith, O Jesus, be mine; let Thy trust, obedience, patience, and humility be my example. May Thy love be the soul of all my actions.

O my Divine Saviour, plant deep in my heart the true spirit of Thy Gospel, and let it become visible in every action of my life, so that my whole life may be a pure offering, and well-pleasing to God as was the pure and spotless Sacrifice which Thou didst offer up to Thy Heavenly Father on the Cross.

In the spirit of charity we are likewise mindful, and

make commemoration before Thee, O best Friend of souls, of our departed brethren, especially our parents, friends, and benefactors. They also are redeemed by Thee; therefore have mercy upon them, O Lord! Purify them from all the sins for which they had not yet made full satisfaction when they entered into eternity. Perfect their holiness and complete their happiness according to Thy mercy and wisdom. Finally, have mercy on us all, and lead us safely through the trials of life up to the dwellings of the Elect—into Heaven, to Thy Father and our Father, Thy God and our God, to whom I now turn full of confidence with the prayer that Thou Thyself hast taught us: Our Father, who art in heaven, etc.

Agnus Dei

Lamb of God, who takest away the sins of the world, have mercy on us and give us peace! [Three times]

O Jesus Christ, our Lord and Saviour, who hast said to Thine Apostles: 'My peace I leave you, My peace I give you,' look not on my sins, but on the faith of Thy Church; preserve her in peace and unity, according to Thy will, who livest and reignest God, world without end. Amen.

O Jesus Christ, Son of the living God, who, according to the will of Thy Father and through the co-operation of the Holy Ghost, hast given life to the world by Thy death, deliver me through this most holy Body and Blood from all my sins and from all evil. Grant that I may always live according to Thy divine precepts, and that I may never be separated from Thee. O my Saviour, come spiritually into my heart, but let not this partaking of Thy Body by Thy unworthy servant be unto my judgment and condemnation, but grant, according to Thy goodness, that it serve unto me as a protection of my body and soul and as a medicine for my weakness. I open my sinful heart to Thee, and penetrated with sorrow and with deep humility, I cry: O Lord, I am not worthy Thou shouldst enter under my roof; say but one word and my soul shall be healed! Lord, I am not worthy that Thou shouldst enter under my roof; say but one word and my soul shall be healed! Lord, I am not worthy Thou shouldst enter under my roof; say but one word and my soul shall be healed!

May the Body and Blood of Jesus Christ preserve my soul unto life everlasting. Amen.

The Communion

O my God, what shall I give Thee in return for all Thou hast given me? How can I hope to repay Thy wonderful goodness, which has given Thine own Body and Blood as a pledge of our eternal happiness? I will give Thee my heart with all its affections and desires; I will bend them all under the yoke of Thy holy law. Graciously accept this thank-offering which I make to Thee, and never let me become unfaithful to Thee. Uphold me by Thy divine grace, so that I may be able to curb my passions and resist all the charms of sin. Give me pleasure and joy in good works, and a constant horror of all wickedness. Destroy in me my predominant passions, and inspire me with such holy thoughts and impulses as may make me worthy to be Thy disciple. Grant me grace to love Thee above all things, and my neighbour as myself, that I may reject and despise all advantages which I might gain by transgressing Thy holy law; that by constant progress in virtue I may render myself fit for that blessed life of which Thou hast given us a pledge in the most adorable Sacrament of the Altar. Let Thy eternal light shine on the souls of the faithful departed, and may they rest in peace with Thy Saints, for Thou art good, and merciful, and loving.

Let Us Pray

Grant, we beseech Thee, O Lord, that the holy Sacrifice of Thy Son, which is ever pleasing to Thee, may obtain the desired reconciliation of the poor souls in Purgatory, Thy servants N. N., with Thee. Purify them from all faults or stains that may still cling to them, and forget them all in the overflowing pleasure which Thou hast in Jesus Christ, Thy Son, our Lord, who with Thee and the Holy Ghost liveth and reigneth one God, world without end. Amen.

The Last Gospel

Eternal Word of God, by which all things were created, most perfect Image of the Godhead, Life and Light of men! With profound adoration I worship Thee and thank Thee for the blessed fruits of Thy redemption. Thou didst come in the form of man, and assume our flesh, and dwell among us, in order to make us children of God. Who can understand Thy love, or fathom Thy compassion? O my God, enlighten me that I may honour Thee as my Lord and God by active charity, and so deserve to be called Thy child. Thou didst walk amongst the children of men full of grace and truth. Grant that I may reproduce in my own life that image of Thine which gave joy to heaven and earth. Son of God, to Thee be honour, glory and praise with the Father and the Holy

Ghost now and for ever more. Amen.

FOURTH METHOD OF HEARING MASS

'I rejoiced at the things that were said to me: We shall go into the house of the Lord.' These words of the royal Psalmist come home to me, and awaken a lively sense of their meaning in my heart, especially when I have the happiness of coming to church, and of assisting at the holy Sacrifice of the Mass. Oh, how much I desire to assist at it worthily and devoutly, and to complete my inward joy by a full participation in the fruits of this most adorable oblation. This holy Sacrifice availeth the living and the dead. Although I am a miserable sinner and stand sadly in need of divine grace, yet I gladly offer up with disinterested love all the merits of this most holy Sacrifice for the benefit of those poor souls who can no longer merit for themselves. With this intention I approach the Altar, where our Lord Jesus Christ is about to offer Himself through the hands of the priest to His Heavenly Father, just as He once offered Himself on Calvary, as a sacrifice for the sins of the whole world. I will forget and not think of myself, but offer all the graces and indulgences and merits of this Mass for the souls, especially those of my poor friends, N. N. Those holy souls will not forget this act of charity. I know moreover that this charity is most pleasing to Thee, my dearest Saviour, as so many Saints and pious servants of God assure us.

At the foot of the Altar

Uniting myself in spirit with the priest, who inclines before the Altar and penitently strikes his breast, acknowledging his sins and asking pardon for them—I, too, prostrate myself and ask pardon for all my sins of thought, word, deed, and omission. Turning with the eyes of faith towards Purgatory, I behold the poor souls who are most urgently asking me to remember them in my prayers, and help to procure their release from that abode of suffering. I am deeply impressed with their misery and helpless condition. I am overcome with sadness and grief in thinking of their dreadful sufferings. I feel irresistibly drawn to compassion, and an ardent desire urges me to do all in my power to succour them. And how could I do so better and more effectually, than by offering up in their behalf the holy Sacrifice of the Mass?

I seem to hear these poor souls saying, as it were by the mouth of the priest: Kyrie eleison,—crying to God to have mercy on them. Therefore I will join my prayers and mingle my tears with theirs, and from the depth of my heart call on the Lord to have mercy on them, saying nine times: 'Lord, have mercy on those poor souls.'

The Epistle

The word epistle signifies a letter, because during Mass the priest always reads some portion from the letters of the Apostles. In the Mass for the Dead, the Angel-guardians of those poor sufferers bring us, as it were, a letter from them, in which it is written: 'We suffer excruciating pains in these flames. We burn in a fire a million times more violent than all the fires of earth together. If you have a spark of love and compassion, come to our rescue, help us by all the means in your power.' It is impossible to think of all this and remain unmoved. Therefore, O my Lord, with renewed zeal and fervour I turn to Thee, and implore Thee to have pity on those poor stricken souls, and to deliver them from their place of woe.

The Gospel

O Jesus, Son of the Living God, Thou hast come upon earth with the message of peace. Send down Thy holy Angels to the poor suffering souls of Purgatory, who are far away from Thee and Heaven, and whose yearning desires become more painful the longer that separation lasts. Grant that the Gospel of the Good Samaritan pouring oil and balsam into their wounds be carried to them. I, also, will try to resemble the Good Samaritan, and not pass by the cries and lamentations of these poor souls. I will bring them the oil of active sympathy, and the wine of powerful intercession. O Jesus, Divine Samaritan, I beseech Thee to break the fetters of those poor prisoners, and lift them out of the burning pit, and bring them into Thy heavenly mansions, where they will find rest and everlasting peace.

Credo

I firmly believe, O my God, that no soul with the smallest blemish of sin, or slightest imperfection, can ever enter the gates of Thy heavenly kingdom.

I firmly believe that Thy divine justice will not allow our most venial sins to go unpunished.

I firmly believe that all the sins which we commit, and neglect to repent of and do penance for, here on earth, must be atoned for by terrible sufferings in Purgatory.

I also believe that it is a holy and a wholesome thought to pray for the dead, that they may be loosed from their sins.

I firmly believe that we may pray for them; that by our prayers we may give them ease and comfort; that it is pleasing to Thy compassionate Heart to hear our prayers for them, and to accept the offering of our good works on their behalf.

I firmly believe also that it is, above all, the holy Sacrifice of the Mass, by which we can most effectually and most powerfully come to their assistance.

Sanctus

When the awful words of 'Holy, Holy, Holy,' are said at Mass, the ever Blessed Virgin and Mother of God falls down before the Throne of God to intercede for the poor souls in Purgatory. The Saints, too, hearing those words of praise on earth, prostrate themselves before the Lamb of God, who taketh away the sins of the world, and also the punishments of Purgatory.

Let us unite our feeble prayers with the all-powerful intercession of the Blessed Virgin and all the Saints, so that they may become irresistible. Let us cry from the bottom of our hearts: Thrice holy God, have mercy on the poor souls in Purgatory!

Consecration

O heavenly Manna! O Bread of Life! he who eateth of Thee will never hunger again. Show Thyself to the poor souls in Purgatory, and still their hunger, lest they succumb to their exhaustion and misery.

O most holy Redeemer! one only drop of Thy most precious Blood would suffice to quench all the burning flames of Purgatory. Oh, let it flow down upon them, that it may soothe and comfort them in their torments until the happy time comes when they will be delivered from their place of woe!

Memento

O Divine Saviour, when Thou wert hanging on the Cross, and consummating the great sacrifice of atonement, the thief on Thy left hand said: 'Lord, remember me when Thou comest into Thy heavenly kingdom.' Thy answer showed that Thou wert moved by his petition. 'To-day shalt thou be with Me in Paradise.' In the same words I now appeal to Thy Divine Heart: Remember the poor souls! oh, forget them not, particularly those poor souls I am more especially bound to pray for. I implore and beg of Thee, O my God, by the infinite merits of this most holy Sacrifice, by Thy most wonderful love and mercy, by Thy most holy Virgin Mother and all Thy beloved Saints, speak now the same consoling words as on the Cross: 'This day shall you be with Me in Paradise; this day I will break their chains and free them from their prison, and bring them with Me into the kingdom of Heaven.'

Agnus Dei

Thou, O Jesus, art the Lamb of God, who taketh away not only the sins of the world, but also all their effects, that is, all distress and suffering. For Thou hast said: 'Come to Me all ye that labour and are distressed, and I will refresh you.' How often have I not, together with thousands of others, experienced the truth of those consoling words? Behold, O compassionate Jesus, those poor souls are also burdened and distressed; their misery, pain, and sorrow is greater than all the concentrated pains and sufferings of the whole world. They appeal through me to Thy goodness; oh, grant them comfort and relief. They are, it is true, no longer living in this world, but Thy compassionate love knows no bounds and has no limits. Lamb of God, shorten the term of their punishment, or mercifully end it altogether.

Communion

Three times the priest strikes his breast in acknowledgment of his unworthiness, before he receives Thee at Holy Communion; yet Thou deignest to enter into his heart. Thou comest also spiritually into mine, which, though full of fear and contrition, is yet ardently longing after Thee; and Thou fillest it with happiness at Thy sacred presence.

I acknowledge the greatness of this grace; I feel the immense happiness bestowed on me. Still, when I think of the poor souls, especially those who are dearest to me, how can I be without sadness? O Jesus, make my joy complete. As Thou hast come spiritually into my heart, so also deign to descend into Purgatory and deliver that poor soul for whom I am most urgently praying, and bring him into Thy holy kingdom! Oh, bring him from exile into his blessed home, from his place of punishment to his place of eternal reward and refreshment.

Last Blessing

The priest, who is Christ's representative, imparts this blessing not only to the living, but also to the dead. They all turn towards him to receive it. They also turn lovingly towards you, to thank you for all you have just now done for them. They know all your labours for them, and will never forget them. Their gratitude increases with the fervour of your compassionate love. Therefore, do not leave the House of God without once more thinking of them; and finish your prayers by saying five Our Fathers and five Hail Marys for the repose of their souls.

FIFTH METHOD OF HEARING MASS

THE MASS FOR THE DEAD ACCORDING TO THE ROMAN MISSAL

At the foot of the Altar

Priest. In the Name of the Father, and of the Son, and of the Holy Ghost. Amen. I will go in to the Altar of God.

Acolyte. To God who giveth joy to my youth.

P. Our ✠ help is in the Name of the Lord.

A. Who made heaven and earth.

P. I confess to Almighty God, to blessed Mary ever-virgin, to blessed Michael the Archangel, to blessed John the Baptist, to the holy Apostles Peter and Paul, to all the Saints and to you brethren, that I have sinned exceedingly, in thought, word, and deed, through my fault, through my fault, through my most grievous fault. Therefore I beseech blessed Mary ever-virgin, blessed Michael the Archangel, blessed John the Baptist, the holy Apostles Peter and Paul, all the Saints, and you brethren, to pray to the Lord our God for me.

A. May Almighty God be merciful to thee, and thy sins being forgiven, bring thee to everlasting life.

P. Amen.

A. I confess to Almighty God, etc., as above, (but instead of 'to you brethren,' he says 'to thee Father').

P. May Almighty God be merciful to you, and, your sins being forgiven, bring you to everlasting life.

A. Amen.

P. May the Almighty and merciful Lord grant us pardon, absolution and remission of our sins.

A. Amen.

P. O God, Thou being turned towards us, wilt enliven us.

A. And Thy people will rejoice in Thee.

P. Show us, O Lord, Thy mercy.

A. And grant us Thy salvation.

P. O Lord, hear my prayer.

A. And let my cry come to Thee.

P. The Lord be with you.

A. And with thy spirit.

The Priest going up to the Altar says, Let us pray.

Take away from us, we beseech Thee, O Lord, our iniquities, that we may deserve to enter into the Holy of Holies with pure minds. Through Christ our Lord. Amen.

Bowing down, with his hands upon the Altar, he says:

We beseech Thee, O Lord, by the merits of those Saints whose relics are here, and of all the Saints, to vouchsafe to pardon all my sins. Amen.

Introit.

Making the sign of the Cross over the book, he says:

Eternal ✠ rest give to them, O Lord, and let perpetual light shine upon them. A hymn, O God, becometh Thee in Sion; and a vow shall be paid to Thee in Jerusalem. O Lord, hear my prayer; all flesh shall come to Thee. Eternal rest give to them, O Lord, and let perpetual light shine upon them.

Going to the middle of the Altar:

P. Lord, have mercy on us.

A. Lord, have mercy on us.

P. Lord, have mercy on us.

A. Christ, have mercy on us.

P. Christ, have mercy on us.

A. Christ, have mercy on us.

P. Lord, have mercy on us.

A. Lord, have mercy on us.

P. Lord, have mercy on us.

The Priest kisses the Altar, and turning to the people, says:

P. The Lord be with you.

A. And with thy spirit.

P. Let us pray.

He then says one or several of the following prayers as appointed
by the Church.

Prayer
On the Day of Decease or Burial

O God, whose property is always to have mercy and
to spare, we humbly beseech Thee for the soul of Thy
servant, N. N., which thou hast this day commanded to
depart out of this world; that Thou mayest not deliver it
into the hands of the enemy, nor forget it unto the end;
but command it to be received by holy Angels, and to be
carried to its country Paradise; that, as in Thee it hoped
and believed, it may not suffer the pains of hell, but
possess eternal joys. Through Jesus Christ our Lord.
Amen.

On the Anniversary

O Lord, the God of mercies, grant to the soul of Thy
servant, whose anniversary we commemorate, the seat of
refreshment, the happiness of rest, and the brightness of
light. Through our Lord, etc.

For Deceased generally

Incline Thine ear, O Lord, to our prayers, by which we humbly beseech Thy mercy that thou wouldst establish the soul of Thy servant which Thou hast commanded to leave this world, in the region of peace and light, and order it to become a companion of Thy Saints. Through our Lord, etc.

For Deceased Parents

O God, who hast commanded us to honour our father and mother, in Thy clemency have mercy on the souls of my father and mother and forgive their sins (if only one be dead, use the singular); and grant that I may see them in the joy of eternal glory. Through our Lord, etc.

For Deceased Brethren, Relations, and Benefactors

O God, the giver of pardon and lover of the salvation of men, we beseech Thy clemency, that Thou wouldst grant the brethren, relations, and benefactors of our congregation who have departed out of this world, to arrive, through the intercession of blessed Mary ever-virgin and all Thy Saints, at the fellowship of perpetual bliss. Through, etc.

Epistle
1 Thess. iv. 12-17.

BRETHREN, we will not have you ignorant concerning them that are asleep, that you be not sorrowful, even as others who have no hope. For if we believe that Jesus died and rose again, even so them who have slept through Jesus will God bring with Him. For this we say unto you in the word of the Lord, that we who are alive, who remain unto the coming of the Lord, shall not prevent them who have slept. For the Lord Himself shall come down from Heaven, with commandment, and with the voice of an Archangel, and with the trumpet of God: and the dead who are in Christ shall rise first. Then we who are alive, who are left, shall be taken up together with them in the clouds to meet Christ, into the air, and so shall we be always with the Lord. Wherefore, comfort ye one another with these words.

A. Thanks be to God.

Or on Ordinary Days.

Apoc. xiv. 13.

ND I heard a voice from Heaven, saying to me, Write, Blessed are the dead who die in the Lord. From henceforth now, saith the Spirit, that they may rest from their labours, for their works follow them.

Gradual and Tract

Eternal rest give to them, O Lord, and let perpetual light shine upon them. The Just shall be in everlasting remembrance; he shall not fear the evil hearing. Absolve, O Lord, the souls of all the faithful departed from every bond of sin. And by the help of Thy grace may they be enabled to escape the judgment of punishment, and enjoy the happiness of light eternal.

SEQUENCE, DIES IRÆ

THE DREADFUL day—the day of ire—
Shall kindle up the avenging fire
Around the expiring world;
And earth, as Sybils said of old,
And as the prophet king foretold,
Shall be in ruin hurled.

How great the trembling and the fear
When the tremendous Judge draws near.
When the great trumpet's blown!

And thundering to earth's utmost bound,
Shall rouse the slumbering nations round,
To stand at God's high throne!

Nature and death shall be amazed;
Poor trembling man for judgment raised;
Leaving the dreary tomb.

Then shall the awful book come forth,
Where stands the saint's recorded worth
And guilty sinner's doom.

He shall be Judge, whose piercing sight
Brings every hidden deed to light
And leaves no thought concealed.

Where then shall be the sinner's place—
When scarcely shall the just find grace
For all his works revealed?

O Thou, most high, tremendous King!
From the eternal mercy's spring
Pure grace flows ever free.

Jesus, my God, to Thee I pray,
Oh, save me in that dreadful day,
By all Thou didst for me!

Thou soughtest me at Sichar's well;
How great Thy torments, who shall tell,
My heavy debt to pay.

O righteous Judge! 'tis Thine to spare—
Let me Thy kind forgiveness share
Before that awful day!

Conscious of guilt, I weep and groan,
I blush my weight of sins to own;
Oh, cleanse my soul's deep stain.

Thou, who wert moved at Mary's tear,
And the repentant thief didst hear,
Let not my hope be vain.

Let my unworthy prayer be heard;
Save me by Thine indulgent word
From hell's dark, dreadful land.

And far from goats, oh, may Thy grace
Grant me among Thy sheep a place,
Ranked on Thine own right hand.

When sinners on that day shall know
Their sentence to eternal woe,
Call me to bliss above.

With broken heart to Thee I bend,
Spare me, Thy suppliant, in the end—
Save me, O God of Love!

A fearful day—a day of tears—
When, to be judged, poor man appears,
Summoned at God's behest.

Spare me, then, Lord; receive my prayer,
Let those who sleep Thy mercy share—
Grant them eternal rest. Amen.

Gospel

P. The Lord be with you.
A. And with thy spirit.

P. The continuation of the Gospel according
to St. John.
A. Glory be to Thee, O Lord.

St. John v. 25-29:

AT THAT TIME, Jesus said to the multitudes of
the Jews: Amen, amen, I say unto you that the
hour cometh, and now is, when the dead shall
hear the voice of the Son of God, and they that hear shall
live. For as the Father hath life in Himself, so He hath
given to the Son also to have life in Himself; and He hath
given Him power to do judgment, because He is the Son
of Man. Wonder not at this, for the hour cometh wherein

all that are in the graves shall hear the voice of the Son of God; and they that have done good things shall come forth unto the resurrection of life, but they that have done evil unto the resurrection of judgment.

A. Praise be to Thee, O Christ.

(Other Gospels are taken from St. John, chapters vi and xi)

Offertory

The Priest kisses the Altar, and turning to the people, says:

P. The Lord be with you.

A. And with thy spirit.

P. Let us pray: O Lord Jesus Christ, King of glory, deliver the souls of all the faithful departed from the pains of hell and from the deep pit; deliver them from the mouth of the lion, that hell may not swallow them up, and they may not fall into darkness; but may the holy standard-bearer, Michael introduce them to the holy light, which Thou didst promise of old to Abraham and to his seed.

We offer Thee, O Lord, sacrifice and prayers: do Thou receive them in behalf of those souls whom we commemorate this day. Grant them, O Lord, to pass from death to that life which Thou didst promise of old to Abraham and to his seed.

The Priest uncovers the chalice, and taking the paten with the Host, says:

Receive, O Holy Father, Almighty, Eternal God, this unspotted Host, which I, Thy unworthy servant, offer to Thee, my living and true God, for mine innumerable sins, offences, and negligences, and for all here present, as also for all faithful Christians living and dead: that it may be available for me and them to life everlasting. Amen.

Putting wine and water into the chalice, he says:

O God, who didst wonderfully constitute the dignity of human nature, and still more wonderfully reform it: grant that by the mystery of this water and wine we may be partakers of His divinity, who vouchsafed to become a partaker of our humanity, Jesus Christ, Thy Son our Lord: who liveth and reigneth with Thee in the unity of the Holy Ghost: world without end. Amen.

Offering up the chalice, he says:

We offer to Thee, O Lord, the chalice of salvation, beseeching Thy clemency, that it may ascend with an odour of sweetness in the sight of Thy Divine Majesty for our salvation and that of the whole world. Amen.

Bowing down, he says:

May we be received by Thee, O Lord, in the spirit of humility and in a contrite mind; and so may our Sacrifice be made in Thy sight this day, that it may be pleasing to Thee, O Lord God.

Raising his hands and eyes, he says:

Come, O Almighty and Eternal God, the Sanctifier, and bless this Sacrifice prepared for Thy holy Name.

Washing his hands, he says the Psalm Lavabo, *without* Glory be, *etc. Then bowing down in the middle of the Altar, he says:*

Receive, O Holy Trinity, this oblation which we offer to Thee, in memory of the passion, resurrection, and ascension of our Lord Jesus Christ; and in honour of Blessed Mary, ever-virgin, and blessed John Baptist, and the holy Apostles Peter and Paul, and of these and all the Saints; that it may be to their honour and our salvation. And may they vouchsafe to intercede for us in heaven whose memory we celebrate on earth. Through the same Christ our Lord. Amen.

Turning to the people, he prays aloud:

P. Brethren, pray [*contin. in a low voice*] that my sacrifice and yours may be acceptable to God, the Father Almighty.

A. May the Lord receive the Sacrifice from thy hands, to the praise and glory of His Name, for our benefit, and that of all His holy Church.

P. Amen.

SECRET PRAYERS
On the Day of Decease or Burial

Be merciful, we beseech Thee, O Lord, to the soul of Thy servant, N., for whom we offer Thee the sacrifice of praise, humbly beseeching Thy Majesty that, by these offices of pious expiation, it may be found worthy to arrive at eternal rest. Through our Lord, etc.

On the Anniversary

Be propitious, O Lord, to our supplications for the souls of Thy servants, whose anniversary is this day commemorated, for whom we offer Thee Thy sacrifice of praise; that Thou mayest vouchsafe to associate them to the company of Thy Saints. Through our Lord, etc.

For Deceased in general

Grant us, we beseech Thee, O Lord, that this oblation may be beneficial to the soul of Thy servant, by offering which Thou didst release the whole world from sin. Through our Lord, etc.

For Deceased Parents

Accept, we beseech Thee, O Lord, the Sacrifice which
I offer for the souls of my father and mother, and grant
them everlasting joy in the land of the living; and
associate me with them in the happiness of the Saints.
Through our Lord, etc.

For Deceased Brethren, Relations, and Benefactors

O God, to whose mercies there is no limit, favourably
receive our humble prayers, and grant to the souls of our
brethren, relations and benefactors, whom Thou didst
grant to confess Thy Name, the remissions of all their
sins. Through our Lord Jesus Christ, Thy Son, who liveth
and reigneth with Thee in the unity of the Holy Ghost,
one Holy God.

Then, in a louder voice:

Preface

P. World without end.
A. Amen.
P. The Lord be with you.
A. And with thy spirit.
P. Raise up your hearts.
A. We have them raised up to the Lord.
P. Let us give thanks to the Lord our God.
A. It is worthy and just.
P. It is truly worthy and just, right and salutary, that
we should always and in all places give thanks to Thee, O
holy Lord, Father Almighty, Eternal God, through Christ
our Lord; by whom the Angels praise Thy Majesty, the
dominations adore, the powers tremble. The heavens and

the virtues of the heavens, and blessed Seraphim celebrate it with exultation together. With whom we beg Thee to command our voices to be admitted, saying with suppliant confession:

Holy, Holy, Holy! Lord God of hosts! The heavens and earth are full of Thy glory, Hosanna in the highest! Blessed is He that cometh in the Name of the Lord. Hosanna in the highest!

CANON

The Priest says in a low voice:

E humbly beg and beseech Thee, therefore, O most merciful Father, through Jesus Christ, Thy Son, our Lord, to accept and bless these gifts, these presents, these holy, undefiled Sacrifices, which we offer Thee especially for Thy holy Catholic Church; which vouchsafe to pacify, preserve, unite and govern throughout the world; together with Thy servant, our Pope N., and our Bishop N., and all orthodox persons and professors of the Catholic and Apostolic Faith.

Commemoration of the Living

Remember, O Lord, Thy servants of both sexes, N. and N. [*he pauses a moment and prays for those for whom he wishes to pray in particular; then continues:*] And all here present, whose faith and devotion are known to Thee, for whom we offer to Thee or who offer to Thee this sacrifice of praise for themselves, and all that belong to them: for the redemption of their souls, for the hope of their salvation and safety: and render their vows to Thee, the eternal, living and true God.

Within the Action *or most solemn part of the Mass*

Communicating, and venerating the memory, in the first place, of glorious Mary, ever-virgin, Mother of our God and Lord Jesus Christ: as also of Thy blessed Apostles and Martyrs, Peter and Paul, Andrew, James, John, Thomas, James, Philip, Bartholomew, Matthew, Simon and Thaddeus; Linus, Cletus, Clement, Xystus, Cornelius, Cyprian, Lawrence, Chrysogonus, John and Paul, Cosmas and Damian, and all Thy Saints; by whose merits and prayers mayest Thou grant that in all things we may be defended by the help of Thy protection. Through the same Christ our Lord. Amen.

Spreading his hands over the oblation, he says:

We beseech Thee, therefore, O Lord, to receive favourably this oblation of our service, as also of all Thy family; and to dispose our days in Thy peace, and command us to be delivered from eternal damnation, and to be numbered in the flock of Thine elect. Through Christ our Lord. Amen.

Which oblation do Thou, O God, we beseech Thee, vouchsafe to make in all things blessed, admitted, ratified, reasonable and acceptable: that it may be made for us the Body and Blood of Thy most beloved Son, our Lord Jesus Christ.

Who, the day before He suffered, took bread into His holy and venerable hands, and with eyes lifted up to heaven to Thee, O God, His Almighty Father, giving thanks to Thee, He blessed, broke, and gave to His disciples, saying: Take and eat you all of this:

FOR THIS IS MY BODY.

In like manner, after He had supped, taking also this excellent chalice into His holy and venerable hands; also giving thanks to Thee, He blessed it and gave it to His disciples saying: Take and drink ye all of it;

FOR THIS IS THE CHALICE OF MY BLOOD, OF THE NEW AND ETERNAL TESTAMENT; THE MYSTERY OF FAITH; WHICH SHALL BE SHED FOR YOU AND FOR MANY UNTO THE REMISSION OF SINS.

As often as you shall do these things, you shall do them in remembrance of Me.

Wherefore, O Lord, we, Thy servants, and likewise Thy holy people, mindful as well of the blessed passion as of the resurrection from the grave, and also the glorious ascension into Heaven of the same Christ, Thy Son, our Lord, offer to Thy excellent Majesty of Thy gifts and presents a pure victim, a holy victim, an unspotted victim, the holy bread of eternal life, and the chalice of everlasting salvation.

Upon which vouchsafe to look with a propitious and serene countenance; and accept them, as Thou didst vouchsafe to accept the offerings of Thy just servant Abel, and the sacrifice of our patriarch Abraham; and that which Thy high priest Melchisedech offered to Thee, a holy sacrifice, an unspotted victim.

Bowing down before the Altar, he says:

We humbly beseech Thee, O Almighty God, command these things to be carried by the hands of Thy holy Angel to Thine altar on high, in the presence of Thy Divine Majesty; that all of us who shall receive the most holy Body and Blood of Thy Son, by this participation of the altar, may be filled with all heavenly blessing and grace. Through the same Christ our Lord. Amen.

Commemoration of the Dead

Remember also, O Lord, Thy servants of both sexes, N. and N., who are gone before us with the sign of faith, and repose in the sleep of peace.

Here he prays for those for whom he wishes to pray particularly, and then continues:

To these, O Lord, and to all who sleep in Christ, we beseech Thee to grant a place of refreshment, light, and peace, through the same Christ our Lord. Amen.

Striking his breast and raising his voice a little at the first words, he says:

Also to us sinners, Thy servants, hoping in the multitude of Thy mercies, vouchsafe to grant some part and fellowship with Thy holy Apostles and Martyrs: with John, Stephen, Matthias, Barnabas, Ignatius, Alexander, Marcellinus, Peter, Felicitas, Perpetua, Agatha, Lucy, Agnes, Caecilia, Anastasia, and all Thy Saints: into whose company do Thou, we beseech Thee, admit us, not considering our merits, but granting us Thy forgiveness. Through Christ our Lord. Amen.

By whom, O Lord, Thou dost always create, sanctify, vivify, bless and grant to us all these good things. Through Him, and with Him, and in Him, is to Thee, O God the Father, in the unity of the Holy Ghost, all honour and glory.

Then in a loud voice:

Pater Noster

P. World without end.
A. Amen.

P. Let us pray. Admonished by salutary precepts, and formed by divine instruction, we presume to say:

Our Father, who art in Heaven, hallowed be Thy Name: Thy kingdom come, Thy will be done on earth as it is in heaven. Give us this day our daily bread, and forgive us our trespasses, as we forgive them that trespass against us. And lead us not into temptation.

A. But deliver us from evil.

P. Amen. Deliver us, we beseech Thee, O Lord, from all evils, past, present, and to come: and the blessed and glorious Mary, ever-virgin, Mother of God, with Thy blessed Apostles Peter and Paul, and Andrew, and all the Saints interceding, grant, in Thy mercy, peace in our days; that, assisted by the help of Thy mercy, we may both be ever free from sin, and secure from all disturbance. Through the same Lord Jesus Christ, Thy Son, who lives and reigns with Thee, in the unity of the Holy Ghost, God,

Holding a part of the sacred Host in his hand, he continues in a loud voice:

P. World without end.

A. Amen.

P. The peace of the Lord be always with you.

A. And with thy spirit.

P. (*Letting the particle fall into the chalice, he continues in a low voice*): May this mingling and consecration of the Body and Blood of our Lord Jesus Christ be to us who receive it effectual to life everlasting. Amen.

Then he says, aloud:

Agnus Dei

Lamb of God, who takest away the sins of the world, grant them rest.

Lamb of God, who takest away the sins of the world, grant them rest.

Lamb of God, who takest away the sins of the world, grant them eternal rest.

Before Communion

O Lord Jesus Christ, Son of the living God, who didst give life to the world by Thy death, by the will of the Father and the cooperation of the Holy Ghost, deliver me, by this Thy most holy Body and Blood, from all my iniquities and all evils; and make me ever adhere to Thy commandments, and never permit me to be separated from Thee; who with the same God, the Father, and the Holy Ghost, livest and reignest God, world without end. Amen.

May the participation of Thy Body, O Lord Jesus Christ, which I, though unworthy, presume to receive, not be to my judgment and condemnation; but in Thy mercy let it avail to the safety of my soul and body, and the reception of a saving remedy. Who livest and reignest with God the Father, in the unity of the Holy Ghost, God, world without end. Amen.

I will take the Bread of Heaven, and call upon the Name of the Lord.

Then raising his voice he says three times, striking his breast:

Lord, I am not worthy that Thou shouldst enter under my roof; but say only the word and my soul shall be healed.

Communion

May the Body of our Lord Jesus Christ preserve my soul unto life eternal. Amen.

<small>Then he communicates; and after awhile he continues:</small>

What shall I return to the Lord for all that He has given to me? I will take the chalice of salvation, and call upon the Name of the Lord. Praising, I will call upon the Lord, and I shall be saved from my enemies.

<small>Receiving the chalice, he says:</small>

May the Blood of our Lord Jesus Christ preserve my soul unto life eternal. Amen.

Ablution

May we receive with a pure mind, O Lord, what we have taken with our mouth; and of a temporal gift may it become to us an eternal remedy.

May Thy Body, O Lord, which I have received, and Thy Blood which I have drunk, adhere to my bowels; and grant that no stain of crimes may remain in me, whom the pure and holy mysteries have refreshed. Who livest and reignest, world without end. Amen.

Post Communion

May light eternal shine upon them, O Lord, with Thy saints for ever, because Thou art merciful; eternal rest give to them, O Lord, and let perpetual light shine upon them. With Thy saints for ever, because Thou art merciful.

P. The Lord be with you.

A. And with thy spirit.

P. Let us pray.

On the Day of Decease or Burial

Grant, we beseech Thee, O Almighty God, that the soul of Thy servant N., which has this day departed out of this world, being purified by this Sacrifice, and delivered from sins, may receive pardon and everlasting rest. Through our Lord, etc.

On the Anniversary

Grant, we beseech Thee, O Lord, that the souls of Thy servants, whose anniversary we commemorate, purified by this Sacrifice, may obtain pardon and everlasting rest. Through our Lord, etc.

For Deceased in general

Absolve, we beseech Thee, O Lord, the soul of Thy servant from every bond of sin, that he may live again among Thy saints and elect in the glory of the resurrection. Through our Lord, etc.

For Deceased Parents

We beseech Thee, O Lord, that the participation of the heavenly Sacrament may obtain rest and light everlasting for the souls of my father and mother (or in the singular as the case may be); and that Thy eternal grace may crown me with them. Through our Lord, etc.

For Deceased Brethren, Relations, and Benefactors

Grant, we beseech Thee, O Almighty and Merciful God, that the souls of our brethren, relations, and benefactors, for whom we offer to Thy Majesty this sacrifice of praise, being purified from their sins by virtue of this Sacrament, may, by Thy mercy, receive the blessing of perpetual light. Through Christ our Lord. Amen.

P. The Lord be with you.

A. And with Thy spirit.

P. May they rest in peace.

A. Amen.

Bowing down before the Altar, he says:

Let the homage of my service be pleasing to Thee, O Holy Trinity, and grant that the Sacrifice which I, unworthy as I am, have offered to the eyes of Thy Majesty may be acceptable to Thee, and, by Thy mercy, be a propitiation for me, and for all whom I have offered it. Through Christ our Lord. Amen.

Last Gospel

P. The Lord be with you.

A. And with thy spirit.

P. The beginning of the holy Gospel according to St. John.

A. Glory be to Thee, O Lord.

N THE BEGINNING was the Word, and the Word was with God, and the Word was God. The Same was in the beginning with God. All things were made by Him, and without Him was made nothing that was made. In Him was life, and the life was the light of men, and the light shineth in darkness, and the darkness did not overtake it. There was a man sent from God whose name was John. This man came for a witness, to bear witness of the light, that all men might believe through Him. He was not the light, but was to bear witness of the light. That was the true light which enlighteneth every man that cometh into this world. He was in the world, and the world was made by Him, and the world knew Him not. He came unto His own, and His own received Him not. But as many as received Him, to them He gave power to be made the sons of God, to them that believe in His Name. Who are born not of blood, nor of the will of the flesh, nor of the will of man, but of God And the Word was made flesh, and dwelt among us (and we saw His glory, the glory as of the only-begotten of the Father) full of grace and truth.

A. Thanks be to God.

Note.—All Catholics ought to bear in mind how very important it is to have the holy Sacrifice offered up for their deceased friends as often as they can. The Church has appointed five Masses, namely, on the day of decease or burial, and on the third, seventh, thirtieth, and anniversary day after a person's burial. She, therefore, supposes that number at least should be said for the repose of the soul of a Catholic.

PRAYERS FOR CONFESSION

Jesus, Thou hast appointed the holy Sacrament of Penance, that we may thereby obtain pardon and remission of all the sins committed since baptism. I desire to avail myself of this grace, but without the help of Thy Holy Spirit I can do nothing. Therefore I call upon Him saying: 'Come, O Holy Ghost, enlighten me, that I may, without the smallest trace of self-love or false shame, see and acknowledge my sins, particularly those I have committed since my last confession.'

I also have recourse to Thee, O most holy Virgin Mary, who, next to Jesus, art my surest hope. I know what great joy it gives thee when thou canst help a poor sinner to convert himself and be reconciled again with God. Obtain for me, therefore, the grace that I may faithfully remember my sins, heartily repent of them, and make a good confession.

Examination of Conscience

O merciful God, how ungrateful and unfaithful I have again been to Thee! How many and grievous sins I have again committed against Thee! I feel ashamed to appear in Thy holy presence. I scarcely dare, O all-knowing God, to raise my eyes to Thee. I am not worthy to be called Thy child. Yet where else can I turn in my misery but to Thy fatherly heart, whose compassion never rejects a sinner! Thou hast lovingly received the penitent

Magdalene; Thou hast looked with pity upon the Apostle who so disgracefully denied Thee; Thou hast pardoned the penitent thief on the cross, and promised him the joys of Paradise. Surely Thou wilt show the same mercy and compassion to me. Well do I know that I have deserved to be cast off by Thee. I see and acknowledge it; but show mercy instead of justice. Look not on my sins, but on the sorrow I feel for having committed them. I promise Thee, O my God, with Thy assistance, never to relapse into my former sins. I sincerely promise amendment now, not in later years; now I will begin. Whatever it may cost me to overcome myself, I will conquer my former passions; I will carefully avoid all occasions of sin, and try to do Thy holy Will in all things. No more shall I wilfully offend Thee! Give me Thy all-powerful grace to keep my resolutions. With these intentions and resolutions I approach Thy holy tribunal of Confession.

After Confession

How great is now my happiness and ease of mind! I feel as if a heavy weight had fallen off my heart; I am as if born anew. As a bath refreshes the weary limbs of the traveller, so is my soul refreshed, invigorated, and soothed by the Sacrament of Penance. Therefore I give Thee most fervent thanks, my God. Truly Thou willest not the death of a sinner, but rather that he be converted and live—live a new and happy life. Had I died in my sins what would have become of my poor soul! True, I have well deserved to be abandoned by Thee, because I have so shamefully abandoned Thee since my last confession. But Thou wouldst not, because Thou lovest me. Thou desirest not my destruction, but rather that I should be holy here and happy hereafter. How can I thank Thee enough! How can I make return for all Thy love and mercy? Thou answerest, and my own heart suggests: by a better life. Yes, my resolution is taken: never more will I commit a grievous sin, never again will I lose Thy love and friend ship. From this day forward I will devote all my thoughts, words and deeds to Thy service, Thy greater honour and glory. I will try, with the help of Thy divine grace to redouble my efforts and make reparations for all the many omissions of my past life. But as all my resolutions are weak and changeable like myself, I beg of Thee, O my God, to assist me with Thy powerful grace. By Thy grace, O God of mighty power, I shall be enabled to conquer mine enemies and myself. Without Thee I can do nothing, and should succumb to the first temptation. Therefore have mercy on me, O God, and give me strength enough to resist all temptations to sin.

O Mary, conceived without sin, and refuge of sinners, thou art also the Mother of final perseverance. It is thy special prerogative to obtain for thy clients this great virtue. I owe it to thy intercession that my conscience is once more purified by a good confession, and I am in the state of grace. Intercede for me, I beseech thee, that I may persevere therein; assist me whenever sin is trying to insinuate itself into my soul; give me grace and fortitude and perseverance in the hour of temptation.

PRAYERS FOR HOLY COMMUNION

Before Communion

BEFORE I approach the Table of my Lord and God in order to receive Him, I will recall to my mind the words which the Eternal Wisdom has spoken concerning it: 'I am the living Bread which came down from Heaven. If any man eat of this Bread, he shall live for ever; and the bread that I will give is My flesh, for the life of the world. Amen, amen, I say unto you, Except you eat the flesh of the Son of Man and drink His blood you shall not have life in you. He that eateth My flesh and drinketh My blood hath everlasting life; and I will raise him up in the last day. For My flesh is meat indeed, and My blood is drink indeed' (John vi.).

Behold, O most loving Saviour, I now come to Thee, and most humbly beg of Thee to increase my faith, that I may worthily receive this most holy Sacrament. Lead me to this holy and pure fountain of life, and refresh me, Thy erring sheep. Give me, through Thy Holy Spirit, the grace of sincere contrition for my sins, and robe me with the nuptial garment of Thy justice, that I may not be an unworthy guest at this holy banquet. Banish from my soul all feelings of enmity, all antipathy against any one of my fellow men. Make me rather love in Thee all men alike, and with all my heart.

O Jesus, Thou hast said that it is not the strong and healthy who require a physician, but the weak and sick. Oh, how weak, how sick am I! No one stands more in need of Thee than I. Be Thou therefore the physician of my soul: cure it from its leprosy; bind up the wounds caused by my sins; save it from all the consequences, and let it never again suffer any relapse into sin.

With a most ardent desire I long to receive Thee, O my Lord; delay not, but come to Thy poor servant who yearns to receive Thee. I will lead Thee into the innermost recess of my heart; there I will love, praise, and worship Thee. Thou alone canst satisfy my hunger and quench my thirst. My God and my all, come and abide with me for ever, as Thou hast promised, saying: 'He that eateth My flesh and drinketh My blood abideth in Me, and I in him, and I will raise him up in the last day'.

After Communion

I have received my Lord and God. Oh, what a blessing! what a grace! He Himself has fed me with the most precious food of His Body, and refreshed me with the most costly drink of His Blood. How can I sufficiently thank Him? what return can I make for His love? Sweet Jesus, I have no words to express my thanks. Dumb and speechless, I rest upon Thy sacred Heart, as did once Thy beloved disciple, and listen in ecstasy to Thy holy communications. From Thy sacred Lips I ever hear the selfsame words saying: 'Love Me! love Me!' Yes, my Divine Lord, I will love Thee, with all the power of my soul, and all the strength of my will. I will never more offend Thee; I will never again fall into mortal sin. I will remain faithful to Thee. This is the best and highest, the worthiest and most pleasing, return of gratitude. Alas! of my own self I can do nothing. Therefore I ask Thee for Thy grace, help and protection, which Thou wilt not refuse me, since Thou hast deigned to come and give Thyself as the food of my soul. Once more I lay upon

Thine altar of expiation all the sins and evil deeds which I have committed since the dawn of my reason, in the sight of Thee and Thy holy Angels. Consume them by the fire of Thy love, and blot out every trace and stain that they have left behind in me.

I likewise lay down upon Thy altar all the good I have done during my life, however little and imperfect it may have been, in order that Thou mayest purify, sanctify and perfect it, and make it worthy of Thy divine acceptance.

I also lay upon this altar the pious intentions and desires of all who have received with me the same heavenly bread. Also all the pious desires and prayers of the faithful; all the secret wants and necessities of my parents, sisters, brothers, relatives, friends, and all those who have done good to me, or others for Thy sake, or recommended themselves to my prayers during this Holy Communion. I pray for all, whether living or dead, that they may obtain Thy grace and consolation; but I pray especially for the poor suffering souls in Purgatory, that Thou mayest soothe their pains and speedily deliver them out of their torments. Oh, forget not those sufferers, most merciful Jesus! Forget not my friends in their place of purification. Comfort them by Thy presence, and make them as happy as Thou hast made me this day.

Lastly I offer Thee, also, this Holy Communion and my unworthy prayers for all those who have offended or injured me, or who may bear me ill-will; also for those whom I may have offended with or without intention, by word or deed. Forgive us all our sins and offences, and banish from our hearts all hatred, jealousy, anger and ill-feeling.

O Jesus, stay with me! I cling to Thee with the arms

of faith and love. Oh, do not abandon me; oh, leave me no more! Now more than ever I feel Thou art my Life and my All.

> O Saving Host, that heaven's gate
> Laidst open at so dear a rate;
> Intestine wars invade our breast,
> Be Thou our Strength, Support, and Rest.
> To God the Father, and the Son,
> And Holy Spirit, Three in One,
> Be endless praise; may He above
> With life eternal crown our love!

Thou hast invited me to Thy holy Feast, and I have come. Thou hast come into my heart: never leave it again. Oh, speak to my soul; I listen to every word. Oh, commune with my heart; inspire it with Thy divine love. I hearken to Thy holy inspirations:

> Jesus, the only thought of Thee
> With sweetness fills my breast;
> But sweeter far it is to see
> And on Thy beauty feast.

> No sound, no harmony so gay
> Can art or music frame;
> No thoughts can reach, no words can say,
> The sweets of Thy blest Name.

> Jesus, our Hope when we repent,
> Sweet Source of all our grace,
> Sole Comfort in our banishment,
> Oh, what, when face to face!

*   *   *   *   *

STATIONS OF THE CROSS
FOR THE POOR SOULS IN PURGATORY

Preparatory Prayer

JESUS SAYS to us: 'Forget not my Passion and death,' and our heart answers back: 'How could we?' For this reason, we love the devotion of the Stations of the Cross, and wish to perform them often and willingly, because they bring so vividly home to our minds the sufferings and death of our dear Lord. The Stations are like so many flowers of the forget-me-not growing on the wayside of His Passion, and glistening with the pearly dew of His tears and Blood. Let us hasten to gather them up! O sweet Jesus, full of sorrow for my numerous sins, which have been the cause of Thy bitter sufferings, I begin to perform the Stations of the Cross. I offer up all the indulgences to be gained by this devotion for the relief of the poor suffering souls in Purgatory—particularly for the soul (souls) of N. N.

I most humbly beg of Thee, that through this devotion I may be able to obtain mercy for my poor departed brethren. I also beseech Thee, sweet Saviour, to deeply impress in my heart the compassionate memory of Thy sufferings, which Thou hast undergone for my sake, as well as for the salvation of all mankind.

O Mary, Mother of sorrows, who hast first taught us to walk on the way of the Cross, obtain for me the grace to follow the footsteps of Jesus with the same feelings that filled thine own heart during that mournful journey. Let me weep and mourn with thee, and make me love thy Divine Son as thou hast loved Him.

71

✠

FIRST STATION

JESUS IS CONDEMNED TO DEATH

V. We adore Thee, O Lord Jesus Christ, and bless Thee. *R.* Because by Thy holy Cross Thou hast redeemed the world.

Meditation

The most innocent Jesus, who committed no sin, nor could commit one, is condemned to death, even to the ignominious death of the Cross. Pilate, fearing that he would not be considered the friend of Caesar, delivers Jesus to the fury of His enemies. Oh, the wicked injustice: to please man he fears not to condemn the innocent and to offend God!

Prayer

How often has not human respect made me fall into sin! How often has it caused me to neglect my holiest duties! There are many souls now suffering, perhaps in Purgatory, for the same sin. I, too, may suffer the same fate if I continue to give way to this weakness. Therefore, O my Jesus, I beg of Thee to make me fear Thee more than men. Have mercy also on those poor souls who are condemned to do penance for this very sin; shorten the term of their banishment through the merits of Thy holy Passion and Death.

Our Father.   Hail Mary, etc.

O crucified Lord Jesus Christ, have mercy on the souls of the faithful departed.

JESUS IS CONDEMNED TO DEATH.

✠

SECOND STATION

JESUS TAKES THE CROSS ON HIS SHOULDERS

V. We adore thee, O Lord Jesus Christ, and bless Thee. *R.* Because by Thy holy Cross Thou hast redeemed the world.

Meditation

Jesus beholding the Cross, with earnest desire stretches forth His arms covered with blood, to embrace it lovingly, to kiss it devoutly, and to take it upon Him joyfully. Although weakened to death, He exults as a giant to run His course.

Prayer

How can I be a friend of Christ if I am an enemy of the Cross! O sweet and holy Cross, I embrace and kiss thee, and gladly I receive thee from the hands of God. Far be it from me to 'glory, save in the Cross of our Lord Jesus Christ, by whom the world is crucified to me, and I to the world' (Gal. vi.). I will be entirely Thine, O Lord Jesus. Have pity also on the poor souls now suffering in Purgatory, for having too reluctantly borne their cross in life. Oh, forgive them their murmurs, and release them.

Our Father. Hail Mary, etc.

O crucified Lord Jesus Christ, have mercy on the souls of the faithful departed.

JESUS RECEIVES THE CROSS.

✠

THIRD STATION

JESUS FALLS THE FIRST TIME UNDER THE CROSS

V. We adore Thee, O Lord Jesus Christ and bless Thee. *R.* Because by Thy holy Cross Thou hast redeemed the world.

Meditation

The most amiable Jesus proceeds loaded with the Cross, and, grievously oppressed by its weight, falls to the ground. It was not the Cross, a light and sweet burden, that dragged my Jesus to the ground; it was my sins and the sins of mankind that bore Him down.

Prayer

O my Jesus, Thou hast taken upon Thee my burden, and hast carried the heavy weight of my sins. Why, then, should we refuse to bear Thy yoke, and by carrying one another's burden fulfil Thy law! Thy yoke is sweet, and Thy burthen light. Therefore I will willingly and gladly take Thy Cross upon me and follow Thee. Do Thou, O Jesus, so strengthen me now to bear the Cross, that I may escape the punishment of Purgatory which those poor souls now suffer who had shrunk from Thy Cross on earth. Oh, have pity on them, console them, and wipe away their burning tears.

Our Father.   Hail Mary, etc.
O crucified Lord Jesus Christ, have mercy on the souls of the faithful departed.

JESUS FALLS THE FIRST TIME

✠

FOURTH STATION

JESUS MEETS HIS MOST AFFLICTED MOTHER

V. We adore Thee, O Lord Jesus Christ, and bless Thee. *R.* Because by Thy holy Cross Thou hast redeemed the world.

Meditation

How sorrowful was the sight to Mary, the most afflicted Mother, when she beheld her beloved Son, Jesus, carrying the Cross through the streets of Jerusalem! What inexpressible grief must she have felt in her loving heart! She desired to die for Him or with Him. Let us beg of the sorrowful Mother that she may also be present with us at the hour of our death.

Prayer

O Jesus, O Mary, O Hearts most loving and afflicted! I am the cause of your many and great sorrows. Oh that my own heart were likewise filled with grief! O Mother, most sorrowful and afflicted, let me share in the bitterness of thy grief; let me weep with thee. Vouchsafe at the hour of my death to come to my assistance. Succour also the poor suffering souls in Purgatory, that through thine intercession, they may derive the benefit of all thou didst suffer at the meeting with thy beloved Son.

Our Father.   Hail Mary, etc.

O crucified Lord Jesus Christ, have mercy on the souls of the faithful departed.

JESUS MEETS HIS MOTHER.

✠

FIFTH STATION

SIMON OF CYRENE HELPS JESUS TO CARRY THE CROSS

V. We adore Thee, O Lord Jesus Christ, and bless Thee. *R.* Because by Thy holy Cross Thou hast redeemed the world.

Meditation

Simon of Cyrene is compelled to bear the cross after Jesus, who is exhausted. Jesus accepts him for a companion. How gladly would He admit also you, my soul, if it were your desire to carry His Cross! He calls you, but you hear Him not; He invites you, but you refuse. Be ashamed, because you only accept your cross by force, and against your will.

Prayer

O Jesus, whoever does not take his cross upon himself and follow Thee, is not worthy to be called Thy disciple. Therefore I will help Thee to carry the Cross, and will accompany Thee on the way of the Cross. I will walk in Thy footsteps and follow Thee, that so I may come to Heaven with Thee, and escape the pains of Purgatory, which cannot be compared to any cross on earth. O Jesus, help also by Thy comfort the poor suffering souls to bear their heavy cross, or, in Thy great mercy, take it from them altogether.

Our Father. Hail Mary, etc.

O crucified Lord Jesus Christ, have mercy on the souls of the faithful departed.

SIMON HELPS WITH THE CROSS.

✠

SIXTH STATION

VERONICA WIPES THE FACE OF JESUS

V. We adore Thee, O Lord Jesus Christ, and bless Thee. *R.* Because by Thy holy death Thou hast redeemed the world.

Meditation

Veronica, inspired with compassion and devotion, presents the veil of her head to Jesus to wipe His face, besmeared with His blood, tears, sweat, and the spittle of His executioners. But He impressed upon it the image of His most adorable Countenance. Oh, how small a service, and how great a reward! But what services do you render to your Saviour for all His many benefits?

Prayer

O Jesus, what return can I make to Thee for all the blessings Thou hast bestowed on me! Behold now, I consecrate myself entirely to Thy service. I offer Thee my whole heart; place Thyself as a seal upon it; impress on it Thine image, that I may always be mindful of Thee. Nor turn away Thine eyes from the pour souls in Purgatory, but let the light of Thy countenance shine upon them, especially upon the soul of N. N., and give them eternal rest.

Our Father. Hail Mary, etc.

O crucified Lord Jesus Christ, have mercy on the souls of the faithful departed.

VERONICA OFFERS JESUS HER VEIL.

✠

SEVENTH STATION

JESUS FALLS UNDER THE CROSS A SECOND TIME

V. We adore Thee, O Lord Jesus Christ, and bless Thee. *R.* Because by Thy holy Cross Thou hast redeemed the world.

Meditation

Again, oppressed by the heavy Cross, the Divine Sufferer falls down, and lies prostrate with His sacred face on the ground. Yet His cruel executioners give Him not a moment of rest. They beat Him with clubs, and force Him to rise and go forward; they drag Him onward with ropes. Our repeated sins were the cause of this fall. Shall I, then, again take delight in sinning?

Prayer

O Jesus, be merciful to me; stretch forth Thy right hand to me that I may not relapse into my former sins. Now I have said it, now I begin; never again will I fall into sin. Do Thou, my Jesus, strengthen me by Thy grace to keep my good resolutions; for Purgatory, I know, is full of souls who have made and not kept such resolutions. O Lord, have mercy on those poor souls, and forget them not in their sufferings.

Our Father. Hail Mary, etc.

O crucified Lord Jesus Christ, have mercy on the souls of the faithful departed.

JESUS FALLS THE SECOND TIME.

✠

EIGHTH STATION

JESUS CONSOLES THE WOMEN OF JERUSALEM

V. We adore Thee, O Lord Jesus Christ, and bless Thee. *R.* Because by Thy holy Cross Thou hast redeemed the world.

Meditation

Women of Jerusalem are weeping over their suffering Saviour; but He turns to them, saying: Weep not over Me, who am innocent, but weep over yourselves and your children, who are guilty. Weep over your sins. Therefore weep also you, my soul, over your past sins. Nothing is more pleasing to Christ, and nothing more useful to you, than the tears of grief shed over your sins.

Prayer

O my Jesus, I beseech Thee so to fill my heart with sorrow that tears of bitter grief may flow from my eyes, and that all my life I may bewail Thy bitter sufferings and my sins, which have been their cause. If the poor souls who are now in Purgatory had repented more of their sins while on earth, they would not now have to weep such bitter tears of anguish. Oh, console them in their grief, most compassionate Jesus, and say to them in Thy mercy: 'Weep no more; the term of your penance is over, and the day of your deliverance has dawned.'

Our Father. Hail Mary, etc.

O crucified Lord Jesus Christ, have mercy on the souls of the faithful departed.

JESUS CONSOLES THE WOMEN.

☩

NINTH STATION
JESUS FALLS UNDER THE CROSS THE THIRD TIME

V. We adore Thee, O Lord Jesus Christ, and bless Thee. B. Because by Thy holy Cross Thou hast redeemed the world.

Meditation

Jesus, weak and weary, having reached the foot of Mount Calvary, falls again, the third time, with great force, under the Cross. It was enough to almost crush His sacred head. Oh, how insupportable a burden is sin! Jesus falls again and again under its weight, and it would have pressed me down to Hell, had not the merits of His sacred Passion preserved me.

Prayer

O most merciful Jesus, I return Thee infinite thanks that Thou hast not permitted me, as I deserved, to die in my sins, and to be hurled into the depths of Hell. Enkindle in me new zeal to love and serve Thee. Keep me constantly in Thy grace, that I may never more fall into sin, but persevere unto the end. Many of my fellow-Christians, alas! are now in Purgatory, because they have not fully repented and done penance for their sins. Have mercy on them, and bring them out of the burning flames into the delights of Thy heavenly kingdom, through the merits of Thy Passion and Death.

Our Father. Hail Mary, etc.
O crucified Lord Jesus Christ, have mercy on the souls of the faithful departed.

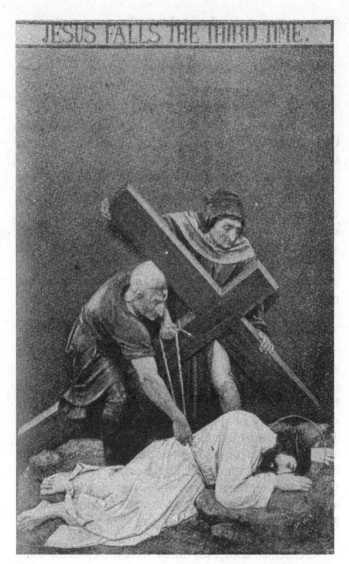

JESUS FALLS THE THIRD TIME.

✠

TENTH STATION

JESUS IS STRIPPED OF HIS CLOTHES

V. We adore Thee, O Lord Jesus Christ, and bless thee. *R.* Because by Thy holy Cross Thou hast redeemed the world.

Meditation

My dear Saviour is stripped of His garments; they are violently torn off from Him. Ah, who can tell the sufferings caused by this new torture! Those clothes, all soaked in blood, were cleaving to the skin, and thus torn off renewed His awful wounds. Jesus is to die stripped and naked. I, too, shall die well if I am stripped of the old man, with all his evil passions and concupiscences.

Prayer

Be it so, O my Jesus! be it so! I will cast off the old man, with his corrupt nature, and put on the new man, created according to Thine image and likeness. However hard and bitter it may seem to me, I will not spare my skin. Despoiled of all earthly things, I will live only for Thee. Oh, how many unmortified souls are now suffering and lingering in Purgatory, because they would not suffer here on earth! O Jesus, in Thy mercy and compassion, take from them their garments of sorrow and penance, and clothe them soon with the robe of Thy heavenly glory.

Our Father. Hail Mary. etc.

O crucified Lord Jesus Christ, have mercy on the souls of the faithful departed.

JESUS IS STRIPPED OF HIS CLOTHES

✠

ELEVENTH STATION
JESUS IS NAILED TO THE CROSS

V. We adore Thee, O Lord Jesus Christ, and bless Thee. *R.* Because by Thy holy Cross Thou hast redeemed the world.

Meditation

Jesus, stripped of His clothes, is now cruelly stretched out on the Cross, and His hands and feet are nailed to it. O torture! O anguish! yet He is silent, because such is the will of His heavenly Father. He suffers patiently, because He suffers for love of me.

O my soul! how do you conduct yourself in your afflictions? How impatiently and with what complaints do you bear them!

Prayer

O most patient Jesus, most meek and gentle Lamb, I detest and abhor all my impatience and anger. Do Thou, then, O Lord, crucify my flesh, with all its concupiscence and vices. Burn and cut in this life as Thou pleasest, that Thou mayest spare me in eternity. Thy holy will be done in all things. Oh, how joyfully would the poor souls now conform themselves to the will of God, against which they so often rebelled, or which they only accepted with murmur and discontent! They are now suffering dreadfully for it. O kindest Jesus, shorten the time of their torments, and gratify their ardent desires to be with Thee in Heaven.

Our Father. Hail Mary, etc.

O crucified Lord Jesus Christ, have mercy on the souls of the faithful departed.

JESUS IS NAILED TO THE CROSS.

O crucified Lord Jesus Christ, have mercy on the souls of the faithful departed.

✠

TWELFTH STATION

JESUS IS LIFTED UP ON THE CROSS, AND DIES

V. We adore Thee, O Lord Jesus Christ, and bless Thee. *R.* Because by Thy holy Cross Thou hast redeemed the world.

Meditation

Behold Jesus raised on the Cross, stripped and naked, covered with many wounds. Behold the bruises which He received for love of me. His whole figure betokens love. His head is inclined to give me the kiss of peace, and His arms extended to embrace me. His sacred Side is opened to let me enter into His loving Heart. In the number of His wounds I may count the pledges of the love of my most affectionate Jesus. Oh, how great is this love! Jesus dies that the sinner may live, and be freed from everlasting death.

Prayer

O dearest Jesus, would that I could die for love of Thee! Grant me at least that I may be dead to the world. Oh, how I loathe the world and all its vanities when I see Thee, stripped and naked, hanging on the Cross! Receive me, O Jesus, into Thine open Heart. I desire to be Thine; I wish but to live and to die for Thee. I also beseech Thee not to close Thy Heart to the poor suffering souls, especially those for whom I particularly appeal. Take them up into Thine everlasting glory.

Our Father, Hail Mary, etc.

O crucified Lord Jesus Christ, have mercy on the souls of the faithful departed.

JESUS DIES ON THE CROSS.

✠

THIRTEENTH STATION
JESUS IS TAKEN DOWN FROM THE CROSS

V. We adore Thee, O Lord Jesus Christ, and bless Thee. *R.* Because by Thy holy Cross Thou hast redeemed the world.

Meditation

Jesus would not descend alive from the Cross at the mocking call of His enemies, but would remain upon it even unto death. But when He was taken down after death, He rested in death as in life—on the bosom of His Virgin Mother. O my soul! be constant in good, and never depart from the Cross. He who perseveres unto the end shall be saved. Reflect at the same time with what purity that heart should shine, into which the Body of Jesus is received in the most holy Sacrament of the Altar.

Prayer

O Jesus, I beseech Thee not to permit me to be withdrawn from the Cross. I desire to live and to die on it. Create in me, O Lord, a clean heart, that I may worthily receive Thy sacred Body in Holy Communion, and that Thou mayest abide in me, and I in Thee, so that I may never be separated from Thee. There are perhaps many souls suffering now in Purgatory for their inconstancy in good, and their want of fervour in receiving Holy Communion.

O Mary, by the merits of that sorrow which thou didst experience when thy beloved Son was laid dead in thine arms, obtain relief for the poor suffering souls.

Our Father. Hail Mary, etc.

O crucified Lord, etc.

JESUS IS TAKEN DOWN FROM THE CROSS

✠

FOURTEENTH STATION
JESUS IS LAID IN THE SEPULCHRE

V. We adore Thee, O Lord Jesus Christ, and bless Thee!

R. Because, by Thy holy Cross, Thou hast redeemed the world.

Meditation

The body of Jesus Christ is buried in the tomb of a stranger. He who on the Cross had not whereon to recline His most sacred Head, had also no tomb or last resting-place of His own on earth, because He was not of this world. Am I, who seem so much attached to it, of this world? O that I may despise the world so as not to perish with it!

Prayer

O Jesus, Thou hast chosen me out of this world; what, then, have I to do with it any longer! Thou hast created me for Heaven. Why, then, do I desire anything on earth? Depart from me, O world, with all thy vanities! I will walk in the way of the Cross which my Saviour has marked with His blessed footsteps, and I will direct my course to my heavenly country, for there is my dwelling-place and my rest for ever. Thither also, I pray Thee, sweet Jesus, conduct the poor souls of Purgatory who are yearning and sighing after Thee, and who in Heaven will praise and glorify Thee for all eternity.

Our Father. Hail Mary, etc.

O crucified Lord Jesus Christ, have mercy on the souls of the faithful departed!

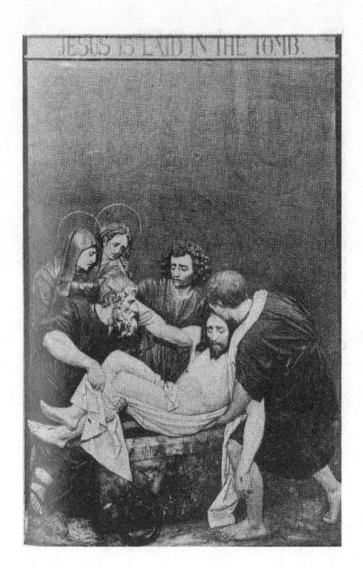

JESUS IS LAID IN THE TOMB

Prayer after the Stations

MOST BENIGN JESUS, I give Thee most humble thanks for the great mercy Thou hast shown to me during this exercise of devotion. I offer it up to Thee in honour of Thy most bitter Passion and Death, for the remission of all my sins, and punishments due to them; also for the relief of the suffering souls in Purgatory, especially those dearest to my heart. Prostrate before Thee, O Jesus, I humbly ask that Thy most precious Blood and Thine innocent sufferings and death may not be lost on my poor soul! Amen.

Three Our Fathers, three Hail Marys, for the repose of the souls of the faithful departed.

ROSARY
FOR THE POOR SOULS IN PURGATORY

I—THE JOYFUL MYSTERIES
The Creed, Our Father, three Hail Marys, Our Father.

FIRST MYSTERY: THE ANNUNCIATION
'The Angel of the Lord said to Mary: Fear not, Mary, for thou hast found grace with God; the Holy Ghost shall come upon thee, thou shalt bring forth a son, and thou shalt call His name Jesus.' (Luke i. 30-35.)

Prayer

Grant, we beseech Thee, O Lord, that also the poor suffering souls in Purgatory may find grace and mercy with Thee. Oh, be to them a Jesus, that is, a Saviour, that they may, without further delay, enjoy the delights of Paradise in company with Thy most holy Mother, all the angels and saints, and there join in their alleluias of praise, love and thanksgiving. I particularly beg this favour for the soul of N. N.

Ten Hail Marys. At the end say: 'Eternal rest give to them, O Lord, and let perpetual light shine upon them.'

SECOND MYSTERY: THE VISITATION
'And Mary, rising up in those days, went into the hill-country with haste, into a city of Juda. And she entered into the house of Zachary and saluted Elizabeth.' (Luke i. 39, 40.)

Prayer

O Mary, hasten also down to Purgatory and visit the

poor souls suffering there. Soothe, console and assist them through the merits of Thy Divine Son. As John the Baptist was sanctified even in his mother's womb when Thou didst visit Elizabeth, so also deign to go and bring good tidings of joy to those poor suffering ones in Purgatory, and they will exclaim with Thee: 'My soul doth magnify the Lord; for He that is mighty hath done great things to me, and holy is His Name, and His mercy is from generation unto generation to them that fear Him.' I beg this grace from Thee particularly for the soul of N. N.

Ten Hail Marys, etc., *as before.*

THIRD MYSTERY: THE NATIVITY

'The Angel said to the shepherds: Fear not: for behold, I bring you good tidings of great joy that shall be to all the people: for this day is born to you a Saviour, who is Christ the Lord, in the City of David; and this shall be a sign unto you: you shall find the infant wrapped in swaddling clothes and laid in a manger.' (Luke ii. 10, 12.)

Prayer

We beseech Thee, O Lord, send down an Angel to those poor suffering souls, and let them also hear the glad tidings, that the time of their redemption is near. Let them also say in the words of the shepherds: 'Come, let us go over to the heavenly Bethlehem and worship Jesus, not as a helpless Infant in His cradle, but as our Lord sitting at the right hand of His Father.' I particularly beg this grace for the soul of N. N.

Ten Hail Marys, etc.

FOURTH MYSTERY: THE PRESENTATION IN THE TEMPLE

'And when His parents brought in the child Jesus, to do for Him according to the custom of the law, he (Simeon) also took Him into his arms, and blessed God and said: Now Thou dost dismiss Thy servant, O Lord, according to Thy word, in peace. ...' (Luke ii. 27, 29.)

Prayer

O Mary, Mother of our Lord Jesus Christ, graciously deign to present Thy Divine Son anew to His Heavenly Father, for the poor suffering souls in Purgatory. Like holy Simeon, they are pining and sighing to see their holy Redeemer, and to be illumined by Him, who was a light to the revelation of the Gentiles, and the glory of the people of Israel. Obtain this grace for them, O Mother of Mercy, and especially for the soul of N. N.

Ten Hail Marys, etc.

FIFTH MYSTERY: THE FINDING IN THE TEMPLE

'And not finding Him, they returned into Jerusalem seeking Him. And it came to pass that after three days they found Him in the temple sitting in the midst of the doctors, hearing them and asking them questions.' (Luke ii. 45, 46.)

Prayer

We pray Thee, O most merciful Lord Jesus Christ, to comfort the poor suffering souls, separated from Thy presence. They long for Thee, and pine after Thee with the most ardent desires! Grant that they may soon arrive at the heavenly Jerusalem, and join with Thine Angels in their hymns of praise, love and thanksgiving to Thee for all eternity. This grace I most especially beg for the soul of N. N.

Ten Hail Marys, etc.

II—THE SORROWFUL MYSTERIES
The Creed, Our Father, three Hail Marys, Our Father.

FIRST MYSTERY: THE AGONY IN THE GARDEN
'And being in an agony, He prayed the longer, and His sweat became as drops of blood trickling down upon the ground.... And there appeared to Him an angel from Heaven strengthening Him.' (Luke xxii. 43, 44.)

Prayer

We beseech Thee, O Lord, to send down Thy holy Angel, to comfort the poor suffering souls in Purgatory, who are plunged into the deepest sorrow. Send them the happy tidings of their redemption. Or grant at least, that the bloody sweat may cool or entirely extinguish the fire in which they suffer. I beg this grace particularly for the soul of N. N.

Ten Hail Marys, ending with 'Eternal rest,' etc.

SECOND MYSTERY: THE SCOURGING AT THE PILLAR
'Then cried they all again, saying: Not this man, but Barabbas. Now Barabbas was a robber. Then, therefore, Pilate took Jesus and scourged Him.' (John xviii. 40; xix. 1.)

Prayer

We pray Thee, O most suffering Jesus, to purify the poor souls in Purgatory, with Thy most precious Blood, which Thou hast shed, when Thou wert so cruelly scourged: Cleanse them from all the remaining stains: and let the day of their deliverance soon dawn for them, particularly for the soul of N. N.

Ten Hail Marys, etc.

THIRD MYSTERY: THE CROWNING WITH THORNS

'And the soldiers plaiting a crown of thorns, put it upon His head; and they put on Him a purple garment. And they came to Him and said, Hail, King of the Jews: and they gave Him blows.' (John xix. 2, 3.)

Prayer

We beg of Thee, O Jesus, crowned with thorns, by the agony then caused Thee, to have compassion on poor suffering souls, and deliver them from their pains. Crown them with honour and glory, and receive them as subjects into Thy heavenly kingdom, where Thou reignest as King of kings. Have mercy particularly on the soul of N. N.

Ten Hail Marys, etc.

FOURTH MYSTERY: THE CARRYING OF THE CROSS

'And bearing His own cross He went forth to that place which is called Calvary, but in Hebrew Golgotha.' (John xix. 17.) 'And there followed Him a great multitude of people and of women who bewailed and lamented Him.' (Luke xxiii. 27.)

Prayer

We beseech Thee, O Lord, through the merits of the painful carrying of Thy Cross, deliver the poor suffering souls from the heavy burden of their torments. Behold, they are bowed down under the weight of their cross, as Thou wert under Thine. O do not suffer them to go to the summit of Calvary; but rather conduct them to the blessed Mountain of Sion, to the heavenly Jerusalem, to the company of the holy Angels and Saints. This blessing I most especially beg for N. N.

Ten Hail Marys, etc.

FIFTH MYSTERY: THE CRUCIFIXION AND DEATH OF OUR LORD

As Jesus hung on the Cross, He said to the thief on His right hand: 'Amen I say to thee, this day thou shalt be with Me in Paradise.' (Luke xxiii. 43.)

Prayer

O Jesus, who on the Cross didst pray for Thine enemies: 'Father, forgive them, for they know not what they do.' We plead likewise for the poor suffering souls of Thine elect. O forgive them as Thou didst forgive the good thief. They also cry out with him: Lord, remember us when Thou shalt come into Thy Kingdom. We most ardently beg of Thee, to say to them as Thou didst to the poor thief: 'Amen I say to you, this day you shall be with Me in Paradise.' I particularly beg this grace for the soul of N.N.

Ten Hail Marys, etc.

III.—THE GLORIOUS MYSTERIES
The Creed, Our Father, Three Hail Marys, Our Father.

FIRST MYSTERY: THE RESURRECTION
'And, behold, there was a great earthquake: for an Angel of the Lord descended from heaven, and, coming, rolled back the stone and sat upon it. ... And the Angel answering, said to the women: Fear not you: for I know that you seek Jesus who was crucified. He is not here: for He is risen, as He said. . . . .' (Matt, xxviii. 2, 5.)

Prayer

We beseech Thee, O Lord, through Thy glorious Resurrection, to deliver the poor souls from their prison, and roll away the stone from their tomb, that they may ascend to, and be with Thee for ever; grant that it may be said of them: they have risen from their grave of sorrow, they are no longer here; the Lord has wiped away their tears; their mourning is turned into joy; the time of their suffering is past. This mercy I particularly request for the soul of N. N.

Ten Hail Marys, ending with 'Eternal rest,' etc.

SECOND MYSTERY: THE ASCENSION
'And the Lord Jesus, after He had spoken to them, was taken up into heaven, and sitteth on the right hand of God.' (Mark xvi. 19.) 'And they adoring, went back into Jerusalem with great joy. And they were always in the temple, praising and blessing God. Amen.' (Luke xxiv. 52.)

Prayer

We beseech Thee, O King of Glory, who didst triumphantly ascend into heaven, remember the poor suffering souls in Purgatory. Thou hast said to Thy Apostles, I go to prepare a dwelling-place for you; and when I have prepared it, I will take you to Me, so that where I am you may be also. Have compassion on the poor suffering souls; their dwelling is already prepared for them: Heaven is open to them. Oh, let them come to Thee that they may offer thanksgiving and praises with the Apostles in the temple of Thy Glory. I beg this great mercy particularly for the soul of N. N.

Ten Hail Marys, etc.

THIRD MYSTERY: THE DESCENT OF THE HOLY GHOST

'And when the days of the pentecost were accomplished, they were all together in one place. And suddenly there came a sound from heaven, as of a mighty wind coming and it filled the whole house where they were sitting. And there appeared to them parted tongues, as it were, of fire, and it sat upon every one of them. And they were all filled with the Holy Ghost. ...' (Acts ii. 1-4.)

Prayer

We implore Thee, O Lord Jesus Christ, to send down Thy Holy Spirit also to the poor suffering souls in Purgatory, in order to be their true Comforter. Grant that Thy Divine Spirit may be to them a mighty wind, wafting them into the haven of rest; a holy fire consuming all that may prevent them from entering the gates of heaven. Then they will sing: Blessed be the God of all consolation, who has comforted us in our tribulation.

Ten Hail Marys, etc.

FOURTH MYSTERY: THE ASSUMPTION OF THE
BLESSED VIRGIN INTO HEAVEN

'Mary is taken up into heaven; the angels rejoice and sing hymns of praise and thanksgivings to the Lord' (Antiphon).

Prayer

O Lord, who hast preserved from the universal corruption the body of the Blessed Virgin Mary, from which Thy Only Begotten Son has taken our human nature unto Himself, we beseech Thee, through the merits of that immaculate Virgin, have mercy on all the poor souls in Purgatory, and deliver them from their sufferings, particularly the soul of N. N. O grant that they may be taken up into heaven, there to love and bless Thy Name for ever and ever. Amen.

Ten Hail Marys, etc.

FIFTH MYSTERY: THE CORONATION OF THE
BLESSED VIRGIN IN HEAVEN

'And the king arose to meet her (his mother) and bowed to her, and sat down upon his throne. And a throne was set for the king's mother, and she sat on his right hand.' (3 Kings ii. 19.)

Prayer

Hail, holy Queen, Mother of Mercy! our life, our sweetness and our hope! To thee do we cry, poor banished children of Eve! To thee do appeal the souls in Purgatory! Turn, then, O most gracious advocate, thine eyes of mercy towards them, and especially upon N. N., and after this their exile show unto them the blessed fruit of thy womb, Jesus, O clement, O loving, O sweet Virgin Mary!

Ten Hail Marys, etc.

THE LITANY OF THE BLESSED VIRGIN

The following indulgences, all applicable to the souls in Purgatory, can be gained by saying this Litany:

1. Three hundred days for each recitation.

2. Whoever says this Litany regularly every day, can gain a Plenary indulgence on her five principal feasts, namely: The Immaculate Conception; the Nativity; the Annunciation; the Purification; the Assumption; after having confessed and received Holy Communion, visited a chapel and prayed for the intention of our Holy Father the Pope. (Rescript, Sep. 30th, 1817.)

Lord, have mercy on us.
Christ, have mercy on us.
Lord, have mercy on us.
Christ, hear us.
Christ, graciously hear us.
God the Father of heaven,
Have mercy on us.
God the Son, Redeemer of the world,
Have mercy on us.
God the Holy Ghost,
Have mercy on us.
Holy Trinity, one God,
Have mercy on us.
Holy Mary, Pray for us.
Holy Mother of God,
Holy Virgin of Virgins,
Mother of Christ,
Mother of Divine Grace,
Mother most pure,
Mother most chaste,
Mother inviolate,
Mother undefiled,

Mother most amiable,
Mother most admirable,
Mother of our Creator,
Mother of our Redeemer,
Virgin most prudent,
Virgin most venerable,
Virgin most renowned,
Virgin most powerful,
Virgin most merciful,
Virgin most faithful,
Mirror of Justice,
Seat of Wisdom,
Cause of our joy,
Spiritual Vessel,
Vessel of honour,
Singular Vessel of devotion,
Mystical Rose,
Tower of David,
Tower of ivory,
House of gold,
Ark of the Covenant,
Gate of heaven,
Morning Star,
Health of the sick,
Refuge of sinners,
Comforter of the afflicted,
Help of Christians,
Queen of Angels,
Queen of Patriarchs,
Queen of Prophets,
Queen of Apostles,
Queen of Martyrs,

Pray for us

Queen of Confessors,
Queen of Virgins,
Queen of all Saints,
Queen conceived without
original sin,
Queen of the most holy Rosary,

Pray for us

Lamb of God, that takest away the sins of the
world,
Spare us, O Lord.

Lamb of God, that takest away the sins of the
world,
Graciously hear us, O Lord.

Lamb of God, that takest away the sins of the
world,
Have mercy on us.

Christ, hear us.
Christ, graciously hear us.

Lord, have mercy on us.
Christ, have mercy on us.

Lord, have mercy on us.

Our Father.   Hail Mary.

V. Pray for us, O holy Mother of God.

R. That we may be made worthy of the promises of
Christ.

Let us pray.

Pour forth, we beseech Thee, O Lord, Thy grace into
our hearts; that we, to whom the Incarnation of Christ
Thy Son was made known by the message of an angel,
may by His passion and cross be brought to the glory of
His resurrection. Through the same Christ our Lord.
Amen.

V. Pray for us, O holy Saint Joseph.

R. That we may be made worthy of the promises of Christ.

Let us pray.

Assist us, O Lord, we beseech Thee, by the merits of the Spouse of Thy most holy Mother, that what our unworthiness cannot obtain may be given us by his intercession with Thee. Who livest and reignest with Cod the Father in the unity of the Holy Ghost, world without end. Amen.

LITANY FOR THE DEAD

Lord, have mercy on us.
Christ, have mercy on us.
Lord, have mercy on us.
Jesus, receive our prayers.
Lord Jesus, grant our petitions.

God the Father of heaven, who hast called the departed unto Thy beatific vision,

God the Son, Redeemer of the world, who hast purchased the souls of the faithful by Thy precious Blood,

God the Holy Ghost, who hast sanctified the elect by Thy grace,

Holy Trinity, one God, and only supreme good of the souls who ardently long to possess Thee,

Holy Mary, comfort in their affliction, refuge in their abandonment, and sure help in their misery,

Saint Michael, appointed prince to receive the souls of the faithful departed, *Pray for them.*

Have mercy on them

Saint Gabriel, especially chosen to announce to the people of God the end of their misery and the beginning of their deliverance,

Saint Raphael, who bearest the sighs of the oppressed to the throne of God,

All ye holy guardian angels, who cannot abandon in the midst of their sufferings the souls entrusted to your care, till they are brought forth unto everlasting rest,

All ye holy angels and archangels, who regard those poor sufferers as your future companions,

All ye holy Patron Saints, for whose assistance they so earnestly prayed, awaiting the dreadful moment on which their eternity depended,

All ye holy Patriarchs and Prophets, who so long and ardently sighed for your redemption,

All ye holy Apostles and Evangelists, who, as princes of the kingdom of Christ, have so much power near the throne of glory,

All ye holy Martyrs, who, purified by the fire of your love in shedding your blood for Christ, were immediately vouchsafed the beatific vision,

All ye holy confessors and penitents, who have gained so much merit, and are so pleasing in the eyes of God,

All ye holy virgins, who, by the splendour of purity and innocence, are permitted to follow the Lamb,

All ye holy saints of God, who desire to see your numbers increased,

Pray for them.

Be merciful to them.
Spare them, O Lord.
Be merciful unto them.
Hear them, O Lord.
From their prison of fire,
From their painful sufferings,
From their gloomy darkness,
From their sadness and abandonment,
From their separation from Thee,
Through Thy coming down from the bosom of
    Thy heavenly Father,
Through Thy conception in the womb of the
    most blessed Virgin,
Through Thy birth in a stable,
Through Thy holy name of Jesus,
Through Thy forty days' fast,
Through Thy sufferings and sorrows,
Through Thy death on the Cross,
Through Thy glorious resurrection and
    ascension into Heaven,
Through the descent of the Holy Ghost,
We poor sinners, *beseech Thee hear us.*
That Thou wouldst spare them, *we beseech*, etc.
That Thou wouldst accept the sacrifice of the Mass, our
    prayers, and good works in expiation for their sins,
    we beseech, etc.
That Thou wouldst soon take them up to *Thee, we*
    beseech, etc.
Son of God, *we beseech*, etc.
Lamb of God, who takest away the sins of the world,
    Give them eternal rest.

Deliver them, O Lord.

Lamb of God, who takest away the sins of the world,
Let perpetual light shine upon them.
Lamb of God, who takest away the sins of the world,
Let them rest in peace.
Lord, have mercy on us.
Christ, have mercy on us.
Lord, have mercy on us.
Our Father.   Hail Mary.
V. O Lord, hear my prayer.
R. And let my cry come unto Thee.

LET US PRAY.

O God, the giver of pardon and lover of the salvation of men, we beseech Thy clemency that Thou wouldst grant the brethren, relations, and benefactors of our congregation, who have departed out of this world, to arrive, through the intercession of the blessed Mary ever virgin and all Thy Saints, at the fellowship of perpetual bliss. Through Jesus Christ our Lord. Amen.

V. Eternal rest give to them, O Lord.
R. And let perpetual light shine upon them.
V. May the souls of the faithful departed, through the mercy of God, rest in peace.
R. Amen.

LITANY OF THE BITTER PASSION

FOR THE REPOSE OF THE POOR SOULS

Lord, have mercy on us.
Christ, have mercy on us.
Lord, have mercy on us.
Christ, hear us.
Christ, graciously hear us.
God the Father of Heaven,
Have mercy on the souls of the faithful departed.
God the Son, Redeemer of the world,
God the Holy Ghost,
Holy Trinity one God,
Jesus, victim of love,
Jesus, who didst drink the bitter chalice for the redemption of mankind,
Jesus, who didst sweat blood in the agony of the garden,
Jesus, who was imprisoned and bound like a common malefactor,
Jesus, who wast mocked aud cruelly beaten,
Jesus, who wast painfully scourged and crowned with thorns,
Jesus, who didst carry the sins of the world on Thy Cross,
Jesus, who was cruelly nailed to the Cross,
Jesus, who, stretched out on the Cross, didst endure the most awful agony,
Jesus, who, when thirsting, wast given gall and vinegar to drink,

Have mercy on the souls in Purgatory.

Jesus, who, in the pangs of death, wast derided
  and mocked,

Jesus, who didst greatly suffer to see Thy
  afflicted Mother under the Cross,

Jesus, who didst commend Thy dearest Mother to
  St. John,

Jesus, who, after three hours of agony on the
  Cross, with a loud cry didst give up the Ghost,

Jesus, who by Thy passion and death, didst open
  for us the gates of Paradise,

    Lamb of God, who takest away the sins of
the world,

    Spare the poor souls in Purgatory.

    Lamb of God, who takest away the sins of
the world,

    Hear the sighs of the poor souls in Purgatory.

    Lamb of God, who takest away the sins of the
world,

    *Have mercy on the poor souls in Purgatory, and give
them eternal rest.*

    Our Father.   Hail Mary.

Prayer

O Lord Jesus Christ, who hast died for us on the
Cross, have mercy on the poor suffering souls in
Purgatory, and purify them, by Thy most precious Blood,
from all stains which may still cling to them and displease
Thy divine goodness. Offer up the prize of Thy painful
sufferings, Thy Blood and many wounds, and, finally, Thy
shameful death on the Cross to Thy eternal Father, that
He may graciously remit their punishments, and
mercifully receive them into His heavenly kingdom.
Through the same Christ our Lord. Amen.

THE LITANY OF THE SAINTS

FOR THE REPOSE OF THE POOR SOULS

Lord, have mercy on us.
Christ, have mercy on us.
Lord, have mercy on us.
Christ, hear us.
Christ, graciously hear us.
God the Father of Heaven,
Have mercy on the souls in Purgatory.
God the Son, Redeemer of the world,
Have mercy on the souls in Purgatory.
God the Holy Ghost,
Have mercy on the souls in Purgatory.
Holy Trinity, one God,
Have mercy on the souls in Purgatory.
Holy Mary,   *Pray for them.*
Holy Mother of God,
Holy Virgin of virgins,
St. Michael,
All ye holy Angels and Archangels,
St. John Baptist,
St. Joseph,
All ye holy Patriarchs and Prophets,
St. Peter,
St. Paul,
St. John,
All ye holy Apostles and Evangelists,
St. Stephen,
St. Lawrence,
All ye holy Martyrs,

Pray for them.

St. Gregory,
All ye holy Bishops and Confessors,
All ye holy Monks and Hermits,
St. Mary Magdalen,
St. Barbara,
St. Catherine,
All ye holy Virgins and Widows,
All ye holy saints of God,

Pray for them.

    Be gracious unto them,
    Spare them, O Lord.
    Be merciful unto them,
    Graciously hear them, O Lord.
From all evil, *Deliver them, O Lord.*
From all their sins,
From their punishment,
From Thy wrath,
From Thy angry justice,
From the power of the enemy,
From the gnawing worm of conscience,
From their weary desires,
From their frightful flames,
From their unbearable cold,
From their horrible darkness,
From their painful tortures,
From their unceasing weeping and lamentation,
From their fearful imprisonment,
Through Thy miraculous conception,
Through Thy holy Birth,
Through Thy painful Circumcision,
Through Thy flight into Egypt,
Through Thy holy Name,
Through Thy holy Baptism and severe Fast,

Deliver them, O Lord.

Through Thy profound humility,
Through Thy spotless chastity,
Through Thy extreme poverty,
Through Thy perfect obedience,
Through Thy great patience and meekness,
Through Thine infinite love,
Through Thy bitter passion,
Through Thy fear and agony,
Through Thy sweat of blood,
Through Thy severe imprisonment,
Through Thy cruel scourging,
Through Thy painful crowning with thorns,
Through Thy weary carrying of Thy Cross,
Through Thy cruel crucifixion,
Through Thy bitter death,
Through Thy five holy wounds,
Through Thy most precious Blood shed for us,
Through Thy glorious Resurrection,
Through Thy wonderful Ascension,
Through the descent of the Holy Ghost,
Through the merits and intercession of Thy most
  holy Mother,
Through the merits and intercession of all Thy
  saints,
We poor sinners, *We beseech thee, to hear us.*
That Thou wouldst spare the suffering souls,
That Thou wouldst forgive them their sins,
That Thou wouldst hear their prayers and
  supplications,
That Thou wouldst save them from their
  torments,
That Thou wouldst free them from their weary

imprisonment,

That Thou wouldst give them part in the good works and prayers of the Christian world,

That Thou wouldst graciously listen to their prayers for us, and ours for them, now and in all times to come,

That Thou wouldst comfort them by Thy holy angels,

That Thou wouldst lead them through St. Michael to eternal light,

That Thou wouldst soon vouchsafe them Thy beatific vision,

That Thou wouldst give to the souls of our parents, friends, benefactors, sisters, and brothers the joys of eternal life,

That Thou wouldst show compassion and mercy to those poor neglected souls, who have no one on earth to remember to them or pray for them,

That Thou wouldst have mercy on the souls of all the faithful departed,

That Thou wouldst graciously hear us,

We beseech Thee to hear us.

Lamb of God, who takest away the sins of the world,
Spare them, O Lord.

Lamb of God, who takest away the sins of the world.
Graciously hear them, O Lord.

Lamb of God, who takest away the sins of the world.
Have mercy on them, O Lord.

Christ, hear us.
Christ, graciously hear us.

Lord, have mercy on us.
Christ, have mercy on us.

Lord, have mercy on us.

V. Eternal rest give to them, O Lord.
R. And let perpetual light shine upon them.
V. From the gates of hell.
R. Deliver them. O Lord.
V. May they rest in peace.
R. Amen.
V. O Lord, hear our prayer.
R. And let our cry come unto Thee.

Prayer

O Lord, to whom it is proper to spare and have mercy, we beg of Thee in all humility to have pity on the souls of Thy poor servants, N. N., whom Thou hast called away from this world. O do not be unmindful of them, and grant that they may not fall into the hands of the enemy. Send down Thy holy angels to conduct them into Thy holy dwellings. Grant that they who have believed and hoped in Thee may not suffer the pains of hell, but obtain the everlasting joys of heaven, through Christ our Lord. Amen.

V. Eternal rest give to them, O Lord.
R. And let perpetual light shine upon them.
V. May they rest in peace.
R. Amen.

AN ACT OF SELF-OBLATION

FOR THE REPOSE OF THE POOR SOULS

O most Holy Trinity, I offer to Thy Divine Majesty all my actions and labours, all my thoughts, words, and deeds, all my crosses and sufferings, my indulgences and other devotions. I desire that all my actions may be performed for the greater honour and glory of God, and united with the holy practices of the blessed Virgin Mary, St. Joseph, and all the Saints. Whatever satisfaction I make, and whatever I may hope from the mercy of God, either here or here after, I offer it up, according to Thy own will and in the spirit of charity, for the solace and release of the poor suffering souls. I pray Thee, have mercy on them, particularly on the soul of N. N. Accept my offering, O God, and vouchsafe to shorten the sufferings of the poor souls, whom I have recommended to Thee, and deliver them entirely from the pains of Purgatory.

SHORT INDULGENCED PRAYERS

APPLICABLE TO THE SOULS IN PURGATORY
Holy, Holy, Holy, Lord God of hosts, the earth is full of Thy majesty. Glory be to the Father, Glory be to the Son, Glory be to the Holy Ghost.

Indulgence of one hundred days, if said once a day. Plenary, once a month for the daily recital, and after reception of the Sacraments. Clement XIV, June 26, 1770.

'May the most just, most high, most adorable will of God be done in all things, and praised and magnified for ever.'

Indulgence of one hundred days, once a day. Pius VII, May 19, 1818.

Eternal Father, I offer Thee the precious Blood of
Jesus in satisfaction for my sins, and for the wants of Thy
holy Church.

Indulgence of one hundred days, each time it is said. Pius VII,
March 29, 1817.

Thanks and praises without end be to the Most Holy
and Divine Sacrament.

One hundred days' indulgence, once a day. Plenary indulgence if
said every day for a month, and under the usual conditions. Pius VI,
May 24, 1776.

My sweet Jesus, mercy!

One hundred days' indulgence each time it is said. Leo XII, 1824,
and Pius IX, September 23, 1857.

Jesus, my God, I love Thee above all things.

Fifty days' indulgence. Pius IX, May 7, 1854.

Sweetest Jesus, be not unto me a Judge but a Saviour.

Fifty days' indulgence, each time it is said. Pius IX, August 11,
1851.

Jesus, meek and humble of heart, make my heart like
unto Thine.

Three hundred days' indulgence. Pius IX, January 25,1863.

Jesus, Mary, and Joseph, to you I give my heart and
my soul.

Jesus, Mary, and Joseph, assist me in my last agony.

Jesus, Mary, and Joseph, may I breathe forth my soul
with you in peace!

Three hundred days' indulgence, each time these prayers are
devoutly said. Pius VII, April 29, 1807.

Acknowledged, blessed, praised, loved, honoured and glorified, be everywhere, and at all times, the divine Heart of Jesus and the most pure Heart of Mary.

Sixty days' indulgence, once a day.

Sweet Heart of Mary, be my salvation!

Three hundred days' indulgence, each time this prayer is said. Plenary indulgence once a month, after having said it daily, and received the Sacraments with the usual conditions. Pius IX, September 30, 1852.

O Angel of God, whom God hath appointed to be my guardian, enlighten and protect, direct and govern me. Amen.

One hundred days' indulgence, each time it is said. Pius VII, May 15, 1821.

OTHER DEVOTIONS FOR THE DEPARTED

REMEMBRANCE OF THE PRECIOUS BLOOD SHED AT SEVEN
DIFFERENT TIMES

1. O sweetest Jesus, the poor souls in Purgatory, so dear to Thee, remind Thee of Thy precious Blood, which Thou hast shed for us at Thy painful circumcision, and cry to Thee, saying: For the sake of that precious Blood do not forget us, but comfort us in our sorrow, and deign to admit us into the kingdom of Thy glory, that we may rejoice and praise and glorify Thee for ever and ever. Amen.

2. O meekest Jesus, I recommend to Thy mercy all those poor souls, for whom I am most bound to pray. In the garden of Olives Thou didst suffer such anguish, that Thy Body was bathed in a bloody sweat, which saturated the earth around. For the sake of that holy Blood, I beseech Thee, remember those poor souls, and forget them not. Alleviate their great sufferings, and grant them quick deliverance. Amen.

3. O sweetest Jesus, the painful scourging at the pillar made Thy Blood flow in streams for our salvation, and it is therefore a Forget-me-not of Thy great love. Oh, forget not the poor souls of my dear parents, brothers, sisters, relations, and friends, and grant that even one drop of that precious Blood may flow down to Purgatory, to quench the burning flames and bring eternal rest to them. Amen.

4. O most merciful Jesus, Thy divine Head, Thy sacred Face, is quite disfigured with the Blood pressed out by the cruel crown of thorns. This Blood was also shed for those poor souls in Purgatory, to whom I may have been an

occasion of sin. I therefore appeal to Thy love and mercy to look down on them, and apply to them the merits of this shedding of Thy precious Blood. Amen.

5. O most gracious Saviour, when Thou wert stripped of Thy garments, Thy painful wounds were torn open afresh, and Blood flowed forth anew from them. Oh, let the blessing of this painful shedding of Thy Blood flow upon those poor souls who have to suffer longest. Show that Thou hast not forgotten them. Shorten their torments, I implore Thee, and give them eternal rest. Amen.

6. O my Divine Saviour, I thank Thee for Thine infinite love and mercy in giving Thyself up to be nailed to the Cross, so that Thy sacred Blood might flow in streams from Thy Hands and Feet. I beseech Thee, apply the merits of that shedding of Thy sacred Blood to the most abandoned souls in Purgatory. Refresh them with Thy divine consolation, and show them that though forgotten by all, they are not forgotten by Thee. Amen.

O most loving Jesus, from the wounds of Thy holy Heart flowed blood and water, to wash away all the sins of the world. Offer up, I beseech Thee, this shedding of Blood for those poor souls who are nearest to their deliverance, that they may obtain full remission of all their debts. Amen.

REMEMBRANCE OF THE FIVE WOUNDS OF CHRIST

DIVINE SAVIOUR, for our sakes hast Thou been wounded, and each wound which Thou hast received is a proof of Thy love for us. Therefore hast Thou retained the marks of those wounds even after Thy death, carried them with Thee into Heaven, and Thou wilt appear with them on the day of judgment, in order to show them to all men. They are for us and for Thee a true Forget-me-not. They remind Thee of what Thou hast done for us, and they will bring to our remembrance all Thy dreadful sufferings, Thy lifelong endurance, and Thy painful death. It is therefore my duty to meditate often on Thy five wounds, to adore them in the spirit of humility and contrition, and in all necessities to fly to them. On these grounds, therefore, I venture to appeal to Thee on behalf of the poor souls in Purgatory. I commend them to Thy holy Wounds, and beg of Thee, through Thy holy merits, to deliver them from their sufferings.

1. With deepest humility I kiss the holy wound of Thy right Hand, and implore Thee, in memory of the pain Thou didst feel when it was cruelly pierced with the rough nail, to be mindful of the poor souls in Purgatory, particularly N. N. Oh, forget them not! Let Thy right Hand open the door of their prison, and give them the freedom of the children of God.

2. With sincere contrition I kiss the wound of Thy left Hand, and beg of Thee to purify with the Blood which flowed from its holy palm the poor souls in Purgatory, particularly N. N., from whatever stains may still be

cleaving to them. Oh, forget them not, and conduct them with Thy pierced left Hand from their place of darkness into Thy blessed kingdom of light!

3. With deepest veneration I kiss the wound of Thy right Foot, and worship the precious Blood which has flowed therefrom for the salvation of the world. Oh, let but one drop of that precious Blood pour into Purgatory, to soothe and comfort the poor souls there, particularly N. N. Oh, forget them not, but hasten to meet them with Thy joyful invitation: 'Come to Me, all ye that labour, and I will refresh you.'

4. With the most ardent love I kiss the wound of Thy left Foot, and, full of confidence in the infinite merits of this wound, I cry from the depths of my heart to Thee for refreshment and freedom for the poor souls in Purgatory, especially N. N. Oh, forget them not, but go and bring them the joyful tidings of their redemption, and they will fall down at Thy Feet with joy and thanksgiving for Thy divine mercy.

5. With glowing devotion I kiss the wound in Thy Side, and recommend to Thee all the poor souls in Purgatory, particularly N. N. It is this wound that reveals to us the depths of Thy great love. We see through it into Thy sacred Heart, which beats and bleeds for us alone. Oh, do not close it against the poor souls, but let it be the gate through which they soon may enter into the joys of Paradise.

THE 'OUR FATHER' FOR THE SOULS OF THE DEPARTED

FROM ST. MECHTILDIS

'Our Father who art in Heaven.' I beseech Thee that Thou wouldst forgive all the souls in Purgatory who have not duly loved nor worthily honoured Thee, their adorable and most beloved Father who of Thine own mere grace didst adopt them to be Thy children, but have thrust Thee forth from their hearts, in which Thou didst delight to dwell. And in satisfaction for this, their sin, I offer Thee that love and honour which Thy beloved Son showed Thee upon earth, and that most abundant satisfaction which He hath made for all their sins. Amen.

'Hallowed be Thy Name' I beseech Thee, O Father of Compassion, forgive the souls of the faithful departed whereinsoever they have not worthily honoured nor duly made mention of Thy holy Name; but have taken it in vain, and by their lukewarm life rendered themselves unworthy of the name of Christians. And in satisfaction for these their sins I offer Thee the consummate holiness of Thy Son, whereby He magnified Thy Name by His teaching, and glorified it by His work.

'Thy kingdom come.' I beseech Thee, O Father of Compassion, vouchsafe to forgive the souls of the faithful departed whereinsoever they have not fervently longed nor ardently striven after Thee and Thy kingdom, in which alone is true rest and abiding glory. And for this and all their sloth in doing good I offer Thee the most holy and longing desires of Thy Son, wherewith He desired to make them heirs together with Him of His

kingdom. Amen.

'Thy will be done on earth as it is in Heaven.' I beseech Thee, O Father of Compassion, vouchsafe to forgive the souls of the faithful departed, whereinsoever they have not preferred Thy will above their own, nor have loved it in all things; but have too often lived and acted only according to their own will. And in satisfaction for this their disobedience I offer Thee the union of the sweetest Heart of Thy Son with Thy will, and all His most ready and loving obedience wherewith He was obedient unto death, even to the death of the Cross. Amen.

'Give us this day our daily bread.' I beseech Thee, O Father of Compassion, vouchsafe to forgive the souls of the faithful departed, whereinsoever they have not received the most blessed and adorable Sacrament of the Altar with pure and perfect desire, devotion, and love; or have received it unworthily, or seldom, or not at all. And in satisfaction for these their sins, I offer Thee the consummate holiness and the devotion of Thy Son, together with that most ardent love and ineffable yearning desire wherewith He bestowed upon us this most inestimable treasure. Amen.

'And forgive us our trespasses, as we forgive them that trespass against us.' I beseech Thee, O Father of Compassion, vouchsafe to forgive the souls of the faithful departed, whereinsoever they have sinned against Thee by any one of the seven deadly sins, and especially wherein they have not forgiven those who had trespassed against them, or have not loved their enemies. And for all these their sins I offer Thee that most tender and sweet prayer which Thy Son made to Thee for His enemies while hanging on the Cross.

'And lead us not into temptation.' I beseech Thee, O Father of Compassion, vouchsafe to forgive the souls of the faithful departed, whereinsoever they have not resisted their concupiscence and evil inclinations, but have again and again consented to the devil and the flesh, and entangled themselves by their own will in many grievous faults. And for all these, their manifold sins I offer Thee the glorious victory wherewith Thy Son overcame the world and the devil, together with His most holy life and conversation, His toil and weariness, His most bitter Passion and His Death. Amen.

'But deliver us from evil.' Deliver us and them from all evil, through the merits of Thy beloved Son, and bring us to the kingdom of Thy glory, which is none other than Thy most glorious Self. Amen.

THE 'HAIL MARY' FOR THE POOR SOULS

'Hail Mary.' O most merciful Mother, look graciously down on thine afflicted and sorrowful children, who are suffering such torments in the flames of Purgatory. We beg of thee, in memory of the great joy thou didst feel at the annunciation of the Angel, that thou wouldst take pity on those poor souls, and send to them likewise an Angel of the Lord to announce to them the joyful tidings of redemption from their gloomy prison.

'Full of grace.' O Mother of Divine Grace, obtain from the Almighty God mercy and complete forgiveness of the heavy punishment which they are now suffering.

'The Lord is with thee!' He will refuse thee nothing; He will hear thy requests, and show mercy to the poor afflicted souls.

'Blessed art thou amongst women!' Yes, truly thou art blessed and exalted above all creatures on earth. Therefore bless and gladden by thy powerful intercession these poor imprisoned souls, and deliver them from their burning chains.

'And blessed is the fruit of thy womb, Jesus,' who is the Saviour and Sanctifier of the whole world, whom thou, a virgin, didst give birth to without pain. O most merciful Jesus, divine fruit of her Immaculate virginity, have compassion on the poor souls! O most merciful Mother, hasten to their assistance!

'Holy Mary, Mother of God, pray for us poor sinners,' and for the poor souls in Purgatory, now and at all times, but particularly at *the hour of our death*; and as thou didst come to those poor souls in their last struggle with death, and in their agony, so I beseech thee to assist them and comfort them in their great suffering and sad imprisonment, that through the merits of thy maternal intercession they may arrive at the heavenly joys of the blessed kingdom, and rejoice for all eternity. Amen.

A PRAYER TO THE MOTHER OF GOD

MOST HIGH and mighty Queen of Heaven, I throw myself at thy feet and solemnly acknowledge thee as the Mother of mercy and the true comforter of the afflicted. Both these titles encourage me to fly to thee, and with unshaken confidence to plead for the poor suffering souls in Purgatory. Therefore in all humility I beg of thee now to exert the whole power of thy intercession with thy well-beloved Son, particularly for the soul of N., whom He has redeemed by His precious Blood, and whom thy merciful love hath protected from so many sins during life. Oh, deliver her from the pains of Purgatory by the word of a Mother who is all-powerful with God. Be her mighty advocate! I implore thee to plead her cause, so that she may soon be delivered from the prison to which the justice of God has condemned her. Break her bonds which still confine her to the dungeon, and fulfil her yearning desires with which she longs to behold thee with thy Divine Son in everlasting contemplation. O Queen of Heaven and of earth, make haste to intercede for her, for thou also hadst a share in the salvation and joy of those souls which Christ has washed in His precious Blood. When Jesus sees thy great anxiety about those souls, surely He will shorten the term of their suffering, or for love of thee admit them to the joys of Paradise. I beseech thee, renew and double thy petitions for the soul I most particularly pray for; and the granting of thy request will bring joy to three hearts: to thine, because thy wishes were so happily fulfilled; to mine, because my ardent request is heard; and to the poor soul who is admitted to the joys of Heaven. Amen.

A PRAYER TO OUR LADY OF SORROWS

MOST SORROWFUL VIRGIN MARY, Mother of my Redeemer, full of compassion and sadness, I recall to my mind the great sufferings of thy maternal heart, which thou didst endure in receiving the martyr's crown on the hill of Calvary. It was there that, according to Simeon's prophecy, a sword did pierce thy most tender heart. O most exalted Mother of God! how great and immovable was thy faith; how firm thy confidence in God's wise providence; how brave thy submission and how persevering thy patience! To thee I now address the most urgent prayer in behalf of the poor suffering souls in Purgatory. I implore thee to use thy powerful intercession for them! Ah, these poor suffering souls cry out piteously for deliverance from their torments. There are few amongst them who, during their lifetime, have not honoured and loved thee as the Mother of God. Canst thou forget thy poor abandoned children, who mourn and lament without ceasing? I particularly commend to thy maternal love the souls of N. N.; through the merits of thy dolours soothe their sufferings, and by thine intercession with God hasten the day of deliverance. Thou hast wept many bitter tears while on earth; many and heavy were thy trials, and thou hast been almost submerged in a boundless sea of sorrows. Therefore thou knowest from personal experience what it is to suffer! For this reason thy maternal heart has more compassion for the sufferings of others. Oh, show it then indeed! Take up thy hands to thy

Divine Son, and ask for their deliverance, so that they
may experience to their great comfort that thou art in
truth the Mother of the poor souls. Amen.

A PRAYER IN HONOUR OF THE SEVEN DOLOURS OF
THE BLESSED VIRGIN

1. O most sorrowful Mother Mary, I remind thee of
the sorrow which filled thy heart when, on presenting thy
Divine Son in the Temple, holy Simeon foretold that a
sword should pierce thy soul, thereby announcing the
share thou wouldst have in the sufferings of thy Divine
Son. I most devoutly compassionate thy grief on this
occasion, and beseech thee, O glorious Queen of Martyrs,
to obtain for me, through the sufferings of Jesus Christ,
which were the great cause of thy dolours, a sincere and
lively horror of sin, an ardent love of God and a practical
devotion to thee. But above all, I beg of thee, through the
merits of thy dolours, to intercede for the poor suffering
souls in Purgatory, that they may be released from their
banishment, and admitted to the joys of Paradise. *Hail
Mary*.

2. O most sorrowful Mother Mary, I remind thee of
the sorrow which filled thy tender heart when thou didst
see thy Divine Son persecuted by His own creatures, and
were obliged to fly into Egypt to save Him from the fury
of Herod. I most devoutly compassionate thy grief on this
occasion, and beseech thee, O glorious Queen of Martyrs,
to protect me on my journey towards eternity. But, above
all, I implore thee to think of the poor souls that suffer
still in the land of exile. Lead them into the blessed home

of the Saints, and to the joys of eternal life. *Hail Mary.*

3. O most sorrowful Mother Mary, I remind thee of the exceeding great sorrow which filled thy maternal heart, when thou hadst lost thy dearest Child, who remained in the Temple of Jerusalem, and wert seeking Him with tears and sighs for three days. I most devoutly compassionate thy grief on that occasion, and beseech thee, O glorious Queen of Martyrs, to obtain for me the grace of never losing my Jesus from my heart, and of never being separated from Him through sin. I implore thee also to use thy influence on behalf of those poor suffering souls in Purgatory. O grant that they may no longer be deprived of the divine presence, and that they may soon enjoy the delights of their heavenly home for ever and ever. *Hail Mary.*

4. O most sorrowful Mother Mary, I remind thee of the unspeakable sorrow which filled thy maternal heart when thou didst meet thy dear Son laden with the Cross, and going out to Mount Calvary to die on it for us sinners. I most devoutly compassionate thy grief on that occasion, and beseech thee, O glorious Queen of Martyrs, to meet me also on my journey towards eternity, and not to suffer me to walk alone and unassisted. I also implore thee, most compassionate Mother, to offer up the rich treasury of all thy tears and dolours to the Divine Justice in satisfaction for the sins of the poor souls who have run their course here, but suffer still hereafter. *Hail Mary.*

5. O most sorrowful Mother Mary, I remind thee of the bitter sorrow which filled thine inmost soul, when thou didst stand by the Cross of Jesus, witness His agony and abandonment, and see Him at length expire for the sins of the world. I devoutly compassionate thy grief on

that occasion, and beseech thee, O glorious Queen of Martyrs, to obtain for me, through the sufferings of Jesus Christ, which were the great cause of thine, a sincere and lively horror of sin, an ardent love of God, a tender and practical devotion to thee. I also implore thee to turn thy pitying eyes on the poor souls suffering in Purgatory. I recommend them to thy love and powerful intercession, as Jesus, dying on the Cross, did recommend thee to the care and protection of His beloved disciple, St. John. I also recommend to thee my own person, and beg thy protection for it in the last awful trial of death, that I may depart this life in the blessed company of Jesus and with thy powerful protection. *Hail Mary.*

6. O most sorrowful Mother Mary, I remind thee of the sorrow which filled thy maternal heart, when the sacred Side of thy beloved Son was pierced by the lance, and the adorable Body of thy Divine Son, all covered with wounds, was taken down from the Cross and laid in thy arms, so that every glance of thine eyes were like so many swords piercing thy soul. I most devoutly compassionate thy grief on that occasion, and beseech thee, O Queen of Martyrs, to take the suffering souls in Purgatory, whose hopes are placed in thee, into thine arms of mercy, and open for them the gates of Paradise. But to me, O Queen of Martyrs, grant that at all times I may have free access to thy motherly heart of mercy. May thy loving heart ever be my refuge, my hope, and my salvation. *Hail Mary.*

7. O most sorrowful Mother Mary, I remind thee of the sorrow which filled thy maternal heart when the sacred Body of Jesus was taken from thine arms and laid in the sepulchre. I most devoutly compassionate thy grief

on that occasion, and beseech thee, O Queen of Martyrs, to obtain for me, through the sufferings of Jesus Christ, which were the great cause of thy dolours, an everlasting remembrance of thy sorrows and of the sufferings of thy Son, that I also may die to all my evil desires. Give me a sincere and lively horror of sin, an ardent love of God, a tender and practical love for thee. I also beg of thee, most afflicted Mother, that thou wouldst offer all thy sorrows, tears, and sufferings to the Divine Majesty, as an expiation for the poor suffering souls. Oh, dry up their tears, deliver them from their pains and torments, and beg of thy Divine Son to admit them into the kingdom of Heaven, and to allow them to become sharers of His divine glory. Amen. *Hail Mary.*

PRAYER IN HONOUR OF THE SEVEN JOYS OF
OUR LADY

1. Hail, Mary, full of grace! suffer me to recall to thy mind the great joy thou didst feel, when the Angel Gabriel saluted thee and announced to thee the joyful tidings of the Incarnation of our Lord Jesus Christ. Through this great joy we beseech thee to pray for us poor sinners, that through the Incarnation of thy Divine Son we may be able to work out our salvation. And oh, remember also in thy prayers the poor suffering souls in Purgatory, that they may be speedily released, and obtain the everlasting rest of eternity. *Hail Mary.*

2. Hail, Mary, full of grace! permit me to call to mind the great joy thou didst feel when thou gavest birth to thy Divine Son in Bethlehem, still remaining a Virgin.

Through this great joy we beseech thee to pray for us poor sinners, that through the blessed Nativity of our Lord Jesus Christ we may persevere in a good life, and continually dwell in a state of grace. We beseech thee to give joy to the poor souls in Purgatory, so that by thine intercession the day of their release may soon dawn upon them, and they may be born to their new life in Heaven. *Hail Mary.*

3. Hail, Mary, full of grace! permit me to remind thee of the great joy thou didst feel when the three kings came to visit thy Divine Son, and, having presented Him with costly gifts, worshipped Him as the true God made man. We poor sinners beseech thee through this great joy that we may daily learn to know and love Jesus Christ better and better, and be made worthy of serving Him. Beg also for the poor suffering souls a shortening of their time of expiation, so that they may offer to God in Heaven their thanksgiving and praise for ever and ever. *Hail Mary.*

4. Hail, Mary, full of grace! permit me to remind thee of that joy which thou didst feel when thou didst find Jesus in the Temple, after having vainly sought Him for three days. Through that great joy we beseech thee to pray for us poor sinners, that in all our necessities and trials we may find Jesus alone our consolation, and thus He may be our comforter and give us strength and grace. Pray also for the poor souls that their time of penance may be soon over, and that they may go rejoicing through the gates of Paradise. *Hail Mary.*

5. Hail, Mary, full of grace! permit me to remind thee of that great joy which thou didst feel on that happy Easter Sunday, when thy Divine Son arose glorious and immortal from the dead, and appeared to thee, saluted

thee, and caressed thee in the most filial and consoling manner. Through this great joy I implore thy prayers for us poor sinners, that the memory of our own future resurrection may incite us to good deeds of piety, so that we may be worthy of the promises of Christ. Oh, think also of the poor suffering souls in Purgatory, and beg of God to break their chains and release them from their fiery prison, that they may also have a glorious resurrection into the joys of eternal life. *Hail Mary.*

6. Hail, Mary, full of grace! permit me to remind thee of the joy which thou didst feel when thy Divine Son went up into Heaven in the presence of the Apostles and thyself. Through this great joy I implore thee to pray for grace for us poor sinners, that we may daily make greater effort to save our souls and make ourselves worthy to enter Heaven. Have compassion also on the poor suffering souls in Purgatory, and pray that they may no longer be detained there, but by the power and mercy of God be speedily allowed to enter Heaven. *Hail Mary.*

7. Hail, Mary, full of grace! Permit me to remind thee of the joy which thou didst feel when thy Divine Son at last called thee to Himself, and raised thy body and soul to the everlasting delights of Heaven, and placed thee as queen above all the choirs of Angels and Saints. Oh, through this joy I implore thee to pray for us poor sinners, that we may lead holy and pious lives, and die in a state of grace, so that we may be worthy of witnessing thy happiness and glory in heaven. And, O most glorious Queen, I beseech thee to use thy great influence at the throne of Heaven in behalf of the poor suffering souls in Purgatory, that they may be released from their sufferings, and admitted into Heaven, to increase the

number of the Saints there, and to rejoice for all eternity. *Hail Mary.*

PRAYER TO SAINT JOSEPH

Hail, holy Joseph, whom God has found just upon earth, and did choose as spouse of the most holy and immaculate Virgin Mary, and foster-father of His only begotten Son Jesus Christ. To thy protection He confided the care of the most exalted of beings who ever lived upon this earth; and to thee He sent the Angel, telling the wonderful mystery of the Incarnation of the Son of God, and deigned to reveal to thee the holy and unsearchable ways of God. How many graces hast thou not received from God, living in such close intercourse with thy holy family and what joy thou must have experienced! And yet how humble thou always wast; how patient and enduring through all thy poverty, sufferings, and labours!

O holy Joseph, I long to follow thee in the path of justice, that, like thee, I may die, blessed by Jesus, the death of the just. Thou wert the foster-father of Jesus; oh, take my soul also under thy protection, and lead it along the path of piety to God, who is the aim and end of all Christian souls.

Oh, I particularly invoke thy help and protection in the last struggle of my life—when I am on my death-bed. Oh, come to me then, with Jesus and Mary, and help me to fight the good fight, that I may die happily under thy protection.

I also recommend to thy protection the poor suffering souls in Purgatory, many of whom venerated thee and loved thee while on earth, and had such confidence in thy intercession. Pray for them to thy

Divine Foster-Son; particularly for the soul of N., for whom I most ardently plead. Oh, pray for her, and all the souls, that thou mayest speedily lead them from the Egypt of their exile into their true home, the heavenly Israel. Amen.

PRAYER FOR A DECEASED FATHER

O my God, Thou hast commanded us to honour our parents: therefore I implore Thee to have mercy on the soul of my deceased father, and purify it from any sins that may still cleave to it. Oh, I beseech Thee to admit that dear soul speedily into Thy blessed presence. He loved me well during his lifetime, and if he was sometimes stern, I know he was so for my own good, and he had my interests at heart. I know I have often caused him trouble and anxiety, and I heartily regret all the pain and uneasiness I may have caused him in the days of my thoughtless youth. Often and often have I made him angry, and caused him, perhaps, to commit many sins of impatience by my wilfulness and folly. I therefore ardently implore of Thee, O my God, to forgive all those sins which he may have committed on my account. Oh, remember how much I have annoyed him, and forgive him for those sins! Oh, shorten the term of his Sufferings, and release him from his banishment from Thee. I willingly offer up for him all my good works, my Masses, prayers, and Holy Communions.

Oh, I implore Thee to have compassion on him, and put an end to his sufferings. The more I think of all my father has done for me, and the great debt of gratitude I owe to him for all his care of me, the more eager am I to redouble my efforts to free him from his place of punishment, and to come to his help by my prayers and petitions. O most merciful Jesus, I beg and implore of Thee, by the merits of Thy precious Blood, which has streamed from the Cross for him and me, to have pity on the soul of my dear father; admit him into Thy heavenly kingdom, and let perpetual light shine upon him for ever and ever. Amen.

PRAYER FOR A DECEASED MOTHER

O loving and merciful God, graciously hear the supplications which I pour forth to Thee for the eternal repose of the soul of my beloved mother. Thou, who hast so highly honoured the Mother of Thine only begotten Son, and placed her above all creatures, wilt willingly lend Thine ear to the voice of the supplications of a child for a beloved mother. Oh, hear, then, my prayer, and lead the soul of my dear mother into everlasting joy. Her loss seems always before me, and is to me a cause of inexpressible grief. When I think of her my eyes fill with tears, and deep sorrow seizes my heart whenever I recall her memory. How tenderly she loved me! how many sacrifices she made for my sake! how much she suffered and withstood! sleepless nights and years of care she passed in rearing me. Oh, how can I ever repay such love? for such sorrows make amends? such sufferings requite? How, but through prayer, through burning, fervent prayer for her repose. I beg and implore of Thee, O my God, to send Thy Angel into Purgatory to announce freedom to my mother with these blessed words: 'Come to Me, all ye that labour and are heavy burthened, and I will refresh you.' I call upon thee, O holy Virgin Mary, Mother of God, to forget not my mother in her helpless state. At thy prayer thy Son turned water into wine: pray again, and He will turn the water of affliction into the heavenly wine of joy. Release the soul of my mother from Purgatory, and admit her to the Marriage Feast. Amen.

PRAYER FOR DECEASED BROTHERS AND SISTERS

O almighty and eternal God, with the deepest veneration I approach Thy throne, and implore Thine infinite charity to turn Thine eyes on the misery and sorrow of the poor souls in Purgatory. Oh, many of those souls are my nearest and dearest relations, brothers and sisters whom Thy justice has condemned to prison until they shall have paid the penalty of their sins. With all the souls in Purgatory I have the deepest sympathy. But the thought of the suffering of those dear to me touches my heart with the keenest pity; and, O my God, Thou hast commanded us to love one another, so I know Thou wilt feel pleased at these petitions for my poor friends. Oh, do not let me cry to Thee in vain! With all the fervour of my heart I implore Thee to hear my prayers for these poor souls! Oh, lighten the sufferings of my departed brethren. Shorten their term of punishment, for they have already suffered much! Forgive all the sins for which they have not yet made satisfaction, and reward my fraternal love by delivering them from the flames of Purgatory and by receiving them into the kingdom of Thy glory. Amen.

PRAYER FOR DEPARTED HUSBAND [OR WIFE]

My departed husband suffers! he is enduring the tortures of Purgatory! My faith makes me think so; for I know nothing impure, nothing with the least stain of sin can enter the doors of Heaven! I know that, like all the children of men, he had little faults and weaknesses, for which he must atone before he is worthy of the divine presence. I know also that I have often been the occasion of sins to him. He suffers, this dear husband, to whom I swore eternal love at the altar of God, with whom I lived united for so many years, who shared so many gifts and joys with me, and spent so many sad and pleasant hours by my side. He is in pain without being able to help himself. How willingly, then, do I come to his assistance by my prayers and good works. I have holy Masses said for his soul, and beg of God through the merits of His precious Blood that it may soothe his poor soul. I assist at the Holy Sacrifice, and unite my petitions with the prayers of the priest. I offer up Holy Communion for the repose of his soul.

I will give all the alms I can, and keep fasts and abstinence for the atonement of his sins. But above all I wish to pray fervently for him every day of my life. Every day shall be a Forget-me-not of his affection and his death. Merciful Jesus, I implore Thee to forget him not. Accept my poor prayers for him. Graciously accept my feeble offerings. Join them to the precious merits of Thy Blood shed for us, and then they will be efficacious, and, having helped to soothe the suffering of my poor husband, will open the doors of his prison. Oh, let me not plead to Thy divine Heart in vain, for Thou Thyself hast said, 'Ask and thou shalt receive; knock and it will be opened unto thee.' Oh, hear my prayers, and let my cry come unto Thee. O Thou who hast blessed our union upon earth, continue Thy blessings, and deliver the soul of my husband from the prison of Purgatory. My God, grant that my ardent petitions may be heard. Oh, hear the request I cry to Thee: I implore of Thee to have mercy on the soul of my departed husband, who, being admitted into the joys of the heavenly kingdom, may dwell there in happiness for all eternity. There he will bless and praise Thee; full of gratitude to his wife upon earth, whose fidelity and enduring love and affection assisted him in his freedom from Purgatory. Amen.

PRAYER FOR DECEASED CHILDREN

O merciful Father of the living and the dead, look graciously down on Thy poor creature here weeping and praying at Thy Feet! Full of grief and sorrow, I am crying and praying for my beloved children who have died, for I know I can help them no longer except by my prayers. The more grieved and heartbroken I am at their loss, the more heartfelt are my wishes and prayers for their eternal welfare. Death has robbed me of them; but it was Thy divine will, without which nothing can happen upon earth! Thou, O God, hast taken them. Thou hast ordained it. Such was Thy divine will, and may Thy adorable pleasure be blessed and praised at all times. I will not loudly lament. I will not murmur even to myself. I will perfectly submit myself to Thy most holy will. I know my submission will make my prayers for my poor children more effective, for I know that Thou art so pleased with an afflicted and submissive spirit that Thou canst not reject these my petitions. Therefore, I raise my hands in supplication to Thee, and implore Thee to hear my sighs, my prayers for my poor children, who perhaps are suffering in Purgatory on my account. Oh, through the merits of the most precious Blood and the great sufferings of Thy Divine Son, purify their souls from any stain of sin, which may render them unworthy of Thy divine presence. Oh, how willingly and heartily do I forgive any annoyance their youthful folly may have given me, while they lived on earth! Oh, do not let them suffer more on my account. They are my children. Flesh of my flesh, bone of my bone, my poor children, whom I love beyond bounds. Agar cried, 'I cannot see my child die,' so I call and cry to Thee from the depths of my suffering heart. I cannot bear to think of my children in agony and in pain, so I call and cry to Thee without ceasing to have pity on them! Oh, soothe their pain. Shorten the term of their sufferings, and through Thine infinite mercy lead them speedily from their prison to their destined home in Heaven. There they will enjoy the perpetual rest and joy of Thy Angels and Saints. Amen.

Prayer for Deceased Relations, Friends, and Benefactors

O most just God, and most loving Father, Thou lovest us, Thy children, and Thou wishest that we should also love each other. Amongst the poor souls suffering in Purgatory are, perhaps, many of my relations and friends. They have ended their pilgrimage on earth, but they have not yet come to their God. I beg of Thee to let them no longer pine and languish in their prison, but purify them perfectly from their sins. In Thy great love Thou dost purify them in the fiery crucible, for Thy justice has ordained that nothing impure can enter Heaven. O infinitely wise and merciful God, well I know that I am not worthy to make a request to Thee; but I venture to plead to Thee for my poor deceased relations, who were bound to me by ties of blood; and also for my benefactors—those dear friends to whose goodness and kindness I owe such a deep debt of gratitude. Oh, I implore Thee to receive their souls into the kingdom of Thy glory! O Jesus, Thou loving Saviour of mankind! Thou hast redeemed these souls by Thy holy death; grant that their souls may find refreshment and light in that holy Sacrifice in which Thy death and Passion in an unbloody manner is commemorated; let them fully experience that Thou art their Redeemer and Saviour. Oh, hear my poor prayers that I offer for them in thanksgiving for their love and goodness to me while on earth. Amen.

PRAYER FOR A DECEASED PASTOR

O Jesus, the Good Shepherd, who hast given to Thy priests upon earth the command to care for and watch over the flocks entrusted to them, and like careful shepherds, to protect them from the wolf and not allow even the smallest lamb to stray from the fold, I pray to Thee for the repose of the soul of my deceased pastor. Oh, remember he was a good shepherd, and lived as Thou wouldst have him live. He has conscientiously taken care of my soul, as well as hundreds of others; preserved the life in them; strengthened them by good advice; protected them when in danger; and when they fell into sin, raised them from their downfall, and helped them to walk again in the paths of virtue. It has pleased Thee to call him away from the midst of us—away from his field of labours. He is dead, and has been judged! No calling is more responsible, none so full of varied temptations, as that of a priest. It is an awful thing to fall into the hands of the living God, before whom even the Angels are not pure, therefore I feel anxious about my late dear pastor. O my God, if he be now in Purgatory, deal lightly with his offences! be not a just but a merciful God; and remember all the good he has done in his priestly life. I beg of Thee to accept my prayers, my tears, my Masses, and all my good actions, in atonement for his little imperfections and his human weaknesses. Oh, deal not with him in Thine anger, but mercifully spare him any future suffering in Thine infinite charity. Take his hand—that hand which was so often raised to bless his congregation, and which so often raised the Sacred Host—and lead him out of the darkness of Purgatory. Place his feet—that, so often weary and tired, led him to the doors of the sick and poor—in the entrance to the holy haven of peace. Let his tongue—which so often preached Thy holy Gospel upon earth—be soon enabled to thank Thee in Heaven, and sing Thy glories and Thy praises for all eternity. Oh, then he will pray for me in Heaven—for me and for many other souls who had been entrusted to his care while on earth—for whose salvation he so frequently prayed. And, oh, may his prayers be pleasing unto Thee, my God! For his sake, may I be preserved from long imprisonment in Purgatory, to be speedily united in Heaven to my dear pastor, and to thank him for his care of me here below, as well as in Heaven. Amen.

ON ALL SOULS' DAY

To-day it is my most holy duty to remember in my prayers all my dear deceased friends. So this holy Feast-day I can truly call a 'Forget-me-not,' for it urges our hearts so remember all our dear dead friends, as well as the souls of all the faithful departed, in all our prayers, the Masses we assist at, as well as all our other acts of piety to-day. With all the fervour and energy of my heart and soul I will pray for them; and, oh, my God! I beg of Thee to give me Thy holy grace, that, with the deepest reflection, I may meditate on the pains of Purgatory, and sincerely pray for the repose of the poor souls.

O Jesus, Thou Good Shepherd! Thou hast lain down Thy life for Thy flock, and dost daily continue the Sacrifice of Thy love, have mercy on Thy poor suffering sheep who are imprisoned in that place of suffering. They still belong to Thy fold, and are patiently waiting to hear Thy much longed-for voice calling them home. O sweetest Jesus, let them hear Thy glad call of their deliverance! Conduct them into the happy home of the blessed, so that Shepherd and flock may be united for ever and ever.

O Holy Ghost, Thou Comforter sent from Heaven! be a comforter also to all the holy souls in Purgatory, for Thou hast received them into Thy holy Church at their baptism, and Thou hast sanctified them by Thy holy grace. Oh, forgive them, Holy Spirit of Peace, all their desecration of Thy holy sanctuary! Extinguish the fire of their suffering with the fire of Thy divine love, and refresh them with the refreshing dew of Thy grace and benevolence.

O most blessed Virgin Mary! thou loving comfortress of the afflicted, forget not thy poor suffering and afflicted children in the depth of Purgatory. By the memory of that sword of sorrow which seven times pierced thy heart—by the memory of all the tears which the sorrows of thy Divine Son caused thee to shed—by all the sighs which the painful work of the redemption of mankind forced from thee—and by all the anxiety thou hast felt for the souls of mankind—I beg and implore of thee to be a good mother also to these poor suffering souls in Purgatory. Pray to thy Divine Son at the throne of grace for pardon for their sins, forgiveness for the rest of the punishment due to them, and an early entrance into heaven, that they may there rejoice eternally, safe under thy maternal protection.

O all ye holy Angels to whose protection these poor souls were once confided, see them now suffering and languishing in their sad prison. Have sympathy with these your late charges. Plead for them at the throne of the Almighty, that He may in His mercy deliver them from the flames of Purgatory as He did three children in the fiery furnace, and that like Peter they may be freed from their prison—the place of sorrow—and be admitted into the heavenly Jerusalem—the happy home of the Elect.

And all ye holy Saints of God! remember that the suffering Church is still united to you by the holy bond of love and faith. Come to the help of your weeping brothers and sisters. Pray that the Lord may give them eternal rest, and let perpetual light shine upon them. May He at last admit them into your midst to enjoy the bliss of eternal happiness. Amen.

PRAYER AT A REQUIEM, OR BURIAL, SERVICE

Filled with deepest sympathy and compassion, I approach Thee, O Father of mercy. I prostrate myself humbly at Thy feet, and pray for this poor soul, who was so near and dear to me, and whose obsequies take place to-day. With all the strength of my heart and soul I beg of Thee to have mercy on this poor soul, who perhaps in the other world may have to undergo some punishment for the sin he may not have atoned for. Oh, how dreadful must it be to dwell in that place of suffering where they have to endure tortures equal to those of hell except that they are not eternal! What agony to have to suffer so much! What misery to be so long cut off from God! What a condition to be in when one can't help one's self! What abandonment to be separated from one's friends! Oh, these poor souls, whose only food is sighs and lamentations, and who drink hot, bitter tears of blood! I should have a heart of stone if I could think of the sufferings without the deepest sorrow and compassion.

Penetrated with the most heartfelt sympathy, I redouble my prayers for them to-day, for to-day are celebrated the obsequies of a dear and well-known friend. Graciously hear my prayer, O Lord, and let my cry come unto Thee. Be merciful to this poor soul, and graciously accept the united prayers of the whole congregation here praying for him. Oh, let our prayers atone for all those sins for which he has not yet satisfied. Grant that our loving prayers may be a comfort to him in his dreadful state of woe. Let it be Thy divine will to send an angel to him with the joyful news that the day of his deliverance has dawned, and the time of his suffering all passed away. I unite my prayers with the holy Sacrifice of the Mass now being offered up for him, and so hope that my poor prayers will reach to Heaven, and will be favourably heard at the throne of the Almighty. Amen.

PRAYER ON THE ANNIVERSARY OF A DEPARTED

We know that the souls of the faithful departed have sometimes to endure long and painful sufferings in the flames of Purgatory. The Church, therefore, admonishes us to remember—to pray for them at all times, but more particularly on the anniversary of their death, as well as during the month devoted to the dead. To-day we commemorate the anniversary of a beloved friend, whose soul, perhaps, may be now undergoing severe pains in Purgatory—that place of purification. Inscrutable are Thy ways, O God, and Thy judgment is just and righteous, though awful. Thou dost not respect persons, or the mighty ones of earth. All are equal in Thy sight.

Oh, therefore, if this poor soul has not yet arrived into the heavenly kingdom, but is still pining in the darksome prison of Purgatory, let my feeble but earnest prayer become the pledge of his deliverance. Grant that the prison doors may be thrown open for him. Remember, most loving Father, he left this world in a state of grace and full of love for Thee. Thy mercy has not banished him for ever from Thy sight, but only for a short time, until he shall become pure and spotless and worthy of Thy divine presence. That shows us here on earth that Thou hast not a lasting anger, but that Thou art glad to be appeased by prayers and good works. Therefore, I offer to Thee in satisfaction for the soul of this poor friend, through the hands of the most blessed Virgin Mary, all the grace which this poor soul may have neglected, as well as all the wonderful works, virtues, and sufferings of Thy Divine Son on earth. I unite them all with the offering of the priest at the Altar during the holy Sacrifice of the

Mass. O my God, I implore of Thee to accept this offering, and graciously vouchsafe to free this poor soul from the woes of Purgatory, and admit it into the kingdom of eternal joy. Amen.

RECORD OF POOR SUFFERING SOULS

E ARE bound not alone to remember in our prayers the souls of our parents, friends, and relations, but we should also pray for the souls of all the faithful who have departed this life. It is just and meet we should pray for them. They are all brothers and co-heirs of the kingdom of Christ. In order to do this effectively, many convents and families have a regular list, or record, in which the different members of the faithful are written, special souls, and all the departed generally. This list reminds the living of praying constantly for all poor souls, more especially for the neglected who have no friends on earth to pray for them.

Here follows a list from which may be chosen every day a few special subjects to be prayed for particularly.

Remember to pray for:
1. Thy parents or grandparents.
2. Thy brothers and sisters.
3. Thy husband (thy wife) and children.
4. Thy friends and benefactors.
5. Thy servants and members of thy house.
6. Thy relations and acquaintances.
7. Thy spiritual directors and pastors.
8. The confessors and priests of thy parish.

9. Those who were members of the Sodalities and Societies to which you belonged.
10. The Bishop of thy Diocese.
11. The teachers who have instructed thee in the Christian doctrine.
12. Those in their last agony who are just about to appear before the throne of God.
13. Those who during their lifetime prayed most for the souls in Purgatory.
14. Those who this year have been sent into Purgatory.
15. Those who have been sent to Purgatory on thy account, and from thy bad example.
16. Those whom thou didst annoy and trouble during their lifetime.
17. Those who endure the bitterest agony.
18. Those who have no one on earth to pray for them, their friends being all dead.
19. Those who have been detained the longest time in Purgatory.
20. The souls who have the longest time to spend in Purgatory, if no one comes to their assistance by prayer.
21. The soul who most longs for thy help.
22. The soul who, while on earth, most loved the Blessed Virgin.
23. The soul who, while on earth, was most devoted to the Holy Family—Jesus, Mary and Joseph.
24. The soul whom God is most anxious to deliver.
25. The soul who has the most ardent desire to behold God Almighty.
26. The soul who is condemned to Purgatory for the

most trifling fault.

27. The soul who had most virtues and graces.

28. The soul who is nearest to its deliverance from Purgatory.

29. The souls of those who have perished at sea, or in the deserts, and are not lying in consecrated ground.

30. The souls of Catholic soldiers who have fallen on the battlefield.

31. The souls who have injured us, and done us harm upon earth.

32. The souls of those who in life could not forgive their enemies.

33. The souls who are doing penance for the sins committed by their eyes.

34. The souls of those who are doing penance for the sins of the tongue.

35. The souls of those who are suffering on account of their pride.

36. The souls of those who are suffering on account of their self-love.

37. The souls of those who are suffering on account of their vanity.

38. The souls of those who are suffering on account of their impatience.

39. The souls of those who have neglected or carelessly said their evening and morning prayers.

40. The souls of those who have neglected to attend Mass and sermons, or who listened distractedly to them.

41. The souls of those who were wilfully distracted

during their prayers.

42. The souls of those who are suffering on account of their bad thoughts.

43. The souls of all the faithful departed of this Diocese.

44. The souls of all the faithful departed of the whole world.

45. The soul of the person who has arranged and got printed this list of the dead.

46. The souls of those who translated this book.

47. The soul of him who first published this book, and for many years laboured to build All Souls' Church at Peterborough.

48. The souls of those who reprinted and edited this book, as well as that funded the work.

MEDITATIONS ON PURGATORY

OUR FAITH IN PURGATORY

'What our Faith has revealed, our Church taught,
Of departed souls, can here be read—
Offered as a small Forget-me-not,
In aid of thee, and of the blessed dead.'

WHAT IS PURGATORY?

AT NO TIME does the human heart stand in greater need of that comfort and peace which the world cannot give than at the painful moment when the grave closes over the remains of those dear to us. Involuntarily we ask ourselves: 'Ah, whither have they gone, these dear souls? where are they whose loss we are now so bitterly bewailing, and whose departure has struck in our hearts a wound that even time can never heal? Where are the souls of our dear father, our never-to-be-forgotten mother, our tenderly loved sisters and brothers? Oh, where are ye now sojourning—ye who have left us in such deep and enduring sorrow? Oh, must we seek ye in that abode of unspeakable sufferings—that sorrowful place of expiation? These are questions which arise in our minds and constantly occupy our anxious thoughts. For love, which asks these questions, is stronger than death, and extends beyond the grave. It finds comfort in the thought that we are still united to the beloved dead, and that our intercourse, begun on earth, continues still; love is happy to know it is our most holy duty to hasten to their assistance, the more so as we can never be certain whether they are still suffering in Purgatory or have

161

reached their blessed goal in Heaven.

Until the end of the world—until the last day of general judgment—there will be an intermediate place between Heaven and hell. Heaven is the place where only the souls of the just and the holy are admitted. Hell is the dungeon into whose depths are plunged the souls of the impious and unrepenting. But Purgatory lies between the two, and is meant to receive for a time those souls of the just who still require some further purification.

Purgatory is a place of punishment, where the souls of the faithful departed must suffer in expiation for those sins for which they did not, or not fully, atone while on earth. Those sufferings consist in pains and torments of the soul in temporary banishment from Heaven and separation from God.

Purgatory is a place of purification where the souls of the departed are cleansed from all such stains as may render them, though not worthy of hell, still unworthy of Heaven, into which nothing impure can enter. There they linger till they are perfectly pure.

Purgatory is a place of divine justice. The justice of God resists and shrinks from being immediately after death united with a soul not perfectly pure, because He is purity itself.

Purgatory is a place of divine mercy. God, who is charity and goodness itself, has made it in order that He should not be obliged for ever to cast from Him His own dear children to whom He has promised peace upon earth, and who, though weak and erring, are of good will.

It is an article of faith that by sacramental absolution from sins the contrite penitent obtains forgiveness as to guilt and eternal punishment; but there remains the temporal punishment due to him, which must be suffered either in this life, or after death in Purgatory, before the doors of Heaven can be opened for him. Moses offended the Lord; David also grievously sinned against Him; and although those great servants of God were by contrition and repentance for their past sins reconciled with God, there yet awaited them a heavy temporal punishment.

The doctrine of faith concerning Purgatory implies, consequently, two truths, which must be particularly borne in mind. First, after a mortal sin is forgiven in the Sacrament of Penance, the eternal punishment due to it is generally changed into some temporal punishment which we must endure either in this life—by deeds of penance—or in the next in Purgatory. Second, even venial sins are a stain which prevent the soul from entering into Heaven. These stains, therefore, must first be wiped off if the soul is to enter the abode of all holiness. Now, Purgatory is precisely the place where the souls predestined to eternal glory are detained for a time, fixed by God's justice for the purpose of expiation and purification, until they are quite worthy of the everlasting bliss prepared for them.

The Church is the mystical body of Jesus Christ, of which He is the Head, and all the faithful are the members. It is divided into three parts: The *Church militant* on earth, consisting of the faithful, who are still fighting for their faith and struggling for their salvation; the *Church triumphant*, consisting of the Saints in Heaven; finally, the *suffering Church*, consisting of the souls in Purgatory.

All the dead, then, who have died in the Lord, belong to the great mysterious body of Christ, either as members glorified already, or as still awaiting the glory to come. But all are united among themselves, and form one great Communion of Saints.

Therefore, when we consider what faith teaches us concerning the suffering Church, or Purgatory, we cannot help exclaiming: 'O faith, how beautiful art thou! how touching is the Communion of Saints!' We children of the Church militant stretch forth one hand towards our brethren of the Church triumphant for help and protection; with the other we pour out our prayers, our alms, and patient sufferings upon our brethren of the suffering Church, who entreat us to alleviate their torments, until they themselves be able to succour us in our infirmities and weakness.

THE OLD TESTAMENT SHOWS THE EXISTENCE OF PURGATORY

The Bible, on its very first pages, shows us that a custom of praying for the dead existed among the people of the earliest ages. But this implies the existence of Purgatory, because it stands to reason that we do not pray either for the Saints in Heaven or for the damned in hell. 'For,' says the angelical Doctor, St. Thomas Aquinas, 'those prayers would be useless and in vain if there were no Purgatory, for they are offered because prayers cannot be offered up for those who have already arrived at their end, but only for those who have not yet reached their final destiny.'

When Jacob and Joseph were about to depart from this world, they earnestly besought those who stood round their deathbed, especially their own children, to convey their mortal remains to Palestine. For those pious patriarchs well knew that their descendants there would offer sacrifices of expiation, and they hoped these offerings would gain for them the longed-for peace and rest. This tradition runs through the whole history of the Jewish people.

On the announcement of the death of Saul all the inhabitants of Jabes imposed upon themselves a seven days' fast. The inspired poet-king takes part, not only in their sorrow, but also in their sacrifices (2 Kings i. 17). He himself sings in touching, elevated strains of the doctrine of Purgatory, when describing the inexpressible joy and delight of those souls who have happily passed through the fire and water of tribulation, and have arrived at the ardently longed-for joy and refreshment of the Lord (Ps. xxxviii. 14). The prophet Micheas contemplated beforehand the consolations of Purgatory: 'I shall arise when I sit in darkness; the Lord is my light. I will bear the wrath of the Lord because I have sinned against Him; until He judge my cause and execute judgment for me: He will bring me forth into the light, and I shall behold His justice' (Mich. vii. 8,9). The prophet Isaias expresses the same thoughts: 'If the Lord shall wash away the filth of the daughters of Sion ... by the spirit of judgment and by the spirit of burning' (Is. iv. 4).

Instructed by such holy and exalted prophets, the people of Israel, from the earliest times, made sacrifices and offerings for the dead, and thereby clearly showed their belief in Purgatory. The records of all the past centuries referring to the subject clearly show that not the smallest doubt can be entertained on this point. When the star of Jewish civilization began to fade, the heroic line of the Machabees gathered all their forces once more

together, in order to inaugurate a new epoch of power
and glory. In the description of their noble and heroic
actions, we come across the unmistakable proof of their
universal tradition and belief. Judas, the mighty hero,
having lost a great number of soldiers in the battle, did
not confine himself to merely giving them an honourable
burial He commanded a collection to be made, and sent
the sum, amounting to 12,000 drachmas, to Jerusalem, for
a sacrifice to be offered for the fallen heroes. Holy
Scripture concludes the narrative with the words: 'It is
therefore a holy and wholesome thought to pray for the
dead, that they may be loosed from sins'—that is, from all
temporal punishment due to those sins (2 Mach. xii. 40).
This thought is justly called holy, because it springs from
a holy source, viz., that of faith and charity. It is called
wholesome, in the first place, to the poor souls
themselves, because it comforts and encourages them in
their sufferings; in the next place, also, to all those who
pray for them, because they increase their own merits
thereby, and gain new faithful friends in Heaven.

The Holy Scriptures, therefore, imply in the conduct
of the great leader, the existence of Purgatory, or some
such place of purification in the next world, where the
souls of the departed can be assisted by our prayers and
sacrifices, and be cleansed from their sins. Certainly it
would have been impossible, in such heavy time of war,
to gather from the people such large sums of money, or to
all at once introduce an innovation in religious practice of
that kind, if this belief in Purgatory had not been long and
firmly planted in their hearts. These passages just referred
to clearly prove the truth of the Catholic doctrine, which
teaches us that there exists a place for the purification of

such souls as die in the state of grace, but have not yet fully expiated all their sins; and that those souls can be delivered by the prayers and good works of the faithful. Jesus, the son of Sirach, also bears witness to the same truth where he says: 'A gift hath grace in the sight of all the living, and restrain not grace from the dead'(Ecclus. vii. 37)—which means, pay them the last respects, and offer up sacrifices for them. But as it is impossible to help either the blessed in Heaven or the damned in hell, nothing remains but to suppose that there is an intermediate place where our charity can be of avail. Finally, the existence of a Purgatory is proved by certain texts of St. Paul (1 Cor. xv. 29), where he writes: 'Otherwise, what shall they do that are baptized for the dead if the dead rise not again at all? Why are they then baptized for them?' 'To be baptized,' here means, according to our Lord's own use of the word, to suffer. 'And I have a baptism, wherewith I am to be baptized: and how am I straitened until it be accomplished?' (Luke xii. 50.)

Thus interpreted, the passage confirms the general belief of the Jews, that we can assist the departed by good works. Wherefore, the words of St. Paul will always be a proof for the belief in Purgatory in the Old Testamental times. Moreover, the Jews even now believe in the existence of some place of purification, and are in the habit of praying for their dead.

THE NEW TESTAMENT SHOWS THE EXISTENCE OF PURGATORY

The Jewish belief in Purgatory rested on a very firm foundation. In the fulness of time the divine Saviour, Jesus Christ, appeared on earth. While disowning in His teaching all the false theories and erroneous traditions of Scribes and Pharisees, while condemning with the greatest decision their errors on the subject of death and resurrection, He never uttered one syllable against the general belief in Purgatory, against the public practice of praying for the dead. On the contrary, He left it just as it existed under the old law. Could the Son of God, who had come down to make known the will of His Father, have acted thus if this were not a holy, just, and pious custom? The Redeemer did not find it necessary to give lengthy proofs for the existence of this place of punishment. It was enough to simply remind the people of it. For, in truth, He addressed a people who had never entertained the smallest doubt on the subject.

In one of His sermons He unmistakably alludes to Purgatory, where He speaks of a prison from which no one can be delivered except on the payment of the full debt. What other prison but Purgatory can here be meant? For Heaven cannot be meant, and out of hell there is no redemption.

Again, the Gospels have preserved another saying of the Son of God, which presupposes the existence of Purgatory: 'And whosoever shall speak a word against the Son of Man, it shall be forgiven him; but he that shall speak against the Holy Ghost, it shall not be forgiven him, neither in this world nor in the world to come ' (Matt. xii. 32).

Therefore, there are sins which can be atoned for in the next world. But in hell there is no hope of forgiveness, no possible chance of expiation.

As their divine Master, so also taught the Apostles. St. Paul, the great Apostle of the Gentiles, says: 'For other foundation can no man lay but that which is laid, which is Jesus Christ. Now, if any man build upon this foundation gold, silver, precious stones, wood, hay, stubble, every man's work shall be manifest, for the day of the Lord shall declare it, because it shall be revealed in fire, and the fire shall try every man's work of what sort it is. If any man's work abide, which he hath built thereon, he shall receive a reward. If any man's work burn, he shall suffer loss: but he himself shall be saved, yet so as by fire' (1 Cor. iii. 12-15).

He who appears before the judgment-seat of God with works still stained and imperfect, will reach indeed his happy end, but not before those stains and imperfections have been cleared away by a process which is like unto the crucible of fire. The fire which the Apostle speaks of cannot be the fire of tribulation, or the sufferings of this life; for he speaks of a fire which burns on the judgment day; that is, after this life. Again, it cannot mean the mere ordeal of the judgment, because here the soul is not only tried, but also burns, and suffers from the burning. Nor can it mean the fire of hell, because he who burns in the fire will come out of it and be saved, which cannot be said of those in hell. The Apostle could only have had the fire of Purgatory in view—that fire which burns for the purification of souls not quite spotless, and which will continue until the day of general judgment.

Again, St. Paul says 'that in the Name of Jesus every knee should bow, of those that are in heaven, on earth, and under the earth' (Phil. ii. 10). By the expression 'under the earth,' according to the general opinion of the holy Fathers of the Church, he pointed to that temporary intermediate place, wherein imperfect souls must abide until they are purified from all stain of sin, but yet, even while still there, are united in common adoration with the Saints who are in full enjoyment of Heaven, as well as with all the Christians of the Church militant on earth.

St. Paul himself has given us the example of praying for the dead. Having enjoyed the hospitality of Onesiphorus at Rome, he reminds his disciple Timothy of the kindness he had received, sends greeting to the friends and the children of his late host, and then adds that he would pray for him, that the Lord would show him grace and favour on the last day of judgment (2 Tim. i. 16-18, and iv. 19). From the whole structure and nature of the phrase, it is clear that Onesiphorus must have been dead already at that time; so St. Paul teaches us by example on that occasion to offer up prayers and petitions to God Almighty for the souls of those who have died in the Lord.

BELIEF IN PURGATORY CONFIRMED BY TRADITION

Tradition excludes every doubt—even the least shadow of doubt—as to the existence of Purgatory. We have a whole cloud of witnesses: testimony from the most renowned writers of the Church, such as St. Augustine, St. Chrysostom, St. Epiphanius, St. Jerome, St. Cyril of Jerusalem, St. Gregory of Nyssa, up to Tertullian, who flourished in the second century, and consequently up to the very beginning of the Church. This tradition is not alone contained in their writings, but also in the practice of the Church, reaching up to the apostolic age, according to which prayers and sacrifices were at all times offered up to God, for the souls of the departed.

Tertullian speaks of the sacrifices for the dead as of an apostolical tradition, and St. John Damascene says, in his sermon on the dead: 'The Apostles and disciples of our Divine Saviour, who had seen the Eternal Word with their own eyes, and had converted the multitudes of the living world, taught that in the awful, immaculate, and life-giving mysteries of the Eucharist, remembrance should be made of those who had died in the Lord.' In confirmation of it he alleges the testimony of St. Chrysostom in these words: 'That John, who on account of the brilliancy of his oratory, was surnamed "Chrysostom," which means golden mouth, teaches that not inconsiderately or accidentally was it ordained by those wise disciples of God and transmitted to the Church, that the priest should offer prayers for the dead in the celebration of the awful Divine Mysteries.' In the same manner St. Gregory of Nyssa writes: 'Not without reason and usefulness was it transmitted from the Apostles, and accepted as a law of the Church, that it is wholesome and well-pleasing to God to make a remembrance, in the most holy Mysteries, for those who died in the true faith.'

The great bishop of Hippo, St. Augustine, in his treatise on the care for the dead, writes thus: 'We read in the book of the Machabees that there were sacrifices offered up for the dead, but even if there had been no mention made of the subject in the pages of the Old

Testament, the authority of the Church would be sufficient, as manifested in her practice, according to which the priest at the Altar makes commemoration of the faithful departed.' By her funeral rites, offices, and commemorations of the dead, as well as her ancient Ordos, the Catholic Church has at all times clearly and definitely testified to, and declared her belief in, the existence of Purgatory. Further, she has solemnly declared it an article of faith in several councils—as, for instance, in two Councils of Carthage, in the fourth General Council of the Lateran, and in the General Council of Trent, which defines that there is a Purgatory, and that the faithful could come to the assistance of the souls suffering therein by their prayers and oblations of the most holy Sacrifice of the Mass. And it even threatens with excommunication from the Church all those who maintain, that every penitent sinner, having received justification, is forgiven as to his guilt and eternal punishment in such a way, that there remains no temporal punishment to be expiated in Purgatory.

A touching proof of the faith in the intercession of the living for the dead is related to us in the story of the life of St. Monica, the mother of St. Augustine. As her son stood by the bedside of his dying mother, and with difficulty tried to restrain his tears, Monica said to him: 'Only one thing I beg of thee, my son, remember me always at the Altar of God, wherever thou dost chance to be!' St. Augustine, therefore, often offered up the holy Sacrifice of the Mass for his mother, and in his Confessions he entreats God in the following touching prayer: 'O God, grant that all Thy servants, who are my brothers, and to whom I have dedicated this book, grant that all who read these prayers may, in their prayers before Thy Altar, think of Thy hand-maid, my dearest mother, and pray for her in loving remembrance.'

THE TESTIMONY OF REASON

Even pure reason may without great difficulty infer the existence of Purgatory from the truths known by faith. Reason enlightened by faith demands it as a necessary postulate.

Our faith teaches us that in the holy Sacrament of Penance our sins are forgiven together with the *eternal* punishment due to them, but not always also the temporal punishment due to them, which consequently often remains to be endured, either in this world or the next. The Holy Scriptures imply this doctrine. We have but to call to mind the examples of Moses, David, Peter, and Mary Magdalen. They were all forgiven their sins and the eternal punishment due to them by the Word of God Himself, or of His Prophets, and yet how much did those dear servants of God, although freed from sin and eternal punishment, bewail their offences during their whole life and expiate the temporal punishment due to them!

The doctrine that sinners, even after the remission of guilt and eternal damnation, have still, as a rule, to satisfy the justice of God in some way, has been acknowledged by the Church both in deed and by express words. By deed because of her severe penitential discipline in the early days of the Church; because of the works of penance enjoined in the confessional, and of granting at all times indulgences. By express words because of the definition of the Council of Trent.

Now, if, according to the certain doctrine of faith,

some temporal satisfaction remains to be made after the remission of sin and eternal punishment, what, we ask, will become of those souls who are suddenly called away before they have done such penance as their sins required? before they have given full satisfaction? Into heaven, where nothing impure can enter, they cannot be received until the full debt be paid. Into hell they cannot be cast because they died in a state of grace, and are the friends and children of God! Therefore, reason says, there must be a place where those just and holy, though not yet thoroughly cleansed, souls must linger till purified completely and fully worthy of God's sacred presence. This, then, is the necessary postulate of reason enlightened by faith. Were it otherwise, our reason would be darkened and troubled by doubts, either as to the justice or the infinite mercy of God.

Again, there is yet another argument and ground on which our reason demands the existence of a Purgatory. It may be that a soul just departed this life is free from all mortal sin, and even free from all temporal punishment due to grievous sins; but perhaps not yet free from certain light and venial sins, which, though not destroying the grace of God in the soul, still darken and stain its full splendour. It may be that all those venial sins are often atoned for and wiped away, by the patiently-borne agony of death; but how often it happens, that the Christian is suddenly surprised by death in many different forms, and when least expecting it! It would be contrary to God's mercy and justice, to cast that soul into hell or to receive it at once into Heaven, as we have shown above, and need not repeat again.

What, then, remains for reason, but to suppose the

existence of a middle state, a place of purification?

Reason tells us, that there is a state of virtue not good enough for Heaven, and a state of vice not bad enough for hell. Common-sense tells us, there is a difference between sin and sin, and that consequently there must be a difference in the punishment, and atonement for those sins! But the result and conclusion from these reasonable principles is no other, than that there must be a place of purification, or Purgatory.

WHAT ARE THE SUFFERINGS OF THE SOULS IN PURGATORY?

The souls in Purgatory *suffer*. They are sent into Purgatory to suffer. They are detained there to suffer. The time of action is gone; the time of passive suffering is come. Their whole existence and life is, as it were, taken up by suffering. And now we ask, What are they suffering? of what kind and character are their sufferings?

The pains of Purgatory are just the same as the torments of hell, with the exception of eternity and despair. The difference between the two is, that the sufferings of Purgatory come to an end, and are not severed from the sweet hope of eternal happiness.

Like the pains of hell, so also are the sufferings of Purgatory of a twofold kind. They are, pains of loss, and pains of sense. These two kinds of pain correspond to the twofold disorder contained in every sin. For every sin is, first of all, an aversion or turning away from God, the highest and uncreated good, either a complete aversion, as in the case of mortal sin, or a partial, as in venial sin; secondly, it is a conversion to, or turning towards, a created, real, or apparent good, as our highest good, which is, of course, a disorderly or inordinate conversion. Now this twofold inordinateness must be expiated and compensated by a twofold corresponding punishment. For wherein a man sins, says Scripture, therein also is he punished. Man sins, and thus turns away from God; the punishment, therefore, must be an eternal or temporary deprivation of God, the highest good of man. He sins, and thus turns towards a created good, and derives pleasure and satisfaction from it; the punishment, therefore, for this illicit, sensual pleasure, is the pain of sense, and pain inflicted by created things.

Now, fire is a pain of sense; and it is the doctrine of the Church, sufficiently warranted by Scripture and Tradition, that the fire of Purgatory is a real fire, by which the souls are chastised and purified. The holy Fathers—among others, St. Augustine and St. Thomas Aquinas—explain that the greatest imaginable sufferings here on earth, the most dreadful martyrdom of the holy confessors of Christ, the worst pains of the most terrible illness, can bear no comparison with the torments and pains suffered by the poor souls in Purgatory. Well-known is the exclamation of St. Augustine: 'Here burn, here cut, here crucify; but spare me, O God, in eternity!' The sufferings of this life can be soothed by consolation; can be softened by many distractions; and now and again there is respite granted to the greatest sufferer; and time heals many woes. But the sufferings of Purgatory continue without interruption or alleviation.

According to the writings of the holy Fathers, the pain of loss is the greatest of all the pains of Purgatory. Together with the bitter remembrance of having done evil, and omitted the good, there is the consciousness of being deprived of the beatific vision of God, than which there can be no greater pain, according to the Council of Florence.

St. Alphonsus says: 'Far greater than the pains of the senses is the pain of loss arising from the deprivation of the presence of God.' Because the poor souls are inflamed with not only natural, but supernatural, love of God, they are almost violently drawn towards union with Him, their Supreme Good; and because they have the consciousness of being debarred from this perfect union with God through their sins and imperfections, they feel such exceeding great pain that it would kill them were it possible for them to die. 'Therefore,' says St. Chrysostom, 'is this pain of loss greater than that of sense, and the worst of all pains. A thousand fires of hell could not produce greater pain than that which is caused by the fully-realized loss of God.'

Here on earth, while confined within their bodies of sin, their souls could not enjoy the delight of the beatific vision; but once delivered from their mortal bodies, the time is come when they are able to see God and would be in their everlasting joy were it not for their own fault. Through their own fault they are detained in Purgatory, as in a dark prison. It is this pain of separation, which makes Purgatory a cleansing fire in the fullest sense of the word. For, however great may be the pains of sense, the pain of loss is greater still. Full of pain and sorrow, even in this valley of tears, are the sighs of holy souls pining after God and Heaven. How painful must have been the burning love and yearning desire in the souls of St. Paul, St. Augustine, and St. Teresa! Yet what was all that, compared to the consuming fire of yearning in the souls of Purgatory? For, however much we may pine after God, our only Good—however we may crave and long for eternal rest—still, while on earth, we have many things that comfort us or deaden our pain. The very burden of our body, the various distracting events of life, the possibility of great age, better preparation, larger store of merit—all these things are so many means of comfort to us. But the poor souls in Purgatory have none of those consolations; there is nothing to assuage their pain of yearning and unfulfilled desire. More than the panting stag do they thirst after the fountain of Eternal Light and Life. This unspeakable thirst is, in their case, all pure pain, unmingled with any soothing substance.

Oh, what a burning sea of sorrow those poor souls are plunged into! Flames within, flames without, flames all round! Were it not that God's omnipotent hand upheld them, their spirit would almost be consumed by those flames of fire!

WHO CAN HELP THE POOR SOULS IN PURGATORY, AND HOW?

That the members of the Church militant here on earth can help the members of the suffering Church in Purgatory, has been a truth recognised and acted upon, from the earliest ages of the Church down to the present time. For it was always the custom to pray to God for the souls of the departed and to offer the holy Sacrifice and other good works for them. The Church, in the great Council of Trent, has defined it as an article of faith, supported by the clear testimonies of constant tradition, and of Jewish Scripture. This truth also follows, as a matter of course, from the other article of faith, according to which we believe in the Communion of Saints. For the members of this community are like the members of one body. Now the members of one body help each other. The members of this community are connected with each other as the members of one family; for, as the children of God, and united with Him by love, they constitute the family of God; but the members of a family have a share in the common goods, as is said in the Psalms: 'I am a partaker with all them that fear Thee' (Ps. cxviii. 63). If Christ could make vicarious atonement to His Heavenly Father for our sins, and the eternal punishment due to them, then, also, the members of the community, founded by Him, can, through His power and merits, assist and make satisfaction for each other with regard to temporal punishment due to their sins; so that, as the Apostle says, the abundance of one may supply the want of the other, that there may be an equality (2 Cor. viii. 14).

The souls in Purgatory, therefore, since they are souls departed in the love of God, belong with us to that great brotherhood, the Communion of Saints; and so we can come to their assistance, and by our efforts help to discharge the debt they are still owing to God's justice. Or united to them by the bonds of love, we form, as it were, one person, and we pass the value of our good works on to them, and our Heavenly Father looks upon the price we pay for them, as if paid by themselves.

Therefore we can greatly and powerfully assist the poor suffering souls. Now let us see by what means. The holy Council of Trent expressly points out to us the means, whereby we can help those poor helpless sufferers. In the twenty-fifth session it declares, that there is a Purgatory, and that the faithful can help the poor souls detained therein by their prayers, and by the most holy Sacrifice of the Mass.

As these means of helping the poor souls will be considered more fully and in detail further on, we shall at present only mention, in a general way, the essential conditions under which, according to the faith of the Church, we can most actively help those poor sufferers.

First of all, it is required that we should have the intention of helping these poor souls by our good works, otherwise these good works are put down to our account, or, if we do not stand in need of them, they are poured into what is called the treasure of the Church, of which we cannot dispose. However, it is not necessary to make a new intention before every action, and to say: 'I will perform such and such an action for the sake of the souls in Purgatory.' It is sufficient to make once for all an intention of doing certain things for the sake of the suffering souls, and not to withdraw it again. Still, it is advisable from time to time to renew the intention, as, for instance, at morning prayers, or at Mass.

Secondly, we must be in a state of grace, if we wish to help the poor souls in Purgatory by good works. 'Without Me,' says our Lord—that is, without My grace—'you can do nothing.' There is, however, a difference in the good works themselves. In one case the merit may depend on the person, not so in another.

Now, good works of the latter kind are always profitable to the holy souls, even if he who performs them is not in a state of grace. Such works are, for example, alms-deeds, of which it is said that they intercede in the hands of the poor; again, the holy Sacrifice of the Mass, which does not receive its value from the priest who offers it, or from him who causes it to be offered, but has it of its own self. But in works of the former kind, such as prayers, penances, indulgences, and so forth, we must be in a state of grace, if we desire to really help the poor souls by them. Bellarmine remarks that he who is in a state of mortal sin, cannot make satisfaction for himself—how then, could he do so for others? How can he, who is captive himself, redeem and give freedom to others?

OFFERINGS AND GIFTS FOR THE POOR SOULS

'Hear ye not from diresome fire
The cry of pity from flames so hot?
Bring offering, appease the ire,
Love pleads: Oh, forget me not!'

ALMSGIVING

he Angel Raphael said to Tobias: 'Alms
delivereth from death, and the same is that
which purgeth away sins, and maketh to find
mercy and life everlasting' (Tobias xii. 8). And in the
Book of Ecclesiasticus it is said: 'Water quencheth a
flaming fire, and alms resisteth sins' (Ecclus. iii. 33).

After these words of sacred Scripture it is not
surprising to see how the holy Fathers, in the most
elevated language, and with all the fire of their eloquence,
exhort the faithful to alms-deeds. St. Leo writes: 'Alms
atone for sins, destroy death, and extinguish the flames of
eternal fire.' St. Chrysostom calls almsgiving the friend of
God, who stands always by His side, obtaining graces
from Him, and tearing asunder the bonds of sin. It is a
heavenly ladder leading to God's right hand, and a sure
refuge for those who give, as well as for those who
receive.

There can be no doubt that almsgiving is a most
meritorious work, and therefore one that can also be
applied to the poor souls in Purgatory. St. Paulinus very
justly praises the Roman nobleman, Pammachius, who, on
the death of his beloved wife, assembled all the poor and
destitute of the city in St. Peter's Church, and distributed
food among them, in order to comfort and help her whose
loss he bewailed. St. Hieronymus remarks that, while

other husbands adorn the graves with violets, roses, and lilies, Pammachius pours the balm of alms over the sacred dust and venerable remains of his beloved wife.

It is therefore a very praiseworthy custom to give alms to all poor people we meet, particularly on Friday, the day on which our Divine Saviour gave His precious Blood in almsgiving to all mankind; or on Monday, the day which is especially dedicated to the memory of the poor souls in Purgatory. The pious Carthusian monk, Landsberg, says, if you hear a beggar knocking at your door, say to yourself, Hark! that is a poor soul in Purgatory asking for my assistance! Say then an Ave Maria, with the pious ejaculation, 'Eternal rest give to them, O Lord! and then give as good an alms as you can afford.

P. Pinelli tells us that Eusebius, formerly Prince of Sardinia, who was a great lover of almsgiving, set aside one of the cities of his kingdom, the revenues of which were annually distributed amongst the poor for the benefit and repose of the souls in Purgatory. Could we not also set aside a certain sum of money for such a noble purpose?—the profits of a certain house or field; the interest of such or such a sum of money? The alms which we give for the poor souls in Purgatory may be likened to so many cheques signed by names dear to God, and which, when presented, He will not dishonour.

When it is difficult or impossible for us to give money in alms, we can, at least, give other things of less value—even things that are no longer of use to us. In the year 1610 there came to one of the missioners in Japan a poor Japanese who had just lost his father by death, and offered him his coat, which he had taken off, imploring him to offer up the holy Sacrifice for the departed soul of his father. The priest was deeply moved, and promised to offer up the holy Sacrifice of the Mass, without, of course, depriving the poor man of his coat. How great was this man's love and devotion! He was ready to deprive himself of his only garment for the sake of one Mass for the repose of his father's soul! Oh, let us not be put to shame by this newly-made convert! Let us open our closets and chests, if not our purses, and bestow on the poor some of the many and superfluous things we have lying by—these things that often are not of the smallest use to us, and yet, when given in alms for the sake of the suffering souls, may be of greatest benefit. Let us give them in charity to those poor and forsaken creatures on earth, that they may benefit them as well as those poor forsaken souls in Purgatory, who, perhaps, may gain freedom and the light of the eternal rest by the alms given on their behalf.

The historian Buzelin relates a very remarkable event which took place in Armentieres, in France. In 1589 a fire broke out in this town, and it was completely destroyed by the flames. One of the citizens—a man named Nikolaus Forcheville—seeing no means of saving his house, exclaimed: 'O my God, I will give up this house to Thee for the use of the poor!' And, behold, that very moment the wind turned, and the house was saved! From such an example we might draw some useful conclusions. We might argue, for instance, in this way: Supposing we glanced at the list of those who owe us money; perhaps there are some, from whom there is little hope of recovering the debt. Well, let us make a promise, for the sake of the poor souls in Purgatory, to give, in case of unexpected payment, half the sum to the poor. It is not at all impossible, that the guardian angel of Purgatory may help to restore to us money otherwise lost.

If a poor person came to us, and begged an alms in the following words, 'Oh, grant my request in the name of thy dead mother, in the name of thy deceased children—I will pray for them,' could we refuse him? Certainly not! Let us, then, accustom ourselves, at the sight of every needy and destitute person, to say to ourselves: 'Alas! perhaps those dear ones I have lost are in just as deplorable a state—perhaps they are just as much to be pitied; and if they happened to be now by my side, they would surely urge me to give an alms to these suffering members of Christ's Church.'

It is not the wealthy alone who can give alms, but also the poor; at least, they can have the goodwill.

At the birth of the Saviour of mankind the Angels sang, 'Peace on earth to men of goodwill.' In truth, God Almighty regards not so much the greatness of the gift, but rather the heart and intention of the giver.

Zacheus, indeed, gave up half of his fortune, and so purchased Paradise; but he possessed great riches. But the poor widow, mentioned in the Scriptures, could only give a mite; and the converted robber could only offer to the Lord his pious intention of stealing no more! Therefore, whoever finds himself in such poor circumstances that he can give only a trifle in alms, let him give that little with a cheerful and loving heart, and it will be as good, if not better, than the large gift of the rich.

In the year 1626, during the Jubilee, a poor servant-maid, having heard it was necessary to give an alms in order to obtain the full indulgence of the Jubilee, divided her whole year's wages amongst the poor, and promised to do the same every ten years of her life. So this poor servant, without knowing it, followed the advice given by the great preacher St. Paul to the Ephesians:

'Let him labour, working with his hands the thing which is good, that he may have something to give to him that suffereth need' (Eph. iv. 28).

Almsgiving, therefore, is a means of helping the poor souls suffering in Purgatory.

FASTING

St. Peter Damian relates, in his 'Life of St. Rambert, Archbishop of Bremen,' of a priest named Arnold, that he lived a careless life, but ended it by a very penitent death. For a very long time he suffered in Purgatory, and at last the Lord gave him permission to appear before St. Rambert and implore his assistance. His confidence was not misplaced. Rambert fasted for forty days on bread and water, and Arnold was delivered from the prison of Purgatory.

Such fasts, of course, are hard indeed, and men of the present age would shrink from them. But the poor souls do not demand any extraordinary fasts or mortifications of us. The offering up of the usual fasts ordained by the Church suffices to shorten the term of their imprisonments. The fast on the vigils of great feasts, the ordinary fast or abstinence on Fridays, or ember-days, or Holy Week, offered up for them may bring them solace, comfort, and deliverance. Perhaps each day's fast may release a soul.

In the Book of Judith it is said, 'Know ye that the Lord will hear your prayers ' [therefore, also, those offered for the dead] 'if you continue with perseverance in fastings and prayers in the sight of the Lord ' (Judith iv. 11).

Vasquez relates a very touching incident which
confirms the truth of the words of Holy Writ. Sancio, the
King of Leon, died from poison, which had been secretly
administered to him. His wife, Queen Guda, who tenderly
loved him, at once laid aside her royal garments and
withdrew into a convent, in order to lead a life of poverty,
and consecrate her remaining days to God, so as to be of
greater help to the soul of her husband. Day and night she
prayed for him, and every Saturday she fasted in honour
of the Immaculate Conception of the Blessed Virgin Mary.
And behold, one Saturday as she was praying for the soul
of her departed husband, he suddenly appeared before her
in mourning garments, and with an expression of intense
sorrow depicted in his mien. He thanked her for her love
and tenderness, but implored her to continue her prayers
for him, even to redouble them. 'Ah!' he exclaimed; 'if I
could only depict to thee all my frightful tortures—those
I have experienced as well as those before me—if I could
only give thee the smallest idea of them, I know thy
compassion would increase tenfold! Beloved Guda,' he
continued, 'by the divine mercy I implore and beseech
thee to remember me.' Then the queen consecrated full
forty days to prayer and fasting. What was her
unspeakable joy, her indescribable consolation, when, at
the end of the forty days her husband once more stood
before her? Vanished were now the garments of
mourning; vanished, every trace of suffering and sorrow!
Sancio stood before her beaming with joy, overflowing
with bliss, and already a foretaste of heavenly light
illuminating his features. 'The hour of my deliverance has
come at last,' he joyfully exclaimed; 'the doors of my

prison have been opened! I have been freed from my sufferings, and to thee, O my good queen, I owe this great happiness! May God eternally bless thee for it! Oh, persevere in thy pious practices! Oh, keep thine eyes fixed on the sufferings of the other world; and always be mindful of the glories of eternity, the joys of paradise, whither I am now going, and where I will intercede for thee before the throne of God!'

All those people who are unable to undergo a bodily fast can yet observe a spiritual fast, viz., by abstaining from everything which might offend God. This moral fast is really the end and purpose of the physical fast. 'Ye fast,' says St. Chrysostom, 'but let it also be seen in your actions.'

St. Augustine asks, What will it avail us to abstain from wine, if we allow ourselves to be drunk with, and carried away by, anger? if we abstain from meat, and yet, like wild animals, delight in tearing to pieces the honour and the good name of our neighbour? What good will it do us to refrain from certain things which are forbidden at one time of the year, if we indulge in the pleasure of sin, which is forbidden at all times?

If the stomach is really too weak—from illness or old age—to fast, and a dispensation from the Church becomes absolutely necessary, see that the other members of the body which have sinned be mortified. If thine eyes have sinned, let them fast by modesty; if thy tongue, let it be silent; if thy ears, make a fence of thorns around them; if thy hands, put fetters on them; if thy feet, do violence to them, and let them not take thee whither thou hast hitherto found pleasure in going.

For the sake of thy parents and near relations, who

may be suffering in Purgatory, curb thy propensity to tell lies, to calumniate, to back-bite. Shorten the hours of thy repose, and rise earlier from thy bed, in order to shorten the painful condition of the poor souls in Purgatory. Deprive thyself of some little extra luxury in eating or drinking, for the sake of those abandoned souls! Consider how many ways thou hast of fasting and abstaining, without doing the smallest harm to thy delicate health or constitution!

By 'fasting' theologians generally mean anything disagreeable which the body voluntarily suffers, and the Council of Trent includes all sickness and misfortune.

Our Divine Saviour said to St. Teresa: 'My daughter, the greater and heavier the trials which My Father allows souls to suffer, the more innumerable are the proofs of divine love, which He shows to them.' Certainly, if our minds were properly penetrated with the truth of this saying, the thorns of life would be sweeter than its roses; we should prefer humiliation to honour, and hard work to rest! We should all exclaim with St. Bernard: 'Oh, how happy should I be to possess the lives of all mankind, that I might bear all their crosses!' We should join in the words of St. Teresa, when she said: 'Let me suffer or die,' or again, those of St. John of the Cross: 'O my God, you ask me what reward I would wish for my labour: I ask for no other reward but to be enabled to suffer more!'

If these were our sentiments, what inexpressible joy and comfort might we not procure for the poor souls in Purgatory! Therefore let us bear with patience and submission all our sorrows, afflictions and trials, for the sake of those poor unhappy beings, and when anything happens to disturb us, let us say, 'I will bear this annoyance patiently and cheerfully, for the sake of my beloved father, my cherished mother, my dear sisters, brothers and relations, that they may the sooner enter into their eternal rest.'

If to love means to suffer and endure, what Christian would refuse to bear and suffer something or other, for the good of the members of his family, especially when he remembers that, by so doing, he can lessen the number, and shorten the term, of their sufferings in Purgatory?

PRAYER

The Holy Scripture says 'it is a holy and wholesome thought to pray for the dead.' It is holy because it is most pleasing to God; it is wholesome because we have reason to believe, that through the infinite mercy and compassion of His sacred Heart, our Lord accepts our prayers, offered in atonement for the sins of those sufferers in Purgatory. If the prayers we offer up for temporal goods are often heard and granted, how much more so when we offer them up for spiritual goods, and for souls so tenderly loved by God, and who are destined to take part in His own glory for all eternity! Oh, surely St. Augustine had good reason to exclaim: 'One cannot conceive a holier and more wholesome practice, than praying for the dead!'

The celebrated Archbishop of Milan, the great St. Ambrose, exclaimed, in his funeral oration on the Roman Emperor Valentinian and his brother Gratian: 'You will both be happy in eternity, if my poor prayers are of any avail; no day will I allow to pass without remembering you. Every night you will be the object of my most fervent intercession, and have a share in all my sacrifices.

May my right hand be forgotten, if ever I cease to remember you!'

St. Bernard exhorts us to pray for the dead in the following words: 'Come, let us help them; let us not delay or hesitate! with lamentations will I beseech the Lord; I will sigh and pray to Him without ceasing. With my ardent prayers I will beseech the Lord, and become the advocate of those poor souls, in the hope that their forlorn condition may be changed to a state of rest and joy, and their frightful sufferings into the infinite bliss of the glory of Heaven. By such intercession can the term of their punishment be shortened and all their torments ended.'

In the 'Imitation of Christ' we meet with the following words, on the subject of prayers for the dead: 'Full of love and charity, we must remember in our prayers the souls of all the faithful departed, but particularly the souls of our parents, friends and relations, and those who have been our benefactors on earth. For that is a work of real love and charity. As we entertain the most earnest hopes, that we shall be remembered when we have departed this life, we ought to make every effort in our power to assist them to arrive speedily at their promised abode of bliss, and by our prayers shorten the weary days of their pilgrimage in Purgatory. And we must remember, that everyone who actively assists in the deliverance of those poor souls, gains for himself the greatest advantages. By offering his prayers for their eternal repose, he by no means loses the fruits of those prayers, for they are remembered to him, and are before him when his time comes to die. And, moreover, one is rewarded even in this life for such prayers—one feels a certain consolation, a certain peace of mind, after having offered up fervent prayers for the dead. For all must know—be the time long or short—that they must go the way of all flesh, and perhaps be soon obliged to undergo the same torments which the poor souls in Purgatory are now enduring. Let us pray, then, for all our dearly-beloved dead, for we must soon follow them; let us pray for them, that they also may pray for us in our need. But let our prayers be fervent, and full of devotion and attention.'

St. Jerome said: 'I would prefer to say one short psalm with ardent devotion, than the whole Psalter with negligence.' If you must content yourselves with short prayers for the dead, you have the *Pater Noster* and the *Ave Maria.* Do not forget to say them, at least once a day, with reverence and devotion for the dead.

A pious bishop once had a dream, in which he saw a youth dragging a woman out of a deep well by means of a golden hook, which was fastened at the end of a silver cord. What was his surprise, the following morning, as he walked through the graveyard, to see the very same youth he dreamt of the previous night, kneeling by a grave! 'What are you doing there, my young friend?' The bishop asked. 'Most reverend sir, I am offering up the *Pater Noster* and the psalm "*Miserere*," for the soul of my departed mother.' The bishop immediately saw the meaning of his dream.

Father Alexis, of Salo, writes thus: 'One of my most favourite practices, when I am very anxious of obtaining a favour, is this— I fold my arms in the form of a cross on my breast, and repeat five "Our Fathers" and five "Hail Marys" for the repose of the souls in Purgatory; and I truly affirm that by these simple means I have obtained many favours and graces for myself, as well as for others. In the midst of my greatest sufferings and annoyances, I have thrown myself down on my knees and appealed to the souls in Purgatory, as to a sure and certain place of refuge; I seemed, as it were, to travel through Purgatory in haste, and to recommend myself to those pious souls. And every time my prayers have been heard.'

The same pious man continues to say:

'In my examination of conscience, for every sin I found myself guilty of, I imposed on myself as penance the recital of the "Rosary for the Dead".'

Besides the 'Our Father' and the 'Hail Mary,' a most efficacious prayer for the dead is the well-known psalm 'De profundis,' which the Church has consecrated to this purpose.

The celebrated Chancellor of England, Thomas More, assembled every evening all the members of his household together, in order to say the night prayers in common; but he always concluded them by the recital of the above-mentioned psalm, 'De profundis.'

Let us consider, that in reciting this psalm we are taking the place of these abandoned souls, and speak the words in their name. Let us acquire the habit of repeating this psalm very often, particularly when we go to bed, for the bed naturally brings home to our mind the bier, which will be our last bed upon earth. Then again, in the morning when we arise from our bed, and as it were, from the grave! Further, we ought to repeat this prayer every time we see a fire, which must remind us of the poor souls condemned to Purgatory; or when we hear a clock striking the hour, which may be the last of the life of some Christian upon earth; or a bell ring, which may perhaps announce a death or burial; or lastly, whenever we pass a churchyard. To this prayer is generally added the short prayer which the faithful so constantly make use of: 'May the souls of the faithful departed, through the mercy of God, rest in peace. Amen.' This short prayer cannot be too often repeated. As a drop of water often falling would finally make up a stream, so the constant repetition of this short prayer, if said with fervour, will not fail to mitigate the great consuming flames of Purgatory.

St. Paul says, Love never can cease (1 Cor. xiii. 8); therefore those who really love each other, can never forget one another, not even in death; and it is said, 'a friend in need is a friend indeed.' Would it not, then, be most cruel to see a brother or a friend cast into prison, or thrown into a flaming fire, and not to be moved to tears nor to hold out to him a helping hand? Or worse still, to pass him by in silence and indifference, when a word would be sufficient to save him?

Therefore let us make use of this simple, agreeable, and most certain means—prayer— to assist the poor souls in Purgatory. Let us frequently raise our hearts and hands in supplication, and do all we can for their deliverance, and do it speedily. Let us consider more and more how much they have to endure, and how impossible it is for them to reach their destined place of rest, before their souls are thoroughly cleansed and purified.

THE HOLY SACRIFICE OF THE MASS

HE HOLY SACRIFICE OF THE MASS is the surest and most effectual means we possess, for procuring the eternal repose and happiness of the departed. St. Augustine, in a moment of inspiration, called this Sacrifice 'The Sacrament of love, the revelation of unity, and the bond of friendship.'

Penetrated with the same ideas as St. Augustine, his holy contemporary, St. Chrysostom, exclaimed: 'No, it is not in vain nor without fruit that the most holy Mystery of the Altar is celebrated for the dead, and prayers said for their repose.'

According to the opinion of St. Gregory the Great, the unbloody Sacrifice of the Altar is the most powerful of all means by which we can help the dead in their sorest need. St. Cyril says: 'We pray for all who have departed this life, with the most confident conviction that the prayers at the Altar are most profitable to them.'

Again, in another place he says: 'Supposing a king, who was offended by a subject has banished him from his kingdom, and the friends of the outlaw wish to restore him to the king's favour, and for that purpose form a deputation to the royal personage, and, presenting a costly gift, venture to plead for pardon for the offender; would not the king comply with their request, and either grant a pardon, or else mitigate the punishment to some extent? Well, in like manner do we, although sinners, plead for pardon from the King of Heaven and Earth for our banished friends, and with much surer hopes of success, for the gift we offer, is not an earthly crown, but

is the Body and Blood of His own well-beloved Son, who
has bled for the sins of the whole world.'

St. Thomas of Canterbury relates that his father,
during a pilgrimage to the Holy Land, after having
confessed his sins to a pious monk, received, before he
was absolved, the following advice: 'I plainly see you will
find it very difficult to appease the divine wrath for all
your dreadful sins, and make sufficient satisfaction for
them; therefore try to make a priest of one of your sons,
that he may frequently offer up the holy Sacrifice of the
Mass, for the repose of your soul.' 'That was what made
me study for the Church, and become a priest,' continues
the Saint; 'and I call on my Lord Jesus Christ to bear
witness, that I speak the truth! On one occasion I was
prevented by some obstacle or other from saying Mass,
and my father appeared to me full of sorrow, and said,
"My son, why do you hesitate? why do you not hasten to
my relief?"' In ancient times there used to be a custom
among the faithful, of having seven Masses said in
different places for the repose of the souls in Purgatory.
They were called St. Gregory's Masses, because it was
thought, that this custom had been introduced by him.
The first of these Masses was offered on Palm-Sunday, in
order to commemorate the voluntary captivity of Jesus
Christ, and to implore Him, by the memory of His own
bonds, to break the chains which detained the poor souls
in Purgatory. The second Mass was said on the following
Tuesday, in memory of our Divine Redeemer's
condemnation to death, in order that He might mitigate
the rigours of His just but terrible judgment,, in regard of
the poor souls. The third was offered on Wednesday in
Holy Week, in memory of the Crucifixion, that by the

unspeakable agony endured by Christ, the condition of the poor souls in Purgatory might be improved, and their suffering alleviated. The fourth—the votive Mass—was offered while the Passion, according to the Gospel of St. John, was being read, in Commemoration of the death of the Redeemer of mankind. The sixth Mass was that of the Resurrection, in order that the poor souls might partake in the glory and triumph of our Saviour. The last of the seven Masses was that of the Assumption of the Blessed Virgin Mary, in order to obtain the powerful help of her special intercession for the poor souls in Purgatory.

The holy Sacrifice of the Mass therefore is the most effectual, the most powerful means we have, for assisting the suffering souls in Purgatory. Let us try, then, to have this most adorable Sacrifice offered up for them as often as we possibly can; and let us join with them our own supplications and prayers, somewhat in the following manner: At the Confiteor let us prostrate ourselves, and penetrate in spirit into the depth of Purgatory, and place ourselves in the midst of those poor souls, imagining them to entreat us, with uplifted hands, to pray with our utmost fervour for them during the oblation of the most holy Sacrifice.

At the Elevation let us raise up our hearts and say: O my God, in memory of Thy painful death have compassion on this poor soul for whom I pray. Let us remember that while we beseech the Lord, all the poor souls unite their prayers with ours. When the Chalice is raised, let us say: O my God, behold Thy precious Blood which was shed for their deliverance. Oh, let the saving fruits of this costly Blood come to the poor souls, let its cleansing streams flow into Purgatory. Remember with what great love Thou didst first shed it for Thy elect, so many of whom are now languishing in the fiery dungeon.

We can also make use of the Crucifix, which is always placed over the Altar, to help us in making our intentions and supplications for the dead. At the sight of the thorn-crowned Head, we may think of and pray for the souls of our deceased superiors, spiritual and temporal; to the wounded right Hand, for the souls of our parents, friends and benefactors; to the left Hand, for the souls of all those who during their lifetime have done or wished to do us harm; to the holy wounds of the right Foot, we can recommend the souls of all those who lie buried in our parish; to the left Foot, the souls of all the faithful departed without distinction of country or time, begging and beseeching the Divine Redeemer, that He might allow the precious Blood of His five Wounds to flow over all the souls of the dead, that they may thereby obtain refreshment and peace. And finally, to the holy wound in the Side of our Saviour, one can more especially recommend one's own soul, saying, if not with the lips, at least in one's heart: O my sweetest Jesus, I know well that my many daily faults must be atoned for in the flames of Purgatory. Therefore, I beg of Thee to have pity on me! Oh, I implore Thee, by the precious Blood which flowed from the loving Heart I now adore. At the Holy Communion, when we see the Sacred Host in the hands of the priest, let us consider, that it is the Body of Him who commanded us to pray for the dead; that it is He who has said: 'If you ask the Father anything in My name He will give it to you' (John xvi. 23). Let us remind Him of His own words—let us implore Him by His love. Let us exert ourselves, and spare no labour. For this is the favourable moment, when our prayers may be heard, and all our requests granted.

St. Jeves, a disciple of St. Dominic and Provincial of Palestine, relates that after the death of his brother, he addressed the following words to the Divine Redeemer while he was celebrating and held the Sacred Host in his hands: 'O my Divine Saviour! if the Turks had taken possession of a prisoner, and his servants had offered to ransom him by as precious a treasure, as I now hold in my hand, without doubt the poor prisoner would be immediately set free. But, Lord, Thou art incomparably more generous. Therefore, I beseech Thee, sweet Jesus, give me the soul of my poor brother.' Three times he repeated this short prayer, and then consumed the Sacred Host; whereupon he saw the soul of his deceased brother ascending to Heaven, full of joy and glory.

At the end of the Mass, when the priest gives the last blessing, we beg in spirit that he who stands in the place of God may impart his blessing also to all the souls in Purgatory.

One day, when St. Francis Borgia was about to ascend the altar steps to celebrate Mass, he thought he distinctly heard the last sigh of a person very dear to him, but far away from him. He immediately offered up the Sacrifice of the Mass for that person, and at the conclusion of it this friend appeared to him and said: 'Just as you were about to begin Mass, I gave up my soul into the hands of my Creator, and I was condemned to Purgatory, and had just arrived at that place of suffering; but the holy Sacrifice of the Mass which you have said for me has opened for me the doors of Heaven. Never shall I forget your love.'

Oh, let us impress this example deeply upon our minds. Let us never neglect an opportunity to have Mass offered for the souls of the faithful departed, and thereby come to their assistance. The Council of Trent tells us, that the holy Sacrifice of the Mass is the surest, the most efficacious of all means, for procuring the release of those poor imprisoned souls from the flames of Purgatory. Let us not grow weary in applying this means again and again, particularly for those souls that are dearest to our Lord, and those that have a special claim upon our love and gratitude.

The efficacy of other means of helping the dead always depends on certain conditions, and we can never be infallibly certain that these conditions are fulfilled. But with the Sacrifice of the Mass it is different. Being the offering of Jesus Christ Himself, it cannot lose its value and power by the unworthiness of the priest, or those who offer it and assist at it; and therefore its effect can never be diminished or lost.

HOLY COMMUNION

At the moment of Holy Communion when we live, indeed not we, but Christ in us (Gal. ii. 20), we may confidently hope to be able to console our departed brethren in their deep sorrow, and to obtain for them, as well as for ourselves, rich treasures of grace—treasures that will bring us, together with them, to life everlasting. Since the holy Sacrifice of the Mass is the best means of helping the poor souls in Purgatory, because it is the constant renewal of Christ's Passion and Death for the atonement of our sins and for our salvation, it follows that the next best means of assisting the poor souls is the personal assistance at, and the actual participation, by Holy Communion, in the Sacrifice of love. United with Jesus in this wonderful Mystery, we need not fear to make the boldest request, for He rests in our hearts as on a throne, waiting, as it were, to hear and grant our prayers and desires. There He will grant us everything and refuse us nothing. Justly, therefore, does the great Doctor of the Church, St. Bonaventure, exhort us to frequent Communion for the repose of the souls departed. 'Love and compassion,' he says, 'should urge you to approach the sacred table, because nothing is more efficacious to obtain the desired peace and rest for the unhappy sufferers.'

Louis Blosius, Abbot of Liessies, who died in the odour of sanctity, confirms the truth of what we have just been saying by the mention of an incident in one of his works (In Mon. Sp., chap. vi.). There appeared once to him, a well-known and most pious servant of God, the soul of a departed completely enveloped in flames, who told him that the reason why he had to endure those terrible torments was, because of his careless manner of preparing for Holy Communion. 'Therefore,' he added, 'I implore thee, my dear friend, by that bond of love and friendship which has always united us, receive once, with devout preparation and great fervour, Holy Communion, for the sake of my poor soul, and I feel confident that it will release me from those frightful torments I am now suffering in punishment for my lukewarmness, towards the most adorable Sacrament of the Altar.' Having spoken these words, he disappeared. His friend lost no time in complying with his request. Having received Holy Communion with perfect preparation and disposition of heart, the soul of his departed friend appeared to him again, but this time resplendent with dazzling light, and soaring swiftly heavenwards.

If you intend to offer up your Holy Communion for the repose of the faithful departed, you may pray during Mass that they should help you in your preparation. For although those poor souls are deprived of the power of helping themselves, they are in a position to help us. With reason remarks St. Ambrose, Bishop of Milan: 'By your prayers and intercession make for yourself friends of those poor souls in Purgatory! Do your best to obtain their release from captivity, that they may pray also for you before the throne of God, and obtain your eternal salvation.' And Pope Adrian VI: 'Whoever prays fervently for the dead, in the sincere hope of helping them (consequently, so much the more he who devoutly offers up Holy Communion for them), obliges them to a return of love and gratitude.'

By Holy Communion, the most sublime act of our religion, we give infinite honour to God, and thereby expiate the offence caused by sin. When we worthily receive Holy Communion, our souls are penetrated with sentiments of humility, contrition, love and zeal. But these acts are already in themselves meritorious, especially when exercised while Jesus Christ, the Sun of love and justice reposes in our heart. Add to this the many indulgences, which, under certain conditions may be gained by Holy Communion. For this reason many commentators apply the words of Tobias: 'Place thy bread and thy wine by the graves of the just,' to Holy Communion offered up for the dead.

The poor souls in Purgatory repeat, as it were, the

words of the Psalmist: 'Lord, Thou hast prepared a table before me against them that afflict me' (Ps. xxii. 5), i.e., against the flames that torture me, against the fire that devours me. In the Churches belonging to the Society of Jesus, there is offered up every month a general communion for the repose of the souls of the faithful departed. Again, theologians agree in regarding 'the tree of life, which stood in the midst of Paradise, and bore twelve fruits, one for each month, whose leaves were for the healing of the nations' (Apoc. xxii. 2), as a symbol of the Blessed Sacrament.

St. Thomas Aquinas, especially, is of this opinion. He says: 'As death and perdition came upon us by the eating of a forbidden food, viz., the apple from the tree of knowledge of good and evil, so also will justification and life come back to us by the sacred food from the tree of life, which is the Body of our Lord.' If, therefore, the fruits of this tree represent the Holy Eucharist, it is clear that monthly Communion must be a most wholesome and salutary practice. The souls thus released will be our intercessors in Heaven.

INDULGENCES

The guilt of mortal sin, and the eternal punishment due to it, are wiped away by the Sacrament of Penance, or also by an act of perfect contrition, while the temporal punishment due to it is taken away, either by the performance of good works here below, or the sufferings of Purgatory in the next world. But, as our works of satisfaction, such as prayers, fasting, alms, etc., are only too frequently insufficient for one reason or another, the Church, like a tender and thoughtful mother, comes to the assistance of her weak children; the Divine Founder having entrusted her with the keys of the kingdom of Heaven, she has power to remove all possible impediments to our entrance into Heaven, and consequently also the remaining temporal punishments. The remission of this temporal punishment, which still awaits the sinner after his sins have been forgiven as to their guilt and eternal punishment, comes under the name of Indulgence. This indulgence, or remission on the part of the Church, which is granted outside the Sacrament of Penance, and under certain conditions only, one of which is that we have previously confessed our sins, repented of them and obtained absolution, supplements the insufficiency of our good works by the overflowing works of satisfaction of Jesus Christ, the Blessed Virgin and the Saints. From this rich treasury at her disposal the Church always takes whenever she grants an Indulgence to her needy children.

Indulgences are of two kinds: plenary, or perfect, when all our temporal punishment is remitted, and partial or imperfect when only a part of it is forgiven. The latter Indulgences correspond to the duration of penances inflicted by the penitential canons of the early Church.

Both the plenary and the partial Indulgences can be applied to the souls in Purgatory, but only when it is expressly so stated. This application to the souls in Purgatory is not a definite and immediate one, because the Church has no longer authority over her deceased members, but is only by way of suffrage, as it is called, which means that the Church asks and beseeches the Lord to accept in His mercy the satisfactory value of the Indulgence for the complete or partial remission of the temporal punishment due to the souls in Purgatory. Of course the degree and measure of this application of Indulgences to the souls in Purgatory depends entirely on the free will of God. All we know is, that Indulgences are of inestimable service to the poor souls.

It is, therefore, as Boudon calls it, a kind of cruelty not to try and gather these heavenly treasures, and bestow them as often as possible upon the poor needy souls. The same writer complains also bitterly of those members of confraternities who are either ignorant or neglectful of the many Indulgences which they might gain and apply to the poor souls in Purgatory.

Segneri relates that on one occasion God allowed the blessed Mary of Quito to see in a vision the great value of Indulgences. He showed her in the centre of a public square a great table laden with a quantity of pieces of gold and silver, of diamonds, and precious stones. 'This treasure,' He said to her, 'is open to every one; each one may take as much as he likes or stands in need of!'

In the life of St. Magdalene de Pazzi we read that during one of her ecstasies she learned that one of the Sisters of the Convent was delivered from Purgatory, after a few hours, in virtue of an Indulgence by which the merits of the life and sufferings of Christ were applied to her. The Popes, as is well known, have bestowed upon the practice of the Stations of the Cross the same rich Indulgences as are gained by visiting those very spots in Jerusalem itself. And since all these Indulgences can be applied to the souls in Purgatory, it is plain that this exercise is of the utmost importance and value for the souls in Purgatory. The life of Catherine of Emmerich furnishes a very touching proof of the great virtue of this devotion. There we read that this pious virgin held through all her life most intimate communion with the poor souls in Purgatory. She offered all her prayers and good works for them, and often felt that they were appealing to her for help, and if she sometimes forgot them they brought themselves to her memory in the most touching manner. When still a young girl she was often roused from sleep at night by a host of poor souls, and then she arose and went with them, barefoot, through the snow on the severest winter nights, in order to do the Stations of the Cross at Koesfeld, which are several miles long.

All our efforts, even the very best, seem poor and deficient; but the least portion of the satisfactory work of Christ is of infinite value. How strongly ought we, therefore, be moved to make use of those heavenly treasures, the Indulgences, in the interest of the poor abandoned souls! The more so as the Church in her motherly care and love has attached sometimes even to the shortest prayer or ejaculation great and extensive graces.

THE HEROIC ACT

It is, no doubt, a proof of great love to offer up all one's good works for the conversion of sinners, particularly of those who are in danger of being eternally lost. But it is a much greater work of charity to offer them up for the repose of the poor souls in Purgatory. And why? Because the chief end of our creation—which is the honour and glory of God—is more perfectly realized if we help the poor souls who are so dear to the heart of God, and for whose deliverance His loving Heart is yearning,

to bring them sooner to God than it would be if we helped
to convert a sinner.

The Heroic Act is nothing else than a voluntary gift
of all our good works—and even of those good works and
Indulgences which may be applied to us after our
death—deposited into the hands of the Blessed Virgin
Mary for distribution among the poor souls according to
her good pleasure.

Father Oliden, a priest of the Theatine Order, is
generally considered as the author of this vow. He always
cherished a particular love for the departed souls, and
repeatedly entreated the Holy See to enrich this Heroic
Act with Indulgences.

Further, this great act of love had been known
already, and also practised in former centuries. In the
17th century it was defended by the S. Congregation in
Rome against the opinions of several divines who had
expressed themselves strongly against it, approved and
enriched with Indulgences by Benedict XIII. These
Indulgences were confirmed by Pius VI and Pius IX in the
following decree, issued on the 20th of November, 1854:

'As it is a holy and a wholesome thought to pray for
the dead, that they may be loosed from their sins, the
Apostolic love of the Roman Pontiffs has never ceased in
its efforts to increase the zeal of the children of the
Church militant for the souls of the departed, and has,
therefore, granted immeasurable Indulgences from the
treasures of the Church, which might be applied also to
the souls detained in Purgatory, bestowing them
(Indulgences) on the recital of certain prayers, as well as
on the performance of certain good works, in order that
those poor souls might be freed from the avenging flames,

and brought sooner into the society of the blessed inhabitants of the city of God.'

In order to assist the poor souls most efficaciously, Father Caspar Oliden, priest of the Order of Theatines, at the time when Benedict XIII, of blessed memory, occupied the Papal Chair, instituted or spread about a pious practice which was called the vow, or gift, in virtue of which the faithful dedicated by a special act of love all the good works of their whole life, and even those that would be offered up for them after death, to the faithful departed. The above mentioned Pope Benedict XIII granted to all those who thus bound themselves special Indulgences, which later, at the request of the same Theatines, were ratified and confirmed on December 12, 1788, by Pope Pius VI, and which our most Holy Father Pius IX, on September 30, 1852, at the earnest request of several priests, not only confirmed, but also defined and determined in the following manner:

1. All priests who make this vow, enjoy, on all the days of the year, the grace of a privileged Altar.

2. To all the faithful who have made this vow a plenary Indulgence—applicable to the dead—is granted on every day they receive Holy Communion, and every Monday of the year on which they hear Mass on behalf of the poor souls, provided that, in both instances they visit a chapel or public oratory and devoutly pray there for some time, according to the intention of our Holy Father the Pope.

3. Moreover, the faithful who have made this vow can apply to the souls in Purgatory all Indulgences without exception which are granted

now, or will be granted at any future time.

4. In order to render more powerful assistance to the souls now suffering in the purifying flames of Purgatory, this (indult) must be regarded as extending to all Christians of every country throughout the world who have taken this vow.

His Holiness, moreover, being mindful also of children unable as yet to receive Holy Communion, of sick and old people, prisoners, farm labourers and all others, who from some lawful cause or other are prevented either from receiving Holy Communion or assisting at Mass on Sunday, has, according to his Fatherly care for all the faithful, provided that those who are lawfully prevented from attending Mass on Monday, may gain the Indulgence attached to the Monday by hearing the obligatory Mass on Sunday. And for all those of the faithful who are either incapable as yet or lawfully prevented from receiving Holy Communion, his Holiness was pleased to give power to the ecclesiastical Superior of each place to delegate, according to their prudence, from among the number of approved confessors, some who would have power to commute, where necessary, the reception of Holy Communion into some other good works.

Given at Rome,
20th November, 1854.
CARDINAL ASQUINI, Prefeet.

This act of love is not a vow in the proper sense of the word, nor does it bind under the pain of sin. Although it is not necessary, we would yet recommend the pious faithful to renew it from time to time, because by so doing we rekindle our zeal and love towards the holy souls, and we feel urged on anew to increase our efforts of help on their behalf. There is no regular formula for making this so-called vow; a firm act of will is sufficient. Nevertheless, we add here a short formula for those who desire it.

All for the greater honour and glory of God!

O most adorable Trinity! one God in three Persons! In order to follow more closely the footsteps of our sweetest Saviour Jesus Christ and to prove my love to the ever Blessed Mother of God, and Mother of the poor souls in Purgatory, I (N. N.) firmly resolve to labour for the release of those poor prisoners in Purgatory who have not yet fully satisfied the divine justice. I sincerely promise, so far as I may do so without binding myself under the pain of sin, to work for the release especially of those souls whose deliverance is particularly desired by the Blessed Virgin. With this intention I commit into the hands of the most faithful Mother all my satisfactory works, as well as that of others which may be applied to me during life or after death.

I most humbly beg of Thee, O my God, to graciously accept this offering which I make. I once more renew my promise for Thy greater honour and glory and for the eternal salvation of my soul.

If my works of satisfaction and penance do not fully satisfy or atone for the sins of those poor-souls, whose deliverence our Lady especially desires, and for my own sins, which I heartily detest, I beg of Thee, my Saviour, to accept and add to them my future sufferings in Purgatory. I commit myself entirely to Thine infinite mercy, and to the compassion of Mary, my dearest Mother.

As witnesses to my vow, I call upon all the Saints in Heaven, as well as all the members of the Church militant and suffering. Amen.

Father Faber relates that Father Ferdinand, of Monroy, a man of great apostolic zeal, made, on his death-bed, a written declaration that he would give to the souls in Purgatory all the Masses that would be said for him after his death, as well as all the Indulgences that would be granted for him. The venerable Chimenes made this vow on the advice of the Blessed Virgin herself. In this he was but following the example of many others distinguished by learning and holiness.

THE SAINTS OF THE POOR SOULS

'The deeds of Saints,
The thoughts of souls,
With love inflamed you here behold!
What they have been,
What they have done,
Do you in turn
For those who're gone.'

OUR LADY

'Let me go to my child, I must see my beloved son once more!' Thus cried, in heartrending grief, the mother of Robert of Flanders, who, on the charge of treason, was cast into a deep dungeon by the cruel Stephen of Blois, with no other entrance to it except a small opening above, and who there was to be starved to death. 'Let me go, let me down!' she cried unceasingly, until at last the hard heart of Stephen was softened and he gave orders that the mother should be let down by means of a rope into the dungeon, to see once more and console her son. That was an earthly mother, and can we imagine that in the tender loving heart of our heavenly Mother there would be less loveless tenderness for her poor imprisoned children in Purgatory? How could she abandon them—she, who never abandons a sinner on earth? How could she refuse to help them, since they can no longer help themselves? How could she not love them, when her love is eternal and does not cease with death? Is she not the Mother of Him who has said, 'I was in prison, and ye visited me,' of Him who loosened the chains which bound His Apostles and miraculously opened the doors of the prison which

213

confined the martyrs? of Him who descended into hell and rose on the third day from the dead?

Therefore it is an opinion well worthy of acceptance and respect, founded on trustworthy revelations and authentic declarations of many papal Bulls, that the Blessed Virgin assists in a most special manner the souls in Purgatory. They are souls and are poor; therefore, the Blessed Virgin loves them. St. Bernard justly calls her the Mother of the poor souls.

They are souls, and are suffering in Purgatory, and that alone would suffice to prove that they are loved by Mary, for souls are the magnet of her heart.

Priceless is the value of a soul, and no one has better shown it than our Lord Himself. The devil persuades Judas to betray Him. But what does not Jesus do to save him?

He prostrates Himself at his feet, and washes them. O Divine Saviour, Thou at the feet of Judas! Thou at the feet of the man who betrays Thee! Thou at the feet of a man already possessed by the devil! How great, then, must be the value of a soul! Of greater value than the whole world. 'Behold, I will give Thee the whole world,' said Satan, 'if, falling down, Thou wilt adore me.' No, not for the whole world could or would our Saviour bend His knee, and yet for the sake of a soul He knelt before a human being, prostrated Himself at the feet of one who was a devil. Satan, by offering the whole world, could not prevail upon Him to fall down; but by trying to rob Him of a soul, he caused Him to bow down even before a man, and such a man!

But after Jesus, who could better know the value of a soul than Mary, who comes next to Him. She had witnessed, how much our Lord did and suffered for souls. She sees these souls red with the Divine Blood, by which they were purchased; she lives in the joys of Heaven, to which all souls are likewise destined. Her Son gave His life for the souls of men; but she, as mother, gave her Son for the same purpose. Therefore the love of her heart embraces also Purgatory; therefore is she also the loving mother of the souls in Purgatory.

The woman in the Gospels who so eagerly and persistently sought after her lost groat, searching and sweeping every corner of her house, is but a faint symbol of the love of Mary for the souls which she has lost, though only for a time, which she sees separated from Heaven, from her Divine Son, and herself, and suffering in the flames of fire. She burns with love for these poor souls, well remembering the words of her Divine Son, when He said, that even a cup of cold water given in His Name would be rewarded with the joy of Heaven. And if Jesus, while hanging upon the Cross, cried out, 'I thirst,' which according to the opinion of the holy Fathers meant, I thirst for souls—and consequently also for the souls in Purgatory—can we suppose that Mary will not try in every possible way to satisfy His desire, and still His thirst?

Both learning and piety conspire in proving the love of the Blessed Virgin for the poor souls in Purgatory. The learned Chancellor, John Gerson, says that, according to a pious tradition, on the day of the Blessed Virgin's Assumption into Heaven, there were admitted also a great many souls from Purgatory, and since that time she has been given the privilege of delivering the souls of her true servants from the burning flames. St. Alphonsus agrees with him, and says: 'Those who love and truly serve the most gentle Mother Mary can indeed be called fortunate, for not alone here on earth, but also hereafter in Purgatory, will she be their helper and comforter.'

St. Bonaventure applies the words of Scripture, 'I have penetrated into the bottom of the deep' (Ecclus. xxiv. 8), and says: she penetrates to the depths of Purgatory, and lightens the sufferings of the souls therein. In like manner, St. Vincent Ferrer says: 'Ah, how loving and kind is Mary towards those poor sufferers in Purgatory! she strengthens them, and refreshes them continually.' Nor does holy Church contradict or disown those sayings of the Saints; but, on the contrary, confirms them, as we can gather from the fact, that on the day of decease she allows a Mass to be sung in honour of our Lady, that through her intercession the departed souls may find eternal rest and peace.

St. Bernardine of Sienna, in his third sermon on the holy Name of Mary, assures us, that this most Holy Virgin helps the poor souls when he says: 'Mary reigns over the kingdom of Purgatory, for the Prophet says of her, "I sojourn over the waves of the sea." The torments and sufferings of Purgatory are compared to waves, because they pass away in time, and to waves of the sea, because of their bitterness. But the powerful intercession of Mary sweetens their bitterness, shortens the torments, and delivers from pains; for she loves these souls because they are poor and helpless. Their poverty consists in a twofold pain—one of the soul, the other of the body—and both are as terrible as those of hell, except that they do not last for ever.' The Divine Saviour passed through the land of the Jews, healing and blessing; He calmed the

storms and the waves; walking on the waters, He cheered
His disciples by His appearance, and saved the sinking
Apostle by His helping Hand. In like manner, Mary, the
Mother of Mercy, passes through Purgatory, gladdening
and calming, blessing and comforting, the afflicted,
announcing to some that the time of their suffering has
been shortened, while others she draws out and delivers
from the flames. Many thousand souls will thank her in
the words of Scripture: 'We have passed through fire and
water, and thou hast brought us out into a refreshment!
(Ps. lxv. 12).

Mary loves the poor souls in Purgatory because she
has also gone through a kind of Purgatory, a fire of
tribulation—not indeed, in punishment of her sins, for she
had none —but that she might have more compassion
with us, and be more fully entitled to the name by which
she is so well known— 'Comforter of the afflicted!' For
this reason she descended into a sea of sorrow, into the
depths of tribulation, into the furnace of poverty, exile,
persecution. For this reason she suffered those pains of
mind and soul, which were caused by the three days' loss
of her Child, and by His absence during the many years
that she lived after His death. All those sufferings were a
real Purgatory to her. Its flames would but increase her
burning love for the poor souls, and make her more truly
the Mother of the Poor Souls.

Let us, therefore, venerate Mary, and beg of her, even
now, while we still sojourn in this valley of tears, to
increase daily our ardour, and give us perseverance in
good works, to obtain for us a happy death and assure us
of her advocacy at the judgment-seat of God. 'If thou dost
truly venerate Mary,' St. Alphonsus says, 'and faithfully

serve her during life, thou canst certainly hope, when thou comest to die, to be led by her at once into Heaven, without having to undergo the pains of Purgatory.'

But the best means to obtain this grace is to imitate the love of the Blessed Virgin for the poor souls. Let us try and be zealous in the cause of the poor souls, and have often recourse to the intercession of the Mother of Mercy, for the same purpose. Let us seek some quiet chapel or altar of our Lady, and there prostrate ourselves, and pray with all our strength and fervour for the repose of the souls of our parents, brothers and sisters, who have preceded us in the great journey to eternity. Or again, to the prayers which we daily address to our Lady let us add a few Aves for the dead, but above all let us say the Rosary for them. Our compassion for those souls will surely be most pleasing to the Mother of Mercy, and when our hour shall come, she will remember us and show herself a true mother of the poor souls.

The ancient Romans ascribed a wonderful power to roses. They not only greatly esteemed them during their lifetime, crowning themselves with roses, but desired also that after their death the tombs should be adorned with them, as is proved by an ancient epitaph of Ravenna, which says: 'He has made the gift under condition that every year roses be placed on his tomb.' They believed, that by the strewing of roses the souls of the departed would receive comfort. Hence the poet Virgil sings: 'With full hands supply me with flowers, with purple roses will I deck the tomb of my grandchild, and with flowers enrich the soul of the departed.' That which was but vain conceit amongst the ancients, is truth and reality among Christians. For the spiritual roses of the rosary can and do help the souls oi the faithful departed. Let us, therefore, with full hands scatter those spiritual roses over the graves of our dear departed parents and friends. Let us lay on their tombs the holy rosary, and Mary the Mother of suffering souls will surely be moved, and not only console and release our dear friends in Purgatory, but will also protect and guard us from falling into it.

ST. AUGUSTINE

This holy Father of the Church makes frequent mention of Purgatory in his writings, and his words clearly reveal how much his heart was filled with love and sympathy for the poor souls suffering therein. He not only strove to assist them himself, but ho also encouraged and excited the faithful, by every means in his power, to this act of charity. 'One day in that dreadful place of purification,' he says, 'could not be compared to a thousand years of suffering in this life,' and he adds, 'the fire there is worse than all the sufferings put together, which could be inflicted in this life.' St. Augustine severely reprimanded the audacity of a Christian of his time, who boldly maintained that Purgatory was not at all to be feared, as it was only a place of temporary punishment, and that it was a matter of indifference to him how long he had to remain there, if at last he could reach Heaven. The Saint answered him: 'Let no man reason in this wise, for the fires of Purgatory are more terrible than all the sufferings of this world, however frightful we may imagine these to be.' In another place he says, the fire of Purgatory exceeds in violence all the pains that can be endured by mankind in this life. According to him, the sufferings of Purgatory surpass the

worst tortures of martyrdom, which so many of the Saints
endured for Christ.

With such authorities on the subject of the awful
pains of Purgatory, by which he exhorted and urged the
faithful to work out their salvation in fear and trembling,
he united a deep sympathy and love for the poor souls,
and made use of all the means which the Church supplies
to assist and comfort them. Very touching is the prayer
which he poured forth to God after his mother's death:
'Grant, O Lord, to Thy servants who are my brothers, to
Thy beloved children who are my friends, and to all who
may chance to read these few lines, that they may
remember at Thine altar my mother Monica, and her
husband Patritius, who gave me life. Oh, grant that they
may with devout charity remember those who were my
parents!'

ST. THOMAS AQUINAS

St. Thomas Aquinas showed a most tender devotion
to the poor souls, making frequent commemoration of
them in Mass, in his prayers and penances. When he was
Professor of Theology at the University of Paris, his
sister—who was Abbess of the Convent of St. Mary of
Capua, and had lately died—appeared to him, and told
him she was suffering great torments in Purgatory. St.
Thomas immediately began to pray and fast and mortify
himself for her; he also asked several of his friends to join
him in prayer. He obtained the release of his sister's soul.
She appeared to him again in Rome, whither he had been
sent; but this time overflowing with heavenly joy and
radiant with glory, and told him of her deliverance, and
happy entrance into Heaven. And she added: 'Thou, my

brother, hasten and finish those writings and works which thou hast begun, for thou wilt soon be called away to eternal life.'

Another time, as this Saint was praying in the Church of St. Dominic, in Naples, he suddenly saw Brother Romanus, who was his successor to the theological chair in Paris. Thomas immediately rose, hastened to greet him, and ask him concerning his health and his journey, believing him to be still among the living; but the good brother kept him hack, told him the days of his earthly life had passed, and that he had already received the crown of heavenly reward, and that God had sent him down to visit him and encourage him to pursue his labours. Thomas was at first quite startled, but after awhile he overcame his fears, and asked him to inform him on one point which he had most at heart. 'Am I in the state of grace,' he asked. The deceased told him he was, and gave him the assurance that God was highly pleased with his labours. Then St. Thomas desired to obtain from that soul some theological explanations, as, for instance, about the Beatific Vision. But the only answer vouchsafed him was that verse of the Psalmist, saying: 'As we have heard it, so we have seen it in the city of the Lord of hosts.' Having said these words, he vanished, leaving in the heart of the evangelical teacher a greater yearning and a more ardent desire for union with his beloved Redeemer, Jesus Christ.

We learn from these two facts that St. Thomas spoke from his own experience when he laid it down, that God at times makes use of the poor souls as messengers, just as He does of Angels.

ST. MALACHY

St. Bernard, in his history of the life of St. Malachy, highly extols the great devotion of that Saint to the souls in Purgatory, while he blames his sister, who was quite of a different mind on the subject. While yet only deacon, he loved to attend above all the funeral services. He used to follow the dead to the graveyard, and often bury them with his own hands. For he considered this work of mercy especially calculated to further humility and charity. This second Tobias was to be tempted by a woman, or rather, by the enemy of mankind. His sister, who was very worldly-minded, thought it a disgrace for the family to have her brother employing himself with such menial work. Full of anger, she came to him and said: 'Infatuated man, what fine handicraft you exercise! You had better let, according to the words of the Lord, the dead bury their dead!' Thus she misused the holy words of Scripture, and loaded her brother with the bitterest reproaches. But Malachy answered her gently, but gravely, and with great determination: 'Poor maiden! what art thou saying? Thou knowest, indeed, the words of the holy Gospels, but understandest not their meaning.'

And he continued to pursue his humble practice. God rewarded him with the greatest consolations. Nor did God allow the frivolous audacity of his sister to escape punishment. She died rather young, and had to appear before the awful Judge who searcheth the hearts and demands an account even of the smallest things. Malachy had suffered much from her during her life, but after her death he only thought of the distress and need of her poor soul. A long time after her death, he seemed to see her in a dream, and how she sighed and lamented. The following morning her pious brother offered up the holy Sacrifice of the Mass for her, and continued to do so for some time, until at last he saw her beaming with light and joy, from which he concluded that she was released from her sufferings. 'We see here once more,' remarks St. Bernard, 'the wonderful efficacy of the holy Sacrifice of the Mass; how it purifies us from sin and makes us acceptable to God.'

We must not pass over in silence the great grace accorded to St. Malachy, in reward for his love and devotion to the dead. One day he invited those under his spiritual guidance to a conference. And as he was conversing with them on the subject of death, he suddenly asked one by one when and where each one would prefer to die! They answered some on such and such a feast, others on another. At last, when his own turn came to say where and when he would like to die, he named as the favourite place of his death the Convent of Clairveaux—then under the direction of St. Bernard—because there the pious monks would say Masses for the repose of his soul immediately after his death. And as to the day on which he would prefer to die, he named the day of All Souls, because of the universal prayers offered up on that day by the Church for the faithful departed. His hopes and wishes were completely fulfilled. While on his way to Rome, to visit Pope Eugene III, he was overtaken by a severe illness at Clairveaux, from which he was not to recover again. As he felt death approaching, he exclaimed with the prophet: 'Here is the place of my rest! I have chosen it, and here will I dwell.' On the very day of All Souls he delivered his soul into the hands of his Creator, and went to receive the eternal reward of his piety and virtue.

ST. PHILIP NERI

This Saint was animated with the most tender love for the poor suffering souls in Purgatory. He prayed constantly for them, and bestowed on them the merits of his good works. He was particularly anxious to help those souls who during life had been under his spiritual care. He considered he owed more to them because, as a priest, he had laboured for the salvation of their souls. Many dead appeared to him, because they hoped to be delivered from Purgatory by his prayers, and indeed he never failed to pray for them forthwith. His biographer assures us that the results of his prayers were most wonderful. The Saint was all the more anxious to pray for the dead, as they often obtained wonderful graces for him.

This devoted love to the souls in Purgatory has passed from the founder on to the whole congregation of the Oratorians. Father Magnanti scarcely ever ceased praying for the dead, and like St. Philip Neri, was often made aware of the happy results of his prayers. This zealous Priest spent the alms which pious Christians gave him, partly in alms to the poor, and partly for Masses in behalf of the suffering souls. He himself loved and practised poverty, but he kept in his cell an alms-box, which he called the 'box of the souls.' He thus followed the example of the Divine Saviour, who, according to the Ven. Bede, gathered the gifts of the faithful in a box in order to distribute them among the poor and sick. To the treasury of his alms Father Magnanti added his prayers, fasts, vigils, and complete retirement from the vain and idle joys of this world. His burning love for the poor souls carried him so far, that he asked our Lord to lay on him some of their sufferings in order to give them relief. His heroic prayer was heard and accepted; he became a prey to the most cruel pains, which hardly allowed him to change from one position to another, and yet, from zeal for salvation of souls, he undertook several long journeys. We may well apply to him the words which a Roman historian pronounced upon a victorious soldier, who, in consequence of a wound received in battle, returned with a limping leg: 'His every step is a mark of his glory.'

The souls of the faithful departed were not ungrateful to him. A great part of the many wonderful graces he had received Father Magnanti ascribed to their intercession. He had the gift of knowing the future, of discovering hidden sins, and of frustrating and escaping the numerous snares of the enemy.

ST. ANDREW AVELLINI

The venerable Theatine Order has always been distinguished by an ardent love of the souls in Purgatory. It was a Theatine Father, Jerome Meaza, who, among other things, published a book, as learned as it was pious, called 'Daily Exhortations to pray for the Dead.' A much better known, and just as zealous a helper of the poor souls, was the great St. Andrew Avellini of the same Order.

He often felt, while praying with angelical fervour for the suffering souls, a secret inward opposition, as if someone were drawing him back from praying; at other times, on the contrary, he would feel a certain inward consolation and impulse, urging him on to prayer. He understood, that in the first case the soul he was praying for was unworthy of pardon, and in hell, while in the second case, they were in Purgatory. He generally offered up the holy Sacrifice of the Mass for the dead, and then he often learned to know the state and condition of the soul, for which he prayed. An invisible hand seemed to draw him back, whenever it was useless to pray for them, while when his prayers were of avail, his heart was filled with heavenly joy and fervour.

ST. LOUIS BERTRAND

The Church is justly praising the great zeal of St. Louis Bertrand, for the conversion of sinners—a zeal which prompted him to resort to all sorts of devices, and even to risk his life. But he showed no less zeal and love for the suffering souls in Purgatory. As master of novices, he exacted from those under him the strictest observance of the rules, and severely punished the smallest deviation from them. He was in the habit of saying, that his love for his novices obliged him to make them atone for their faults now by light penances, lest they should have to severely suffer for them in Purgatory.

For the deliverance of the poor souls in Purgatory, he imposed on himself prayers, fasts, and mortifications. The souls frequently appeared to him, either to thank him for their release, or else to implore him to continue his prayers for them. Great indeed was his joy, when he heard that such and such a soul was released; but deep was his sorrow, when he heard that others had to suffer still longer. Now, if the prayers of Father Bertrand were already so powerful, we may gather how much more efficacious must be the oblation of the holy Sacrifice! His zeal and fervour were always redoubled on All Souls' Day—a feast on which every priest in Spain is allowed to say three Masses. It was then especially, that souls would appear to him, and implore him to offer them up for their repose.

THE VEN. GRATIAN PONZONI

Gratian Ponzoni was a member of the congregation founded by St. Charles Borromeo, and, later on, also Archpriest at Arona. All through his life, he showed the greatest active sympathy for the poor suffering souls. Like all pious Christians anxious to appease the anger of God, and obtain the release of the poor souls in Purgatory, he prayed much and fervently; chastised himself by scourgings, fasts, and nightly watchings, and wore a hair shirt. Besides that, he performed other and more extraordinary works of piety.

His charity urged him to follow the example of Tobias in burying the dead. Ponzoni took great pleasure in burying with his own hands the poor, the abandoned, and neglected. A frightfully infectious disease broke out amongst the Neapolitan soldiers stationed in Arona, and carried off a great number of them. The grave-digger refused to bury them, from fear of infection. When the good priest heard this, he reproached him for his weakness, encouraged him as well as he could, and gave him good advice, and then accompanied him in the night to the dead, and helped him to bury them. He was filled with that holy zeal, which, as St. Paul says, drives away fear. And, therefore, his prayers, like those of his holy model Tobias, were pleasing to God, and wafted by angels to His heavenly throne.

He was not satisfied with cherishing a most fervent charity in his own heart for the poor souls, but sought also by every means in his power—by sermons, conversations, and so forth—to instil it into the hearts of all the faithful, and especially priests. Therefore, he built a little mortuary chapel in that part of the cemetery which touched the church, wherein everything reminded the visitor of the dead, and exhorted him to pray for them. All his piety was centred in this favourite devotion, and he hoped thereby to please the Lord. During the time of recreation in his house, he allowed even some simple games, under condition that all the winnings should go to pay for Masses for the dead. No one could refuse so pious a request; and thus all the winnings were cheerfully put into a small alms-box placed upon the table.

ST. BRIDGET

In the revelations of St. Bridget, we have wonderful accounts of the appearances of the poor departed souls. Nor are they untrustworthy, because they have been examined by learned divines, and recognised by them as authentic, so that the words spoken of Judith, 'All things which thou hast spoken are true, and there is nothing to be reprehended in thy words' (Judith viii. 28), might fitly be applied to St. Bridget, and put at the foot of her portrait.

Once St. Bridget saw in a vision the souls of the faithful departed being purified, as it were, in a crucible before they reached their place of eternal rest. And at the same time she heard the voice of an Angel saying, 'Blessed are those who dwell upon earth, and who by their prayers and other good works hasten to the relief of the souls in Purgatory. For the justice of God demands that their sins be atoned for either by their sufferings or else by the prayers and good works of their friends on earth.' Then the Saint heard a great number of voices praying in piteous tones, 'O Lord Jesus Christ! O great and just Judge! We implore Thee in Thine infinite mercy to regard not the number and magnitude of our offences, but to look on the merits of Thy most precious Passion and Death. Oh, let the streams of Thy great charity flow into the hearts of all Thy priests, monks, and all the faithful, that by their Masses, prayers, and alms, they may come to our relief. If they wish, they can help us greatly by their prayers and indulgences, and can shorten the term of our awful sufferings. They can hasten our happy reunion with Thee, O God.' At other times, St. Bridget heard appeals from Purgatory like the following: 'O Lord, send down Thy grace a thousandfold to those charitable Christians, who have helped us in our affliction by their prayers!'

Then she saw a certain light, half clear, half obscure, coming down, as it were, like the dawn of day, whereby she knew was meant, that the day of deliverance had dawned for some. And she heard new voices singing, 'O God, whose power is infinite, we beg of Thee to reward a thousandfold all those, who pray for our deliverance, and help us to come to Thine everlasting light.'

From all this we can easily see, what great rewards all those will receive, who pray for the dead and obtain their release, and what grateful friends they make for themselves near the throne of God. They are souls who owe their eternal happiness to those, who by their prayers released them from Purgatory: and that they can never forget. God grant, that there may be instilled into the hearts of a great many Christians even a small portion of the love and sympathy which St. Bridget, in consequence of her visions, felt for the poor souls as long as she lived.

ST. CHRISTINA

What is related of the penances and mortifications, undergone by this great Saint, for the souls in Purgatory, would almost seem incredible, were it not that we have it on the authority of the most trustworthy biographers. It is related, that on one occasion the soul of this pious virgin was borne by Angels down to Purgatory, to make her a witness of their terrible sufferings, and that this sight was the cause of her indescribable compassion. Thence she was led before the throne of God, where she heard the following words addressed to her: 'Christina, thou art in the abode of everlasting bliss; I give thee free choice either to remain here for ever amongst the elect, or to return to earth for a few more years, in order to help the poor souls by thy good works. If thou dost choose the first, thou wilt be safely in the haven of rest, and have no more to fear. In the other case, thou wilt return to earth and suffer a martyrdom, console the unhappy, and thus merit a more beautiful crown.' The generous maiden immediately replied: 'My Lord, allow me to return, in order that I may suffer and pray for the poor departed souls. I fear no misery, no sufferings, where they are concerned.' She then awoke from her trance and found herself again amongst her friends, who, believing her dead, were about to bury her. She immediately began to practise the most terrible penances, which one can scarcely read of without shuddering. She considered it quite a trifling matter to go for several days without food, and to chastise her tender flesh by the most terrible scourgings. In her holy ardour she used every means to mortify her own senses, and to atone for the self-indulgence of others. God frequently permitted the souls released by her to appear to and thank her. Her delight in suffering was thereby greatly increased. Sometimes a whole host of delivered souls appeared to her, which filled her with new supernatural strength. It will suffice to mention but one of those apparitions. Count Louis of Leon had a great veneration for Christina, and bore with the meekest patience the reproaches and admonitions she gave him, on account of the irregularities of his life. He was attacked by a severe illness, and, fearing his life was in danger, he sent a messenger to Christina, entreating her to come and talk to him about the affairs of his soul, and help him to prepare for death. She came immediately. With tears and sobs, he addressed her thus: 'Oh, great servant of God, thou knowest already what a sinner I am. In a few hours, perhaps, I must appear before the supreme Judge, to render Him an account of my many sins. Do, then, thou, who hast served the Lord so faithfully, appeal for me to His divine mercy, and obtain for me the grace of true contrition for my sins, that they may be forgiven me. Moreover, I implore thee in thy charity, to procure for my poor soul at least a diminution of the punishment which it deserves.' The compassionate virgin began at once to pray with all the fervour of her soul, and Louis, fully penitent, gave up his soul into the hands of his Creator, having been reconciled to Him by a good confession. Soon afterwards he appeared to Christina, and said to her: 'Oh, most faithful servant of Jesus Christ, if thou didst only know to what awful torments I am condemned, how great would be thy sympathy! I beg of thee once more to redouble thy prayers and supplications to the most merciful and compassionate God, that I may be delivered from my sufferings.' Full of sympathy, St. Christina answered him:

'Depart in peace, poor suffering soul; I am ready to suffer in my own body one half of the punishment, ordained for thee by God's justice.' She would even go to the places where Louis during his lifetime had given himself up to his sinful pleasures, and atone by her tears, and even her blood, for his sins. To the horror of all who saw her, she continued her frightful penances, until at last Louis again appeared before her, beaming with light, and thanking her in the most touching manner, for all the sufferings by which she had paid his debts. The holy maiden followed him with her eyes, as he hastened towards his heavenly home. This joy more than compensated her for all her pains and privations.

ST. ELIZABETH

St. Elizabeth, daughter of King Andrew of Hungary and Queen Gertrude, had an extraordinary affection for the souls of the faithful departed. She frequently sewed with her own hands the shroud for the dead body, or defrayed the funeral expenses of the poor; she also followed the funeral processions to the grave, praying fervently all the time, that the Lord might be a merciful Judge to His poor creatures. If any of her relations died, she redoubled her prayers and supplications. After the death of her mother, Queen Gertrude, she never ceased offering up her fervent prayers and good works for the repose of her soul. One night her dead mother appeared to her, with the most sorrowful expression of countenance, and said to her: 'My dear daughter, come to the assistance of thy poor suffering mother. Oh, help by the increase of thy prayers, for I am suffering frightful tortures, on account of the many sins for which I have not done penance. I implore thee, by all which I have ever done and suffered for thee, to do all thou canst to release me.'

Grieved and horrified, Elizabeth immediately arose from her couch, and, with many tears and prayers, appealed to the mercy of God. After a time she was overcome by sleep in this act of charity. Then she had a second vision of her mother, but this time she was quite different to behold. She was overflowing with joy and happiness, and from her lips poured words of thanks and blessings upon her daughter, because her fervent prayers had opened for her the gates of Heaven.

Even while still a child, St. Elizabeth had the habit of leading her little playmates to the churchyard, saying: 'Just think, one day we, too, shall be dust.' Then she would lead them to the charnel-house, and say: 'Those people once lived and breathed as we do, and are now dead. We, too, shall die. Therefore we ought to love God very much, and constantly pray to Him.' Then she would make them kneel around her, and she would say, 'O my God, in memory of Thy painful death, and for the love of Thy most Blessed Mother, deliver the souls of the departed from their sufferings. O God, deliver them for the sake of Thy five holy wounds!'

ST. TERESA

Speaking of the prophet Elias, the writer of the Book of Ecclesiastes says: 'By the word of the Lord God, thou didst call the dead back to life.' The prayers of Elias, according to St. Augustine, were powerful keys to open the doors of Heaven, especially when he restored to life the son of the widow of Sarepta.

These words may also be applied to those charitable Christians, who exert themselves to deliver the souls of the faithful departed from the pains of Purgatory, and open for them the gates of Paradise. Foremost amongst them stands St. Teresa, whose intercession was of extraordinary efficacy. She herself tells us, that the devil had made great efforts to prevent her from practising this work of piety. 'Once, on the eve of All Souls' Day,' she says, 'when I retired to my oratory to say the Office for the Dead, the demon suddenly appeared before me, and tried to prevent me. I made the sign of the Cross, and threw some holy water at him, whereupon he made off with the greatest speed, and left me to finish my prayers in peace. After I had finished this prayer, I saw a number of souls leaving Purgatory; they had only required those few prayers to release them, and that was the reason why the wicked one endeavoured to prevent me from saying them.'

The fact of her prayers being thus rewarded, inflamed St. Teresa with still greater zeal for the poor souls. Not alone did she pray for them herself, but she spread this devotion through all the houses of her Order. Every year, on the second of November, after the *Requiem* had been sung, the members of the community met together, to listen to an instruction upon the ways and means of assisting the dead. Each member of the assembly gave a written promise that during the coming year she would say such and such prayers, or do some specified good works, either in the way of mortification or other spiritual works of mercy.

Bernardin of Mendoza had drawn up a regular deed, by which he left a house and beautiful garden, in Valladolid, for the purpose of a convent in honour of Our Lady. He then sent for St. Teresa, and begged of her to take possession of the property at once, and to begin the work forthwith, acting as if he had a presentiment of his approaching death. This good work was destined to be most salutary for his poor soul. St. Teresa, at that time much pressed by other affairs, could only commence the new building after some months. But meanwhile the poor donor was attacked by a violent fever, which deprived him of the power of speech, so that he was unable to confess his sins.

He died with every appearance of the most heartfelt contrition and resignation. Teresa was in Alcala, when the sad news first reached her. She felt the greatest pain on hearing that the poor dying man had been unable to receive the last Sacraments, and began directly to offer up the most fervent prayers for the repose of his soul. The Lord revealed to her, that the departed friend had had a happy death, and that his brotherly love for his neighbours had obtained for him many favours, through the intercession of Our Lady, to whom he had dedicated the new convent. But the soul of Mendoza would not be released from Purgatory, until the day when the first Mass was said, in presence of the community, in the new convent. This revelation deprived her of all rest and peace. She had difficulty in awaiting the time when she could go to Valladolid, open the new chapel, and release the soul of her benefactor. When, some days later, she arrived in Valladolid, she plainly saw that the building could not be ready for a very long time yet; therefore she earnestly begged of her superiors to allow her to erect a temporary chapel, where the members of the community could assist at Mass together. Permission was granted to her. As Father Avila, who said the first Mass at the new Altar, was just about to give Holy Communion to the Saint, he perceived, as he had often before, during that holy moment, that she was in an ecstasy. He learned afterwards that, during that time, just as she was about to go to Holy Communion, she saw the soul of Mendoza shining like the sun, and resplendent with the glory of the elect. He saluted her respectfully, and with an expression of deepest gratitude, and then, before her eyes, ascended into Heaven. The joy of the Saint at this occurrence was almost indescribable, for she had scarcely dared to hope, that the Mass offered in the temporary chapel would be accepted by God, as the one that would satisfy the claims of His divine justice.

ST. MARGARET OF CORTONA

Margaret was a great sinner in her youth. She lost her mother when quite young, and so was mostly left to herself. Her extraordinary beauty and lively temperament soon led her away from the right path into a frivolous and sinful life, which lasted for some considerable time. God brought her back to Himself in a wonderful manner. The violent death of her companion in sin—whose corpse she saw in the last stage of corruption—opened her eyes at last. She was so horrified at his appearance, that she immediately renounced sin, and became such a sincere penitent, that in a short time she attained the summit of piety and sanctity. She lived henceforth for God alone. She spent her days in the strictest retirement from the world, and in the exercise of the severest penances, in perfect self-denial and mortification. Amongst the many virtues which she practised after her conversion, the most striking was her love and devotion for the poor suffering souls in Purgatory, for whose deliverance she sacrificed time and rest, and everything. Great was her reward for it! As she lay on her death-bed, she saw a crowd of souls, released by her, hastening to her side, to form, as it were, a guard of honour, escorting her to the heavenly kingdom.

An intelligent love of the dead will, above all and in the first place, embrace one's own parents. Margaret always remembered her parents first, in all her supplications for the dead. Her father and mother were both dead, and for their repose she offered up Communions, Masses, and other good works. God revealed to her, that she had very much shortened their term of punishment by her fervour, and delivered their souls from Purgatory much sooner than it was at first determined. With like affection, Margaret also remembered a faithful servant of the name of Julia. She prayed for her with such intense zeal, that she delivered her, as was told her by revelation. In the next place, Margaret prayed with great ardour for all the dead, whether known or unknown to her. In fact, we might say that praying for the dead was her special daily occupation. Her every thought and desire was tending towards the deliverance of the souls in Purgatory: to hasten the day of their deliverance, to shorten the term of their punishment, to soothe their pains, was her one aim and object. She seemed to completely forget her own self, for all the merits which she gained by her virtuous, penitential life, she bestowed with heroic and most unselfish love on her poor suffering brethren in Purgatory.

THE FLOWERS OF THE POOR SOULS

THE CARNATION

LOWERS are grateful beings; how richly they repay us for the labour and care we bestow upon them! The sweet fragrance which they send forth is the expression of their gratitude. Their grace and beauty of form, their brilliancy of colour, by which they charm our eyes and gladden our hearts, are, as it were, so many expressions of thanks for our love of them. To them we owe the beauty of our gardens and pleasure grounds; they are willing to grow and bloom in pots or vases, to adorn our windows and cottages; they let themselves be gathered into bouquets, to fill our dwellings with their sweets perfumes, or made into wreaths, to adorn our pictures and Altars; lastly, they sweetly bloom upon the tombs of our beloved dead.

The souls of the faithful departed are equally grateful; nay, infinitely more so, and in the true sense of the word. They repay a thousandfold the sympathy, compassion and love, which we feel and bear towards them. Their gratitude expresses itself by the spiritual gifts, the heavenly treasures of grace, with which they reward us, just as the flowers repay us by their sweet fragrance and exquisite colour. Let us, therefore, under the symbol of some particular flowers, consider the great advantages we may gain, by our sympathy and compassion for poor souls in Purgatory.

Amongst all the flowers, the carnation seems to us to

be the most appropriate emblem of the *gratitude* of the poor souls in Purgatory.

We shall not easily find a more grateful flower than the carnation. It thrives in the cold air, as well as in the hot greenhouse: it spreads around a perfume, which in sweetness and power surpasses almost every other flower. Jesus called the Samaritan, whom He had healed from leprosy, blessed, because he returned, fell down on his knees and thanked Him. 'Go,' He said to him, 'for thy faith has made thee whole.' Nothing, says St. Chrysostom, is so pleasing to God as a grateful soul; nothing brings man nearer to God than the virtue of gratitude; this virtue is an inexhaustible treasure of riches, and a strong armour of defence. But how many Christians are there not of whom our Lord could complain, in the words of the Prophet: 'What shall I do with thee, O Ephraim, and with thee, O Juda, for your love is as the cloud of the morning, as the dew which is quickly dried up!' But if the virtue of true gratitude be rare among Christians, it abounds with the poor souls in Purgatory. And why? Because the torments which they have to endure are so terrible, and their pains so intense, that every alleviation, and much more complete deliverance from them, which we may obtain by our prayers for them, fills their hearts with the most ardent gratitude. The amount of gratitude depends on and corresponds to the favour received. How thankful would you not be to one who cured you from a violent toothache, or, again, to him who, at risk of his own life, rushed into a burning house and saved you from a certain and horrible death! But what is the pain of a toothache compared with the sufferings of Purgatory? What are the most violent tortures of an earthly fire, in comparison with the supernatural flames of that place of purification? Imagine, then, what must be the gratitude of the poor souls!

The leaves of the carnation are acute and pointed, and the colour is generally red, reminding us of the flames of Purgatory, where the virtue of gratitude thrives and flourishes most. For Purgatory is the *home* of gratitude! And why? The poor souls are the beloved children of God, and as such they must resemble Him. But is not gratitude a peculiar attribute of God? Does He not reward with divine life every cup of cold water given in His Name? Does He not repay the smallest service with graces and blessings innumerable? Therefore the poor souls will try to please God, by imitating Him in the virtue and perfection of gratitude.

The poor souls are in the state of sanctifying grace, which enhances, preserves, and perfects all their other good qualities and virtues. How perfect, then, must be the virtue of their gratitude towards us when, by our intercession and good works, we procure relief or deliverance!

The poor souls no longer abide in this world, of which it has been truly said that ingratitude is its reward. They are in the next world, and although in a place of suffering, yet surrounded by a thousand examples of the most fervent gratitude. For all those souls are Saints, destined for the glory of Heaven; and it is not likely that they would be ungrateful to us, who have shown them love and compassion. The cupbearer of King Pharaoh might forget Joseph, who foretold him his deliverance and restoration to office, and asked him to remember him then; but the poor souls do not act thus, says St. Bernard.

Ingratitude can only dwell in the heart of a wicked and vicious person but is not found in the Saints of God.

The flower of the carnation, which is the emblem of gratitude, is sometimes simple, and sometimes double. In like manner does Gratitude sometimes double her gifts and pour them out in their fulness upon her benefactors, as it were a horn of plenty. And where can gratitude be greater and fuller, than in the hearts of the dear departed—in hearts that are perfectly purified from all earthly dross and weakness, and ripe for Heaven? Lastly, there are carnations of various colours and shapes. So also are there various kinds of gratitude, by which the poor souls repay us for our love of them, as will be shown in the sequel.

THE TULIP

The tulip is one of the fairest flowers, and though it emits no fragrance, yet it enraptures the eye by the beauty of its colours. It rears its head on the top of a solid straight stem, and is surrounded by longish leaves. It closes up its calyx at night, and opens it again at sunrise. As the peculiarities of this flower have great analogy with prayer, it is often taken as the emblem of prayer.

The tulip closes her calyx at the approach of night. When we think of the poor souls, we say: Let perpetual light shine upon them. Why? Because they are suffering in darkness, far from the heavenly sun, far from the light, which is Jesus Christ. In this darkness of night they can no longer work for themselves, but they can do everything for us. They pray for us in Purgatory. Many learned divines and Doctors of the Church maintain, that the souls in Purgatory can pray for us; for they are not in a worse condition, in this respect, than the sinners and enemies of God; they are confirmed in the grace and friendship of God; they possess the most perfect love and charity, and can remember all they owe to our prayers, of which their Guardian Angels may inform them. St. Alphonsus Liguori says: 'It is probable that we can ask and obtain the prayers of the poor souls; for it is reasonable to suppose, that God reveals to them our prayers for them, in order that they may pray for us in return, and so form a bond of love and mutual assistance between them and us.' In like manner, the learned Father Suarez, of the Society of Jesus, says: 'These souls are holy and much loved by God; they also love us with the most perfect love; they know, at least in general, our dangers, and how much we stand in need of God's assistance. Surely, then, they will pray for us, although they have still their own faults to atone and do penance for.' We can pray for each other during our lifetime, although we are sinners and debtors to God. The Saints of old also, who were in Abraham's bosom, or in limbo, have prayed for those on earth, as we learn from the example of Jeremias and Onias, the High Priest (2 Mach. 15). Cardinal Bellarmine expresses himself in almost the same words: 'And why should not those souls pray for us who have so often invoked our prayers, as we read in the life of St. Bridget, to whom her husband appeared, begging of her to have Mass offered up and alms given for the repose of his soul?' St. Catherine of Bologna often invoked the souls in Purgatory, and assures us, that through their intercession she had obtained most wonderful favours from God. 'Often even,' she adds, 'that which I could not obtain by earnest prayers to the Saints in Heaven, I immediately obtained by having recourse to those poor suffering souls in Purgatory.'

A certain holy person of our own time, and well versed in the spiritual life, says, when every other means fails me, I have recourse to the poor souls, and my prayers are heard.

The tulip unfolds its calyx when the sun appears. As soon as the eternal light of heaven shines on the poor souls in the darkness of their dungeon, and brings them out of the gloom of night into the brightness of everlasting day, they remember us before the throne of God, pray for us, returning love for love, and recommend us to the divine mercy. We are certain of having in them most faithful and loving patrons and protectors in Heaven, and most powerful advocates pleading for us before the throne of God. Although they cannot merit any longer or make satisfaction for us in Heaven, still by their prayers they can obtain all the graces necessary for our salvation. Should we, then, think little of this great and powerful protection! When there is question of our material interests, and temporal advantages are at stake, how we busy ourselves, and how anxious we are! No sacrifice is too great or burden too heavy; then we are ready to forget our ease and comfort, and submit to the hardest privations. Shall we, then, altogether neglect our true and easily-attainable advantages? Shall we not endeavour to make friends with patrons so powerful as to be able to open for us the gates of Heaven? Truly a greater folly could not be well imagined. Let us, then, unceasingly pray for the poor souls, because they also, in Purgatory as well as in Heaven, can efficaciously pray for us.

Tulips are of different colours; some are red, some yellow, some purple, but generally they are variegated. In like manner the souls of the departed pray for all kinds of gifts and blessings for us. They pray that we may obtain health of body, success in our affairs, prosperity in our labours, and temporal happiness; but above all, they pray for the salvation of our souls. For they well know what it means to suffer and expiate in the next world. Who can know better or more keenly appreciate the supreme bliss of Heaven than they who have so long and bitterly felt the pains of separation from God? Therefore, they reward our charity by their prayer to God to give us grace to attain our eternal salvation.

THE IRIS, OR SWORD-LILY

The iris has a dark-blue colour, with leaves shaped like a sword. Therefore it is often called 'the sword-lily,' and has been chosen as the emblem of warfare. If thou dost aspire to be a lily of purity, thou must seize the sword! If thou wouldst live chaste and spotless, thou must not fear the battle, but must stand armed and prepared to fight! After the fall of our first parents and expulsion from the Garden of Paradise, a cherub with a flaming sword was placed at the entrance of it in order to guard it. St. Michael also was armed with a sword, and with it drove Lucifer and his followers out of Heaven.

What relation has the sword-lily to the souls of the faithful departed? For them there is no more warfare—their fight is past, they can but submit and suffer whatever is laid upon them; to guard them has no meaning since they are kept in prison; they can no longer do wrong, or struggle for good.

And yet for all that there is room in a spiritual sense for the sword, and the sword-lily has every claim to be regarded as a flower of the poor souls.

The flower of the sword-lily is of a dark-blue or purple colour—the emblem of sorrow and penance. In time of Advent, when we are sighing for the coming of Christ, and purify our sighs and yearnings by penance, or in Lent, when with sorrow and contrition we contemplate the bitter sufferings and passion of our Saviour, the Church assumes purple colour; the priest at the altar wears purple vestments; altars, statues, pictures, and crosses are covered with purple cloth.

When any of our dear friends depart this life, we are clad for some time in garments of mourning. But internally we ought never to cease to mourn for the poor suffering souls of the departed. Our hearts should ever be like the flower of the sword-lily, clad with the garment of sorrow and compassion for the dead, who are always so grateful for our love, and repay our remembrance of them a thousandfold.

The leaves of the iris are sword-shaped, and the poor souls in Purgatory show their gratitude to us by fighting for us, by defending and protecting us from perils, and delivering us from dangers of every kind.

The venerable servant of God, Father Martin Boa, of the Society of Jesus, says: 'I can testify myself that many times when I was in the greatest trouble and anxiety of soul, or afflicted by the most severe sickness, or again during long and dangerous travels through countries infested by robbers, or high up in the rough and steep mountains, or low down in the depth of dangerous valleys and in the midst of dreary deserts, I have always experienced the wonderful protection of those holy souls. Under their protection I felt secure and courageous, and often escaped the greatest dangers almost before I had time to fear or guard against them.'

If the holy souls are so very ready and willing to help their benefactors in their temporal needs, and preserve them from every kind of danger, how much more anxious will they be for the spiritual welfare of their souls! The following example will show it, as related by Pope Benedict XIII, in one of his religious discourses: 'Christopher Ugo, before he joined the Dominican Order, was a young man full of levity, quite blinded by his passions and love of pleasure, and seemed to hurry onward to the abyss of perdition. One trace of piety, however, was still left in his heart. He recited daily the penitential psalms for the repose of the departed. And behold! One day, without understanding how or wherefore, he felt his heart suddenly changed and converted; and feeling drawn by a divine light, he joined the Dominican Order, and there made wonderful progress in spiritual perfection.' The same Pope relates likewise the following fact: 'The pious Alphonse Cortesi, of the Society of Jesus, was, like St. Paul, buffeted by an angel of Satan, that is, the sting of the flesh. As the poor priest had tried every means in vain to free himself of this persecution, he had recourse at last to Mary, the Mother of Chastity, who appeared to him and recommended him to pray ardently for the poor souls in Purgatory. Having done so he was freed from those temptations.' A man of our time was greatly addicted to drink, and could not free himself from this fatal habit. At last he made a resolution that every night, instead of going to the tavern, he would go to the churchyard or a mortuary-chapel, and pray for the repose of the poor souls buried there. By this means he was perfectly cured of his dreadful vice.

These examples prove clearly what care the poor souls take of all those who are mindful of them; they guard them in peril and protect them from danger. Hence St. Ambrose, a Father of the Church, and Archbishop of Milan, says on this subject: 'Through thy prayers and intercession procure the deliverance of the poor souls from Purgatory; make friends of them that they also may pray for thee before the throne of God, and obtain for thee the joy of eternal happiness.' We may also quote the well-known sentence of Pope Adrian VI, who says: 'Whoever prays with the intention of assisting the souls in Purgatory, lays on them the obligation to help him in return, and earns their gratitude; they will fight for him, defend, protect, and deliver him from all dangers.'

THE ROSE

The rose is the queen of all flowers, therefore we can take it as the emblem of the love of God, which is the first, the highest, the queen of the virtues. St. Paul, in his first Epistle to the Corinthians (chap. xiii.), says: 'And now there remain faith, hope, and charity, these three; but the greater of these is charity.' In order to increase in us this love and charity, there is no better means than compassion and zeal for the poor souls in Purgatory. An increase in our hearts and strengthening of the love of God is, as it were, the reward of the grateful souls for our love of them.

The rose is of the most marvellous grace and beauty—it is a masterpiece of the Creator: its beauty awakens in us a love of our Heavenly Father. But what could nourish and strengthen this love more than compassion with the sufferings of souls in Purgatory; for thereby we fulfil the great desire of our Heavenly Father, and promote most perfectly His greater glory. It is the nature of true charity to prompt and urge us to all that is pleasing and acceptable to God. Now we easily understand that God, whose hands are bound by the measures of His inflexible justice—desires nothing more ardently than that we should make atonement for the souls who are so very dear to Him for many reasons, but are, by some slight stains, still separated from Him, although He longs to receive them into His sacred embrace. Do not our works of atonement, then, appear like so many beautiful means of letting His goodness shine forth without diminution of His justice?

We justly admire the apostolic zeal of men who, in their great love for the salvation of souls, cross the wide and stormy seas in search of pagan lands and people, in order to convert and win them for God. But let us not forget what the learned Blosius says: 'Charity and zeal in relieving and releasing the poor souls in Purgatory, is in no way inferior in its object to the conversion of the heathen, nay, it even surpasses it in some respects.' And why? Because those souls are holy and confirmed in grace, and therefore incomparably more precious in His eyes than the souls of heathens. They are dearer to God, and in a condition to promote and contribute to the glory of God much more than the heathens. The great aim of the Saints was ever to seek, in all their actions, the greater glory of God. Our Divine Saviour willed that to be always the first petition addressed to our Heavenly Father, 'hallowed be Thy Name.' In like spirit the Church says, in the Gloria of the Mass, 'We give Thee thanks for Thy great glory.' And, 'singing the praises of the Almighty' is the chief joy of the Saints and elect in Heaven. Therefore our chief end and object in our works of charity for the poor souls, ought likewise to be the glory and honour of God. There could be no better and more effective way of increasing His glory, than by helping to deliver the poor souls from Purgatory, and bring them there where alone God is perfectly known, loved and glorified.

The rose has a deep red colour, which reminds us of the Blood of Jesus Christ shed for our salvation on the tree of the Cross. St. Christina was once conducted in spirit before the throne of the Son of God. Jesus gave her her choice to remain in Heaven with Him, or else to return to earth for some time longer, to assist the souls in Purgatory by her prayers and other good works. 'If thou dost choose to return to earth, thou wilt give Me much joy,' our Lord said to her. She begged to be allowed to return to earth. Then she began a life of such extraordinary and superhuman penance, that it seems almost incredible, in spite of the most trustworthy contemporary evidence. But she was so filled with intense love of Jesus, that in the midst of her penances she felt the greatest joy and comfort, to see thousands of souls released by her prayers and mortifications ascend into Heaven. Our Lord once said to St. Gertrude: 'Whenever anyone through prayers and good works delivers a soul from Purgatory, he gives Me as much joy and shows Me the same charity, as if he had taken Me down from the Cross!'

The rose has an exquisite perfume. Divine grace is the

sweet fragrance which the Holy Ghost sends forth, and He pours it out especially upon those who charitably assist the dead. To them He imparts the fullest measure of love and grace. The Holy Ghost is the comforter of all souls. How pleasing must it therefore be to Him when we imitate Him in that office, and seek to comfort the sufferers of Purgatory! He is the loving Spouse of those souls, which He sees adorned with His seven gifts. He consequently desires nothing more ardently, than that those chosen ones of His heart be delivered from their bitter woes, and united to Him in the closest bond of union.

From all that has been said it is clear, that our compassion with the poor souls in Purgatory is calculated to promote the honour and glory of the Father, Son, and Holy Ghost, and to obtain and secure for us the love and grace of the Most Blessed Trinity. Thus the rose of divine love will bloom in our heart, and make sweet with its fragrance the whole course of our lives, in grateful reward for our sympathy and compassion for the suffering souls, who, by our prayers and good works, have obtained everlasting peace, joy and rest.

THE LYCHNIS
(BURNING LOVE, OR LOVE IN A MIST)

This flower is composed of a group of tiny star-shaped flowerets, growing close together on a solid pale green stem. It is called the 'burning love,' on account of its flaming-red colour, and is generally regarded as the emblem of charity or love of our neighbour. 'I have come to cast fire upon earth,' says our Lord, 'and what do I will but that it be kindled!' This fire which He wishes to burn in all the hearts of the faithful, is no other than the fire of love which burned in His own Heart, and of which He Himself has given the most beautiful example by dying for us on the Cross! It is that love of which He said: 'By this will they know that you are My disciples, if you love one another.' Brotherly love, this most characteristic mark of the true Christian, is peculiarly ennobled and exalted by compassion with the poor souls. *The poor souls sanctify our charity*, make it purer and more pleasing to the eyes of God, and thereby prove their gratitude to us.

The 'burning love' has a fiery-red colour. When we succour the poor souls burning in the flames of Purgatory we show that our hearts are aflame with the love of our neighbour. It is said in the Book of Proverbs that a friend loves at all times. A true friend never forgets his friend, though he be removed from earthly sight. Father Diego Lainez, the second General of the Jesuits, was never tired of repeating this saying to those under him! He wished that their love and zeal for the salvation of souls should also reach beyond the grave. He used to say if we give alms to the poor we see about us, if we comfort the sick and dying whom we can visit, if we console the afflicted who can come in person to tell us their troubles, it is certainly a great act of charity; but still it is natural and of less value than that exercised towards the souls in Purgatory. The love of our neighbour may be glowing like fire even when its object is removed from human sight and can only be grasped by the eye of faith, as in the case of the souls in Purgatory. To help and assist them is an act of charity of infinite value and merit, the purest and most perfect act of love not blurred by considerations of nature, not weakened by self-love or worldly interests and motives.

*The 'burning love' is composed of a group of starlike
flowerets.* Stars are only visible at night, and the darker
the night the brighter they shine. In the gloom and
darkness of their dungeon, the poor souls languish after
light, the light of God and of eternal life. In the night of
their prison they sigh after deliverance, after the star of
redemption and freedom. Again, when we pray for the
poor souls, we walk in the darkness or twilight of faith.
We do not see them; we hear not their voices; we are all
ignorant as to whether our prayers have been heard, or
whether they have given solace to those for whom they
were intended. It is precisely this darkness which purifies,
ennobles, and sanctifies our love of our neighbour, just as
the stars shine the brighter the darker the night.

The 'burning love ' consists of a number of flowerets
united into one. In like manner charity towards the poor
souls presents many different points of view, and can be
exercised in many ways. St. Francis of Sales speaks thus
of works of charity for the dead: 'By every act of charity
done for the relief of the poor souls, the whole fourteen
works of mercy are practised. For is it not like visiting the
sick when we try to obtain for these souls relief from
their pain? Is it not like giving drink to the thirsty when
we help to shorten the term of suffering of those who are
burning with thirst for the beatific vision? Do we not feed
the hungry when, by the use of all the means suggested
by faith, we obtain their release? Do we not truly redeem
from captivity prisoners detained in the direst bondage,
when by our offerings we satisfy the claims of God's
justice? Is it not clothing the naked when we procure the
garment of light and glory for those who can no longer

merit for themselves? Is it not true hospitality when we use all our influence to obtain for them an entrance to the Heavenly Jerusalem, and assist them to become fellow-citizens with the Saints and Angels and servants of God in the heavenly and everlasting Sion? Is it not as great a work of mercy—and even greater—to bring one soul into Heaven than to bury dead bodies? And as for the spiritual works of mercy, is it not as meritorious a work to help the poor souls to gain their eternal rest, as to give counsel to the doubtful, to instruct the ignorant, to correct sinners, to comfort the afflicted, to forgive offenders, and bear injuries patiently? And what is the greatest comfort that one can bestow on the afflicted of this earth, in comparison with the comfort given to the poor souls in Purgatory?'

To exercise charity towards the suffering souls is, in truth, to cultivate a burning love in one's heart. But the grateful souls are also amply rewarding us for our affection and love towards them. For our love is made perfect, noble, sublime, and is rendered much more meritorious, and one that makes us truly children of God: 'By this will I know that you are My disciples, if you love one another.'

THE MARIGOLD

What are the thoughts that come to our mind whenever we pray or labour for the poor souls in Purgatory? We think of death, which has separated us from our beloved ones; of the last moment which was so awful for the dying and the assistants; of the tomb which encloses those who were so dear to us. We think of the poor souls, and how much they are suffering; of

Purgatory, whose torments and pains differ not from those of hell except in duration. But these are all thoughts in harmony with the divine admonition, saying: 'Remember thy last end, and thou shalt never sin.' Now, I ask, is not this a great blessing and reward for our love to the poor souls?

The marigold is a simple yellow flower, with a hollow stem containing milk; it grows almost like a weed, and is chiefly found on the graves of the dead, For this reason the Germans call it the 'Death-flower,' regarding it as a symbol of death.

The poor souls in Purgatory, too, constantly remind us of death. The thought of them is a continual *memento mori*, which no one can fail to hear and feel.

Marigolds grow like weeds. They need no planting or sowing; they require no care and cultivation; they thrive everywhere, no matter what soil or clime or atmosphere. And in this it most resembles death, which is in every place and common to every country, every clime, and every man without exception. Death is everywhere at home—in the palaces of kings as well as the huts of the peasants. Therefore, it is almost incredible that there are people who forget that they must one day die. Lest we should belong to this class of thoughtless Christians, let us pray diligently for the souls in Purgatory. To remember them is as good as to think of death. But the thought of death keeps us back from sin, urges us on to the practice of virtue, disengages our heart from the world, banishes from it all levity and frivolity, makes us grave and firm of character, shows us the shortness of time, and inspires us with love of Heaven. Is not all this an exceedingly great reward for our small love of the dead?

The marigold has a bitter taste; alas, how bitter is death! Bitter, even for those who have lived a pious and holy life when they have to sever themselves from those whom they love. But far more bitter is it for those who are surprised by death, who have never given the subject a thought during their lives, and who are so strongly attached to the things of this world, and who have only lived for its pleasures and vanities.

St. Ephraim calls death a bitter medicine, the bitterness of which, however, may be sweetened in some measure. Think and meditate often on death, and death will lose its bitterness. You become familiarized with and prepared for it; you will calmly await it, and peacefully look forward to the future with no fear of being suddenly surprised, and perfectly resigned to the will of God. This constant remembrance of death, which is so useful to the soul, the pious Christian can acquire as it were praying, if he will but accustom himself to pray daily, and even several times during the day, and offer up his good works for the repose of the souls departed. The remembrance of death; and the poor souls suffering in Purgatory, go hand in hand and cannot be separated. Whoever prays fervently for the dead is not likely to forget death. 'The thought of death,' says St. Cassian, 'is the shield of virtue, the buckler of the Christian, the sword of zeal and the lance of salvation.' The frequent meditation on death robs it of all its pain and bitterness.

The marigold is chiefly to be found on the graves of the dead, and is, therefore, in a special manner the flower of the holy souls. Those flowers on the grave are, as it were, like the hands of our departed friends stretched forth in supplication to us, saying: 'Have pity on us! have pity on us! at least you, our friends.' Perhaps it is the hand of a beloved parent, so often raised to bless and caress us, or the hand of a beloved wife with her wedding-ring; or again, the hands of our cherished children, or those of dear friends which we so often clasped in ours during life. Oh, who could coldly pass by a grave and not remember the blessed dead! Who can look at those flowers without thinking of those arms extended in supplication to us? If it happened that some person were buried alive, would not everyone on hearing it rush to the grave, and with all his strength tear away the stones and clay that cover him, so that the unhappy captive might be released? Surely, then, there is no Christian with any spark of faith and feeling left in his breast who could push away from him the pleading hands of the poor souls without assisting them.

Therefore, set this little flower—this token of death and of the poor souls in Purgatory—upon thy breast. Let it grow upon thy heart and multiply in it. It is a most grateful flower. It invites thee to compassionate and active love for the poor souls; it keeps the thought of death before thy mind, and thus helps thee to fulfil the words of the Holy Ghost: 'Remember thy last end, and thou shalt never sin.'

THE FORGET-ME-NOT

A lovely little flower is the forget-me-not. It seems to smile at us with its sky-blue eyes; it grows in thousands by the banks of river and stream; its very name secures for it a lasting place in our memory and heart.

Now, if we turn our eyes from the green fields of this earth to the burning sea of Purgatory, we behold countless souls who are ever calling out to us, 'Forget-me-not! forget-me-not!' Let us listen to their cries, and come to their assistance by our prayers and good works. They, in return, will show themselves grateful to us. They will not forget us at the hour of our death, and at the awful judgment-seat of God. Nor will they ever forget us when once in Heaven.

The forget-me-not grows and thrives best in damp and watery places, generally by the banks of streamlets. In like manner, when the hour of death has come for the good Christian, and the cold sweat runs down from his brow, and all his limbs are moistened by the dews of death, and the last tears are flowing from his dying eyes, then, indeed, if he has been a good friend to the poor souls in life, will grow up by his side the sweet flower of the forget-me-not. For the souls of those whom he has comforted in or released from Purgatory, do not forget him at the last moment. They come gratefully around him, because he has not forgotten them, and they help him in his last struggle.

Cardinal Bellarmine affirms that the poor souls delivered from Purgatory gather round the death-beds of their benefactors to defend them from the assaults of the devil, to diminish their fears of death, and by their presence to comfort and strengthen them. St. Thomas Aquinas says: 'No king is so well protected by his bodyguard as a Christian by the souls which he has delivered from Purgatory.' It seems quite natural that those souls could never forget the great act of charity done for them, least of all at that dread moment when the soul most requires help and protection.

Another feature of the forget-me-not is that, wherever it grows, it grows in great numbers. But numberless will be the sins and offences which we have committed, and which we shall have to render an account of on the last day; innumerable will be the accusations brought against us on the day of judgment. Who will then, at that decisive moment, come to speak for us and take our part? who but the souls who owe their deliverance to our prayers and efforts; they will not forget to come and stand by us in our need. As St. Gertrude says, the poor souls have often to cry long and loud in their misery, imploring us not to forget them, before we heed their cries and hasten to help them. But the poor souls are more grateful than we; they fly to our assistance even before we call on them, they precede us to the judgment-seat; they are there before us, uniting their prayers with those of our Angel-Guardians and Patron-Saints! We shall then experience, indeed, that a good friend is a strong defence, a powerful protection, a costly treasure. We shall then rejoice in the prayers, Masses, Communions by which we released those poor souls, who now so generously return our love!

The forget-me-not is blue, and blue is the colour of the sky or Heaven! Surely the souls that reach Heaven sooner by the help of our prayers will never forget us in that happy land. They, in turn, will pray for our admittance there; they will lead us into Heaven, and receive us there with indescribable joy and jubilation.

When the Emperor Charles V conquered Tunis he delivered 20,000 Christian slaves from a most cruel captivity. Filled and penetrated with gratitude towards their great benefactor, they gathered round him and blessed and thanked him for their liberty.

Like this great man so do all who give life and happiness and freedom to the sick, the poor, the prisoners, earn their blessings and gratitude. But where shall we find a deeper gratitude than that of the poor souls whose captivity surpasses in harshness every earthly bondage? They hasten to the bedsides of their dying benefactors, in order to lead them in triumph to Heaven. St. Margaret of Cortona experienced this, as we will briefly relate.

St. Margaret was once a great sinner, but, through the mercy of God, she was converted and then became as great a saint. Amidst the many virtues which she exercised, after her conversion, with great ardour and zeal, her love of the poor souls was the most remarkable. For them she would sacrifice everything. Great was her reward for it. As she lay on her death-bed awaiting her last moment, she perceived a great multitude of the souls she had released from Purgatory by her prayers and penances, hastening towards her in order to form, as it were, a guard of honour escorting her in triumph to her heavenly home. A great servant of God, living in the city of Castello, was favoured with a vision of this wonderful and consoling spectacle.

In like manner, if we have shown pity and zeal for them during our lifetime, they will come and bring us out of this valley of tears, and lead us out of a strange land into our true heavenly home. They will be our true and real forget-me-nots.

OFFICE OF THE DEAD

HEN the Office for the Dead is said through devotion at any other time of the year, and when it is daily performed for the souls departed in general, the rite is simple, viz., the invitatory psalm is omitted, only one Nocturn is recited according to the day of the week, the first words only of the anthems are said before the psalms, but the anthems are repeated entire after them, the shorter responsory is said after the third lesson on Wednesdays and Saturdays; at the end of Vespers and Lauds the respective psalm is said, with the versicles, kneeling, and the three prayers are recited under one short conclusion, thus: Who livest and reignest world without end. Amen. When only one Nocturn is recited at Matins, the order of the Nocturns is as feollows: the 1st Nocturn is said on Mondays and Thursdays, the 2nd Nocturn on Tuesdays and Fridays, and the 3rd Nocturn on Wednesdays and Saturdays.

His Holiness Pope Pius V, of holy memory, has granted one hundred days of indulgence to those who are obliged by duty to recite the Office for the Dead; but to those who perform it through devotion he has granted forty days of indulgence, in order to encourage all pious Christians to this devout practice of offering prayers and suffrages for the souls of the faithful departed.—July 9th, 1568.

261

AD VESPERAS

Ant. Placebo Domino.

Psalmus cxiv.

ilexi, quoniam exaudiet Dominus * vocem orationis meæ.

Quia inclinavit aurem suam mihi: * et in diebus meis invocabo.

Circumdederunt me dolores mortis: * et pericula inferni invenerunt me.

Tribulationem et dolorem inveni: * et nomen Domini invocavi.

O Domine, libera animam meam: * misericors Dominus et justus, et Deus noster miseretur.

Custodiens parvulos Dominus: * humiliatus sum, et liberavit me.

Convertere anima mea in requiem tuam: * quia Dominus benefecit tibi.

Quia eripuit animam meam de morte, * oculos meos a lacrymis, pedes meos a lapsu.

Placebo Domino * in regione vivorum.

[*In fine omnium Psalmorum dicitur.*]

Requiem aeternam * dona eis, Domine.

Et lux perpetua * luceat eis.

Ant. Placebo Domino in

Vespers

Anthem. I will please the Lord.

Psalm cxiv.

have loved, because the Lord will hear * the voice of my prayer.

Because He hath inclined His ear unto me: * and in my days I will call upon Him.

The sorrows of death have compassed me; * and the perils of hell have found me.

I met with trouble and sorrow: * and I called upon the Name of the Lord: O Lord, deliver my soul.

The Lord is merciful and just, * and our God sheweth mercy.

The Lord is the keeper of little ones: * I was humbled, and He delivered me.

Turn, O my soul, into thy rest; * for the Lord hath been bountiful to thee.

For He hath delivered my soul from death, * mine eyes from tears, and my feet from falling.

I will please the Lord * in the land of the living.

[At the end of every Psalm is said.]

Eternal rest * grant to them, O Lord.

And let perpetual light * shine upon them.

Ant. I will please the Lord in

regione vivorum.

Ant. Heu mihi, Domine.
    Psalmus cxix.

d Dominum cum tribularer clamavi * et exaudivit me.

Domine, libera animam meam a labiis iniquis * et a lingua dolosa.

Quid detur tibi, aut quid apponatur tibi, * ad linguam dolosam?

Sagittae potentis acutae, * cum carbonibus desolatoriis.

Heu mihi, quia incolatus meus prolongatus est! habitavi cum habitantibus Cedar: * multum incola fuit anima mea.

Cum his, qui oderunt pacem, eram pacificus: * cum loquebar illis, impugnabant me gratis.

Requiem aeternam, etc.

Ant. Heu mihi, Domine, quia incolatus meus prolongatus est!

Ant. Dominus custodit te.
    Psalmus cxx

evavi oculos meos in montes: * unde veniet auxilium mihi.

Auxilium meum a Domino,* qui fecit coelum et terram.

Non det in commotionem

the land of the living.

Ant. Woe is me, O Lord.
    Psalm cxix.

n my trouble I cried to the Lord, * and He heard me.

O Lord, deliver my soul from wicked lips * and a deceitful tongue.

What shall be given to thee, or what shall be added to thee,* to a deceitful tongue?

The sharp arrows of the mighty, * with coals that lay waste.

Woe is me, that my sojourning is prolonged! I have dwelt with the inhabitants of Cedar: * my soul hath been long a sojourner.

With them that hated peace I was peaceable:* when I spoke to them, they fought against me without cause.

Eternal rest, etc.

Ant. Woe is me, O Lord, that my sojourning is prolonged!

Ant. The Lord keepeth thee.
    Psalm cxx

have lifted up mine eyes to the mountains: * from whence help shall come to me.

My help is from the Lord, * who made heaven and earth.

May He not suffer thy foot to

pedem tuum:* neque dormitet, qui custodit te.

Ecce non dormitabit, neque dormiet, * qui custodit Israel.

Dominus custodit te, Dominus protectio tua:* super manum dexteram tuam.

Per diem sol non uret te,* neque luna per noctem.

Dominus custodit te ab omni malo: * custodiat animam tuam Dominus.

Dominus custodiat introitum tuum et exitum tuum: * ex hoc nunc, et usque in saeculum.

Requiem aeternam, etc.

Ant. Dominus custodit te ab omni malo: custodiat animam tuam Dominus.

Ant. Si iniquitates.

Psalmus cxxix

e profundis clamavi ad te, Domine: * Domine, exaudi vocem meam.

Fiant aures tuae intendentes, * in vocem deprecationis meæ.

Si iniquitates observaveris, Domine, * Domine, quis sustinebit?

Quia apud te propitiatio est: * et propter legem tuam sustinui te, Domine.

Sustinuit anima mea in verbo ejus: * speravit anima mea in

be moved: * neither let Him slumber that keepeth thee.

Behold, He shall neither slumber nor sleep, * that keepeth Israel.

The Lord is thy keeper, the Lord is thy protection * upon thy right hand.

The sun shall not burn thee by day, * nor the moon by night.

The Lord keepeth thee from all evil; * may the Lord keep thy soul.

May the Lord keep thy coming in and thy going out, * from henceforth now and for ever.

Eternal rest, etc.

Ant. The Lord keepeth thee from all evil: may the Lord keep thy soul.

Ant. If Thou wilt mark our iniquities.

Psalm cxxix

ut of the depths I have cried to Thee, O Lord: * Lord, hear my voice.

Let thine ears be attentive * to the voice of my supplication.

If thou, O Lord, wilt mark iniquities; * Lord, who shall stand it?

For with Thee there is merciful forgiveness: * and by reason of Thy law I have waited for Thee, O Lord.

My soul hath relied on His word: * my soul hath hoped in

Domino.
A custodia matutina usque ad noctem, * speret Israel in Domino.
Quia apud Dominum misericordia: * et copiosa apud eum redemptio.
Et ipse redimet Israel, * ex omnibus iniquitatibus ejus.
Requiem aeternam, etc.
Ant. Si iniquitates observaveris, Domine, Domine, quis sustinebit?

Ant. Opera.
Psalmus cxxxvii.

onfitebor tibi, Domine, in toto corde meo: * quonian audisti verba oris mei.
In conspectu Angelorum psallam tibi: * adorabo ad templum sanctum tuum, et confitebor nomini tuo.
Super misericordia tua, et veritate tua: * quoniam magnificasti super omne nomen sanctum tuum.

In quacumque die invocavero te, exaudi me: * multiplicabis in anima mea virtutem.

Confiteantur tibi, Domine, omnes reges terrae: * quia audierunt omnia verba oris tui.

Et cantent in viis Domini: * quoniam magna est gloria

the Lord.
From the morning watch even until night * let Israel hope in the Lord.
Because with the Lord there is mercy: * and with Him plentiful redemption.
And He shall redeem Israel * from all his iniquities.
Eternal rest, etc.
Ant. If Thou wilt mark our iniquities, O Lord, Lord, who shall stand it?

Ant. The works.
Psalm cxxxvii.

will praise Thee, O Lord, with my whole heart: * for Thou hast heard the words of my mouth.
I will sing praise to Thee in the sight of the Angels: * I will worship towards Thy holy temple, and I will give glory to Thy Name.
For Thy mercy and for Thy truth: * for Thou hast magnified Thy holy Name above all.

In whatever day I shall call upon Thee, hear me: * Thou shalt multiply strength in my soul.

May all the kings of the earth give glory to Thee: * for they have heard all the words of Thy mouth.

And let them sing in the ways of the Lord, * for great is the

Domini.

Quoniam excelsus Dominus, et humilia respicit: * et alta a longe cognoscit.

Si ambulavero in medio tribulationis, vivificabis me: * et super iram inimicorum meorum extendisti manum tuam, et salvum me fecit dextera tua.

Dominus retribuet pro me:* Domine, misericordia tua in saeculum; opera manuum tuarum ne despicias.

Requiem aeternam, etc.

Ant. Opera manuum tuarum Dómine ne despicias.

V. Audivi vocem de coelo dicentem mihi:

R. Beati mortui, qui in Domino moriuntur.

Ant. Omne.

MAGNIFICAT

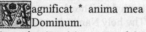agnificat * anima mea Dominum.

Et exultavit spiritus meus * in Deo salutari meo.

Quia respexit humilitatem ancillae suae: * ecce enim ex hoc beatam me dicent omnes generationes.

Quia fecit mihi magna qui potens est:* et sanctum nomen ejus.

glory of the Lord.

For the Lord is high, and looketh on the low: * and the high He knoweth afar off.

If I shall walk in the midst of tribulation, Thou wilt quicken me: * and Thou hast stretched forth Thy hand against the wrath of my enemies, and Thy right hand hath saved me.

The Lord will repay for me: * Thy mercy, O Lord, endureth for ever: O despise not the works of Thy hands.

Eternal rest, etc.

Ant. Despise not the works of Thy hands, O Lord.

V. I heard a voice from Heaven, saying to me:

R. Blessed are the dead who die in the Lord.

Ant. Whatever.

MAGNIFICAT

y soul doth magnify * the Lord.

And my spirit hath rejoiced * in God my Saviour.

Because He hath regarded the humility of His handmaid: * for behold from henceforth all generations shall call Me Blessed.

Because He that is mighty hath done great things to me, * and holy is His Name.

Et misericordia ejus a progenie in progenies * timentibus eum.

And His mercy is from generation unto generations * to them that fear Him.

Fecit potentiam in brachio suo: * dispersit superbos mente cordis sui.

He hath shewed might in His arm: * He hath scattered the proud in the conceit of their heart.

Deposuit potentes de sede, * et exaltavit humiles.

He hath put down the mighty from their seat, * and hath exalted the humble.

Esurientes implevit bonis, * et divites dimisit inanes.

He hath filled the hungry with good things, * and the rich He hath sent empty away.

Suscepit Israel puerum suum * recordatus misericordiae suae.

He hath received Israel His servant: * being mindful of His mercy.

Sicut locutus est ad patres nostros: * Abraham, et semini ejus in saecula.

As He spoke to our fathers, * to Abraham and to his seed for ever.

Requiem aeternam, etc.

Eternal rest, etc.

Ant. Omne, quod dat mihi Pater, ad me veniet: et eum qui venit ad me non ejiciam foras.

Ant. Whatever My Father giveth Me, shall come to Me: and I will not reject him who cometh to me.

Pater noster, *secreto*.

Our Father, *in silence*.

V. Et ne nos inducas in tentationem.

V. And lead us not into temptation.

R. Sed libera nos a malo.

R. But deliver us from evil.

AD MATUTINUM
INVITATORIUM

MATINS
THE INVITATORY

Regem, cui omnia vivunt, Venite adoremus.

Come, let us adore the King, to whom all things live.

Regem, cui omnia vivunt, Venite adoremus.

Come, let us adore the King, to whom all things live.

Psalmus xciv

Psalm xciv

enite, exultemus Domino, jubilemus Deo

ome, let us praise the Lord with joy: let us

salutari nostro: praeoccupemus faciem ejus in confessione, et in psalmis jubilemus ei.

Regem, cui omnia vivunt, Venite adoremus.
Quoniam Deus magnus Dominus, et Rex magnus super omnes deos: quoniam non repellet Dominus plebem suam, quia in manu ejus sunt omnes fines terrae, et altitudines montium ipse conspicit.
Venite adoremus.
Quoniam ipsius est mare, et ipse fecit illud, et aridam fundaverunt manus ejus: venite adoremus, et procidamus ante Deum: ploremus coram Domino, qui fecit nos: quia ipse est Dominus Deus noster, nos autem populus ejus, et oves pascuae ejus.
Regem, cui omnia vivunt, venite adoremus.
Hodie si vocem ejus audieritis, nolite obdurare corda vestra, sicut in exacerbatione secundum diem tentationis in deserto: ubi tentaverunt me patres vestri, probaverunt et viderunt opera mea.
Venite adoremus.
Quadraginta annis proximus fui generationi huic, et dixi: Semper hi errant corde: ipsi vero non cognoverunt vias meas: quibus juravi in ira mea,

joyfully sing to God our Saviour: let us come before His presence with thanksgiving: and make a joyful noise to Him with Psalms.
Come, let us adore the King, to whom all things live.
For the Lord is a great God, and a great king above all gods: For he does not cast off his people, because in His hands are all the ends of the earth, and the heights of the mountains are His.
To whom all things live.
For the sea is His, and He made it: and His hands formed the dry land. Come, let us adore and fall down and weep before the Lord, who made us: for He is the Lord our Lord: and we are His people, and the sheep of His pasture.
Come, let us adore the King, to whom all things live.
To-day if you shall hear His voice, harden not your hearts, as in the provocation, according to the day of temptation in the wilderness: where your fathers tempted me; they proved me and saw My works.
To whom all things live.
Forty years long was I offended with this generation, and I said: These always err in heart; but they have not known My ways and I swore to them in My

si introibunt in requiem meam.

Regem, cui omnia vivunt, Venite adoremus.
Requiem aeternam dona eis, Domine: et lux perpetua luceat eis.
Venite adoremus.
Regem, cui omnia vivunt. Venite adoremus.

IN I. NOCTURNO.
[Pro Feria ii. et v.]
Ant. Dirige.

Psalmus v

erba mea auribus percipe, Domine, * intellige clamorem meum.
Intende voci orationis meae: * Rex meus, et Deus meus.

Quoniam ad te orabo: * Domine, mane exaudies vocem meam.
Mane astabo tibi, et videbo: * quoniam non Deus volens iniquitatem tu es.

Neque habitabit juxta te malignus: * neque permanebunt injusti ante oculos tuos.
Odisti omnes, qui operantur iniquitatem: * perdes omnes, qui loquuntur mendacium.
Virum sanguinum et dolosum abominabitur Dominus: * ego autem in multitudine

wrath that they shall not enter into My rest.

Come, let us adore the King, to whom all things live.
Eternal rest grant to them, O Lord: and let perpetual light shine upon them.
To whom all things live.
Come, let us adore the King. To whom all things live.

FIRST NOCTURN
[For Monday and Thursday.]
Ant. Guide.

Psalm v

ive ear, O Lord, to my words, * understand my cry.
Hearken to the voice of my prayer: * O my King, and my God.

For to Thee will I pray, O Lord: * Thou, in the morning, shalt hear my voice.
In the morning I will stand before Thee, and will see * that Thou art not a God that willest iniquity.

Neither shall the wicked dwell near Thee: * nor shall the unjust abide before Thy eyes.
Thou hatest all the workers of iniquity: * Thou wilt destroy all who speak a lie.
The Lord will abhor the bloody and deceitful man: * but as for me, in the multitude of Thy

misericordiae tuae.

Introibo in domum tuam: * adorabo ad templum sanctum tuum in timore tuo.

Domine, deduc me in justitia tua: * propter inimicos meos dirige in conspectu tuo viam meam.

Quoniam non est in ore eorum veritas: * cor eorum vanum est. Sepulchrum patens est guttur eorum, linguis suis dolose agebant: * judica illos, Deus.

Decidant a cogitationibus suis, secundum multitudinem impietatem eorum expelle eos, * quoniam irritaverunt te, Domine.

Et laetentur omnes, qui sperant in te: * in aeternam exultabunt: et habitabis in eis.

Et gloriabuntur in te omnes, qui diligunt nomen tuum:* quoniam tu benedices justo.

Domine, ut scuto bonae voluntatis tuae * coronasti nos.

Requiem aeternam * dona eis, Domine.

Et lux perpetua * luceat eis.

Ant. Dirige, Domine, Deus meus, in conspectu tuo viam meam.
Ant. Convertere.

Psalmus vi

mercy,

I will come into Thy house: * I will worship towards Thy holy temple in Thy fear.

O Lord, lead me in Thy justice: * and. because of my enemies guide my way in Thy light.

For there is no truth in their mouth:* and their heart is vain. Their throat is an open sepulchre, they dealt deceitfully with their tongues: * judge them, O God.

Let them fall from their devices: according to the multitude of their wickedness cast them out: * for they have provoked Thee, O Lord.

But let all them be glad who hope in Thee: * they shall rejoice for ever: and Thou shalt dwell in them.

And all they who love Thy holy Name shall glory in Thee: * for Thou wilt bless the just.

O Lord, Thou hast crowned us as with a shield: * of Thy good will.

Eternal rest * grant to them, O Lord.

And let perpetual light * shine upon them

Ant. Guide my way, O Lord, my God, in Thy sight.
Ant. Turn to me.

Psalm vi

omine, ne in furore tuo arguas me: * neque in ira tua corripias me.

Miserere mei, Domine, quoniam infirmus sum; * sana me, Domine, quoniam conturbata sunt ossa mea.

Et anima mea turbata est valde: * sed tu Domine usquequo?

Convertere, Domine, et eripe animam meam; * salvum me fac propter misericordiam tuam.

Quoniam non est in morte qui memor sit tui * in inferno autem quis confitebitur tibi ?

Laboravi in gemitu meo, lavabo per singulas noctes lectum meum: * lacrimis meis stratum meum rigabo.

Turbatus est a furore oculus meus: * inveteravi inter omnes inimicos meos.

Discedite a me omnes, qui operamini iniquitatem: * quoniam exaudivit Dominus vocem fletus mei.

Exaudivit Dominus deprecationem meam, * Dominus orationem meam suscepit.

Erubescant, et conturbentur vehementer omnes inimici mei: * convertantur et erubescant valde velociter.

Requiem aeternam, etc.

Ant. Convertere, Domine, et eripe animam meam: quoniam

Lord, rebuke me not in Thy indignation: * nor chastise me in Thy wrath.

Have mercy on me, O Lord, for I am weak; * heal me, O Lord, for my bones are troubled.

And my soul is exceedingly troubled: * but Thou, O Lord, how long?

Turn to me, O Lord, and deliver my soul; * O save me for Thy mercy's sake.

For there is no one in death mindful of Thee; * and who shall confess to Thee that is in hell?

I have laboured in my groanings, every night I will wash my bed: * I will water my couch with my tears.

My eye is troubled through indignation; * I am grown old amidst all my enemies.

Depart from me, all ye workers of iniquity; * for the Lord hath heard the voice of my weeping.

The Lord hath heard my supplication:* the Lord hath received my prayer.

Let all my enemies be ashamed, and be very much troubled; * let them be turned back, and be ashamed very speedily.

Eternal rest, etc.

Ant. Turn to me, O Lord, and deliver my soul, for there is no

non est in morte, qui memor sit tui.

Ant. Nequando.

Psalmus vii.

omine, Deus meus, in te speravi: * salvum me fac ex omnibus persequentibus me, et libera me.

Nequando rapiat ut leo animam meam,

dum non est, qui redimat, neque qui salvum faciat.

Domine, Deus meus, si feci istud, * si est iniquitas in manibus meis:

Si reddidi retribuentibus mihi mala: * decidam merito ab inimicis meis inanis.

Persequatur inimicus animam meam, et comprehendat, et conculcet in terra vitam meam, * et gloriam meam in pulverem deducat.

Exurge, Domine, in ira tua: * et exaltare in finibus inimicorum meorum.

Et exurge, Domine, Deus meus, in praecepto quod mandasti: * et synagoga populorum circumdabit te.

Et propter hanc in altum regredere: *
Dominus judicat populos.

Judica me, Domine, secundum justitiam meam. * et secundum

one in death that is mindful of Thee.

Ant. Lest at any time.

Psalm vii.

Lord my God, in Thee have I put my trust: * save me from all them that persecute me and deliver me.

Lest at any time he seize upon my soul like a lion: * while there is no one to redeem me nor to save.

O Lord my God, if I have done this thing: * if there be iniquity in my hands:

If I have rendered to them that repaid me evils: * let me deservedly fall empty before my enemies.

Let the enemy pursue my soul, and take it, and tread down my life on the earth: * and bring down my glory to the dust.

Rise up, O Lord, in Thy anger: * and be Thou exalted in the borders of my enemies.

And arise, O Lord my God, in the precept which Thou hast commanded: * and a congregation of people shall surround Thee.

And for their sakes return Thou on high: * the Lord judgeth the people.

Judge me, O Lord, according to my justice: * and according to

innocentiam meam super me.
Consumetur nequitia peccatorum, et diriges justum: * scrutans corda et renes, Deus.

Justum adjutorium meum a Domino, * qui salvos facit rectos corde.
Deus judex justus, fortis, et patiens: * numquid irascitur per singulos dies?
Nisi conversi fueritis, gladium suum vibrabit: * arcum suum tetendit, et paravit illum.

Et in eo paravit vasa mortis: * sagittas suas ardentibus effecit.

Ecce parturiit injustitiam: * concepit dolorem, et peperit iniquitatem.

Lacum aperuit, et incidit effodit eum: * et incidit in foveam, quam fecit.
Convertetur dolor ejus in caput ejus: * it in verticem ipsius iniquitas ejus descendet.

Confitebor Domino secundum justitiam ejus: * et psallam nomini Domini altissimi.

Requiem aeternam, etc.
Ant. Nequando rapiat ut leo animam meam, dum non est qui

my innocence in me.
The wickedness of sinners shall be brought to nought, and Thou shalt direct the just: * Thou, O God, who searchest the hearts and reins.

Just is my help from the Lord, * who saveth the upright of heart.
God is a just judge, strong and patient: * is He angry every day?
Unless you be converted to Him, He will brandish His sword: * He has bent His bow and made it ready.

And in it He hath prepared the instruments of death: * He hath made ready His arrows for them that burn.

Behold, he hath been in labour with injustice: * he hath conceived sorrow, and brought forth iniquity.

He hath opened a pit and dug it: * and he is fallen into the hole he made.
His sorrow shall be turned upon his own head: * and his iniquity shall come down upon his own crown.

I will give glory to the Lord according to His justice: * and I will sing to the Name of the Lord the most high.

Eternal rest, etc.
Ant. Lest at any time he seize on my soul like a lion, while

redimat, neque qui salvum faciat.

V. A porta inferi.
R. Erue Domine animas eorum.
Pater noster, etc., totum secreto.

Lectio I. Job vii.

Parce mihi, Domine, nihil enim sunt dies mei. Quid est homo, quia magnificas eum? aut quid apponis erga eum cor tuum? Visitas eum diluculo, et subito probas illum. Usquequo non parcis mihi, nec dimittis me, ut glutiam salivam meam? Peccavi, quid faciam tibi, o custos hominum? quare posuisti me contrarium tibi, et factus sum mihimetipsi gravis? Cur non tollis peccatum meum, et quare non aufers iniquitatem meam? ecce, nunc in pulvere dormiam: et si mane me quaesieris, non subsistam.

R. Credo quod Redemptor meus vivit, et in novissimo die de terra surrecturus sum: * Et in carne mea videbo Deum, Salvatorem meum.

V. Quem visurus sum ego ipse, et non alius: et oculi mei conspecturi sunt.

there is none to redeem me or to save.

V. From the gates of hell.
R. Deliver their souls, O Lord.
Our Father, etc., all in silence.

The First Lesson. Job vii.

Spare me, O Lord, for my days are nothing. What is man that Thou shouldst magnify him? or why dost Thou set Thy heart upon him! Thou dost visit him early in the morning, and thou provest him suddenly. How long dost Thou not spare me, nor suffer me to swallow down my spittle? I have sinned, what shall I do to Thee, O keeper of men? why hast Thou set me opposite to Thee, and I am become burdensome to myself? Why dost Thou not remove my sin, and why dost Thou not take away my iniquity? Behold I now shall sleep in the dust: and if Thou seek me in the morning, I shall not be.

R. I firmly believe that my Redeemer is living, and that I shall rise again from the earth on the last day: * And that in my own flesh I shall see God, my Saviour.

V. Whom I myself in my own person shall see, and with my own eyes contemplate.

R. Et in carne mea videbo Deum, Salva torem meum.

Lectio II. Job x.

aedet animam meam vitae meae, dimittam adversum me eloquium meum, loquar in amaritudine animae meae. Dicam Deo: Noli me condemnare: indica mihi cur me ita judices. Numquid bonum tibi videtur, si calumnieris me, et opprimas me opus manuum tuarum, et consilium impiorum adjuves? Numquid oculi carnei tibi sunt: aut sicut videt homo, et tu videbis? Numquid sicut dies hominis dies tui, et anni tui sicut humana sunt tempora, ut quaeras iniquitatem meam, et peccatum meum scruteris? Et scias quia nihil impium fecerim, cum sit nemo, qui de manu tua possit eruere.

R. Qui Lazarum resuscitasti a monumento foetidum: * Tu eis, Domine, dona requiem, et locum indulgentiae.
V. Quid venturus es judicare vivos et mortuos, et saeculum per ignem.

R. Tu eis, Domine, dona requiem, et locum indulgentiae.

R. And that in my own flesh I shall see God, my Saviour.

The Second Lesson. Job x.

y soul is weary of my life. I will let go my speech against myself. I will speak in the bitterness of my soul. I will say to God: Do not condemn me: tell me why Thou judgest me so. Doth it seem good to Thee to calumniate me, and oppress me, the work of Thy hands, and to help the designs of the wicked? Hast Thou eyes of flesh, or shalt Thou see as man seeth? Are Thy days as the days of man? and are Thy years as the times of men? that Thou shouldst inquire after my iniquity, and search after my sin? And shouldst know that I have done no wicked thing, whereas there is no man that could deliver out of Thy hand.
R. Thou didst raise Lazarus fetid from the grave: * O Lord, grant to them a place of rest and of comfort.
V. Thou art to come to judge the living and the dead, and to consume the whole world by fire.
R. O Lord, grant to them a place of rest and comfort.

Lectio III. Job x.

Manus tuae fecerunt me, et plasmaverunt me totum in circuitu: et sic repente praecipitas me? Memento, quaeso, quod sicut lutum feceris me, et in pulverem reduces me. Nonne sicut lac mulsisti me, et sicut caseum me coagulasti? Pelle et carnibus vestisti me: ossibus et nervis compegisti me: Vitam et misericordiam tribuisti mihi, et visitatio tua custodivit spiritum meum.

R. Domine, quando veneris judicare terram, ubi me abscondam a vultu irae tuae? * Quia peccavi nimis in vita mea.

V. Commissa mea pavesco, et ante te erubesco: dum veneris judicare, noli me condemmare.

R. Quia peccavi nimis in vita mea.
Requiem aeternam dona eis, Domine, et lux perpetua luceat eis.
R. Quia peccavi nimis in vita mea.

The Third Lesson. Job x.

Thy hands have made me, and fashioned me wholly round about, and dost Thou thus cast me down headlong on a sudden? Remember, I beseech Thee, that Thou hast made me as the clay, and Thou wilt bring me to dust again. Hast Thou not milked me as milk, and curdled me like cheese? Thou hast clothed me with skin and flesh: Thou hast put me together with bones and sinews: Thou hast granted me life and mercy, and Thy visitation hath preserved my spirit.

R. O Lord, when Thou shalt come to judge the world, where shall I hide myself from the view of Thy wrath? * For I have sinned exceedingly during my life.

V. I am seized with fear at my offences, and I blush for shame before Thee: do not condemn me, when Thou shalt come to judge.
R. For I have sinned exceedingly during my life.
Eternal rest grant to them, O Lord, and let perpetual light shine upon them.
R. For I have sinned exceedingly during my life.

IN II NOCTURNO
[Pro Feria iii. et vi.]
Ant. In loco pascuae.
Psalmus xxii.

ominus regit me, et nihil mihi deerit: * in loco pascuae ibi me collocavit.

Super aquam refectionis educavit me: animam meam convertit.

Deduxit me super semitas justitiae: * propter nomen suum.

Nam et si ambulavero in medio umbrae mortis, non timebo mala: * quoniam tu mecum es.

Virga tua, et baculus tuus: * ipsa me consolata sunt.

Parasti in conspectu meo mensam: * adversus eos, qui tribulant me.

Impinguasti in oleo caput meum: * et calix meus inebrians quam praeclarus est!

Et misericordia tua subsequetur me: * omnibus diebus vitae meae.

Et ut inhabitem in domo Domini, * in longitudinem dierum.

Requiem aeternam, etc.

Ant. In loco pascuae ibi me collocavit.

SECOND NOCTURN.
[For Tuesday and Friday.]
Ant. In a place of pasture.
Psalm xxii.

he Lord ruleth me, and I shall want nothing: * He hath set me in a place of pasture.

He hath brought me up on the water of refreshment: * He hath converted my soul.

He hath led me on the paths of justice: * for His own Name's sake.

For though I should walk amidst shadows of death, I will fear no evils: * for Thou art with me.

Thy rod and Thy staff * they have comforted me.

Thou hast prepared a table for me, * against them that afflict me.

Thou hast anointed my head with oil: * and my chalice which inebriateth (me), how goodly is it!

And Thy mercy will follow me, * all the days of my life:

And that I may dwell in the house of the Lord * unto length of days.

Eternal rest, etc.

Ant. In a place of pasture He hath set me.

Ant. Delicta.

Psalmus xxiv.

d te, Domine, levavi animam meam:

Deus meus, in te confido, non erubescam,

Neque irrideant me inimici mei: * etenim universi, qui sustinent te, non confundentur.

Confundantur omnes iniqua agentes * supervacue.

Vias tuas, Domine, demonstra mihi: * et semitas tuas edoce me.

Dirige me in veritate tua, et doce me:

quia tu es Deus, salvator meus, et te sustinui tota die.

Reminiscere miserationum tuarum, Domine, * et misericordiarum tuarum, quae a saeculo sunt.

Delicta juventutis meae, * et ignorantias meas ne memineris.

Secundum misericordiam tuam memento mei tu: * propter bonitatem tuam, Domine.

Dulcis et rectus Dominus: * propter hoc legem dabit delinquentibus in via.

Diriget mansuetos in judicio: * docebit mites vias suas.

Universae viae Domini misericordia et veritas, * requirentibus testamentum ejus et testimonia ejus.

Ant. The faults

Psalm xxiv.

o Thee, O Lord, have I lifted up my soul: * in Thee, O my God, I put my trust, let me not be ashamed.

Neither let my enemies laugh at me: * for none of them that wait on Thee shall be confounded.

Let all them be confounded, * that act unjust things without cause.

Shew, O Lord, Thy ways to me, * and teach me Thy paths.

Direct me in Thy truth, and teach me: * for Thou art God, my Saviour; and on Thee I have waited the whole day long.

Remember, O Lord, Thy bowels of compassion: * and Thy mercies, that are from the beginning of the world.

The sins of my youth and my ignorances, * do not remember. According to Thy mercy remember Thou me: * for Thy goodness' sake, O Lord.

The Lord is sweet and just: * He will therefore give a law to sinners in the way.

He will guide the mild in judgment: * He will teach the meek His ways.

All the ways of the Lord are mercy and truth, * to them who seek after His covenant and His testimonies.

Propter nomen tuum, Domine, propitiaberis peccato meo: * multum est enim.

For Thy Name's sake, O Lord, Thou wilt pardon my sin, * for it is great.

Quis est homo, qui timet Dominum? * legem statuit ei in via, quam elegit.

Who is the man that feareth the Lord? * He hath appointed him a law in the way He hath chosen.

Anima ejus in bonis demorabitur: * et semen ejus haereditabit terram.

His soul shall dwell in good things: * and his seed shall inherit the land.

Firmamentum est Dominus timentibus eum; * et testamentur ipsius ut manifestetur illis.

The Lord is a firmament to those who fear Him: * and His covenant shall be made manifest to them.

Oculi mei semper ad Dominum: * quoniam ipse evellet de laqueo pedes meos.

My eyes are ever towards the Lord: * for He shall pluck my feet out of the snare.

Respice in me, et miserere mei:* quia unicus et pauper sum ego.

Look down upon me, and have mercy on me; * for I am alone and poor.

Tribulationes cordis mei multiplicatae sunt: * de necessitatibus meis erue me.

The troubles of my heart are multiplied: * deliver me from my necessities.

Vide humilitatem meam, et laborem meum, * et dimitte universa delicta mea.

See my abjection and my labour, * and forgive me all my sins.

Respice inimicos meos, quoniam multiplicati sunt: * et odio iniquo oderunt me.

Consider my enemies for they are multiplied, * and have hated me with an unjust hatred.

Custodi animam meam, et erue me: * non erubescam, quoniam speravi in te.

Keep Thou my soul, and deliver me: * I shall not be ashamed, for I have hoped in Thee.

Innocentes et recti adhaeserunt mihi:* quia sustinui te.

The innocent and the upright have adhered to me: * because I have waited on Thee.

Libera, Deus, Israel, * ex omnibus tribulationibus suis.

Deliver Israel, O God, * from all his tribulations.

Requiem aeternam, etc.

Eternal rest, etc.

Ant. Delicta juventutis meae, et ignorantias meas ne memineris, Domine.

Ant. Credo videre.

Psalmus xxvi.

ominus illuminatio mea, et salus mea, * quem timebo?

Dominus protector vitae meae, * a quo trepidabo?

Dum appropiant super me nocentes * ut edant carnes meas.

Qui tribulant me inimici mei: * ipsi infirmati sunt, et ceciderunt.

Si consistant adversum me castra * non timebit cor meum.

Si exurgat adversum me praelium, * in hoc ego sperabo.

Unam petii a Domino, hanc requiram, * ut inhabitem in domo Domini omnibus diebus vitae meae.

Ut videam voluptatem Domini, * et visitem templum ejus.

Quoniam abscondit me in tabernaculo suo: * in die malorum protexit me in abscondito tabernaculi sui.

In petra exaltavit me: * et nunc exaltavit caput meum super inimicos meos.

Circuivi, et immolavi in tabernaculo ejus hostiam vociferationis: * cantabo et psalmum dicam Domino.

Ant. The faults of my youth, and my sins of ignorance, O Lord, do not remember.

Ant. I believe to see.

Psalm xxvi.

he Lord is my light and my salvation, * whom shall I fear?

The Lord is the protector of my life: * of whom shall I be afraid?

Whilst the wicked draw near against me, * to eat my flesh.

My enemies that trouble me, * have themselves been weakened, and have fallen.

If armies in camp should stand together against me, * my heart shall not fear.

If a battle should rise up against me, * in this will I be confident.

One thing I have asked of the Lord, this will I seek after, * that I may dwell in the house of the Lord all the days of my life.

That I may see the delight of the Lord, * and visit His temple.

For He hath hidden me in His tabernacle: * in the day of evils He hath protected me in the secret place of His tabernacle.

He hath exalted me upon a rock; * and now He hath lifted up my head above my enemies.

I have gone round, and have offered up in His tabernacle a sacrifice of jubilation: * I will sing and recite psalms to the

Exaudi Domine vocem meam, qua clamavi ad te: * miserere mei, et exaudi me.

Tibi dixit cor meum, exquisivit te facies mea: * faciem tuam, Domine, requiram.
Ne avertas faciem tuam a me; * ne declines in ira a servo tuo.

Adjutor meus esto; * ne derelinquas me, neque despicias me, Deus salutaris meus.
Quoniam pater meus et mater mea dereliquerunt me: * Dominus autem assumpsit me.
Legem pone mihi Domine, in via tua * et dirige me in semitam rectam propter inimicos meos.
Ne tradideris me in animas tribulantium me; * quoniam insurrexerunt in me testes iniqui, et mentita est iniquitas sibi.
Credo videre bona Domini: * in terra viventium.

Expecta Dominum, viriliter age: * et confortetur cor tuum, et sustine Dominum.
Requiem aeternam, etc.
Ant. Credo videre bona Domini in terra viventium.

V. Collocet eos Dominus cum

Lord.
Hear, O Lord, my voice, with which I have cried to Thee: * have mercy on me, and hear me.
My heart hath said to Thee, My face hath sought Thee: * Thy face, O Lord, will I still seek.
Turn not away Thy face from me: * decline not in Thy wrath from Thy servant.
Be Thou my helper: * do not forsake nor despise me, Thou O God, my Saviour.
For my father and my mother have left me; * but the Lord hath taken me up.
Set me, O Lord, a law in Thy way, * and guide me in the right path, because of my enemies.
Deliver me not over to the will of them who trouble me; * for unjust witnesses have risen up against me, but iniquity hath belied itself.
I believe to see the good things of the Lord * in the land of the living.
Wait on the Lord, do manfully; * and let thy heart take courage, and wait thou for the Lord.
Eternal rest, etc.
Ant. I believe to see the good things of the Lord in the land of the living.

V. May the Lord place them

principibus.
R. Cum principibus populi sui.

Pater noster, totum secreto.

Lectio IV. Job xiii.

Responde mihi: quantas habeo iniquitates et peccata, scelera mea et delicta ostende mihi. Cur faciem tuam abscondis, et arbitraris me inimicum tuum? Contra folium, quod vento rapitur, ostendis potentiam tuam, et stipulam siccam persequeris: Scribis enim contra me amaritudines, et consumere me vis peccatis adolescentiæ meae. Posuisti in nervo pedem meum, et observasti omnes semitas meas, et vestigia pedum meorum considerasti: Qui quasi putredo consumendus sum, et quasi vestimentum, quod comeditur a tinea.

R. Memento mei, Deus, quia ventus est vita mea, * Nec aspiciat me visus hominis.

V. De profundis clamavi ad te Domine: Domine, exaudi vocem meam.
R. Nec aspiciat me visus hominis.

with princes.
R. With the princes of His people.

Our Father, all in silence.

The Fourth Lesson. Job xiii.

Do Thou answer me. How many are my iniquities and sins? make me know my crimes and offences. Why hidest Thou Thy face, and thinkest me Thy enemy? Against a leaf that is carried away by the wind Thou shewest Thy power, and pursuest a withered straw. For Thou writest bitter things against me, and wilt consume me with the sins of my youth. Thou hast put my feet in the stocks, and hast observed all my paths, and Thou hast examined my footsteps, who am to be consumed as rottenness, and as a garment that is moth-eaten.

R. Remember me, O God, for my life is like the fleeting wind: * nor shall the eyes of man behold me.

V. From the depths I have cried to Thee O Lord, hear my voice.
R. Nor shall the eyes of man behold me.

Lectio V. Job xiv.

Homo natus de muliere, brevi vivens tempore, repletur multis miseriis. Qui quasi flos egreditur et conteritur, et fugit velut umbra, et numquam in eodem statu permanet. Et dignum ducis super hujuscemodi aperire oculos tuos, et adducere eum tecum in judicium? Quis potest facere mundum de immundo conceptum semine? Nonne tu, qui solus es? Breves dies hominis sunt numerus mensium ejus apud te est; constituisti terminos ejus, qui praeteriri non poterunt. Recede paululum ab eo, ut quiescat, donec optata veniat, sicut mercenarii, dies ejus.

R. Heu mihi, Domine, quia peccavi nimis in vita mea! Quid faciam miser? Ubi fugiam, nisi ad te, Deus meus? * Miserere mei dum veneris in novissimo die.

V. Anima mea turbata est valde, sed tu, Domine, succurre ei.

R. Miserere mei dum veneris in novissimo die.

The Fifth Lesson. Job xiv.

Man born of a woman, liveth but a short time, and is burthened with many miseries. He is likened to a flower which is nipped as soon as it comes forth; he disappears like a shadow, and never continues in the same state. And deignest Thou to cast Thy eyes on such a being, and to cite him to judgment? Who can make pure and righteous him that was conceived in iniquity? Is it not Thou who alone canst do it? The days of man are short, Thou hast fixed the number of his months, and hast prescribed the term of his life, which he cannot go beyond. Cease then a little to afflict him, that he may rest, until the wished-for day come to him, as to the hired servant, for receiving his wages.

R. Woe to me, O Lord, for I have grievously sinned during my life! What shall I do, unhappy wretch? Whither shall I flee, but to Thee, O my God? * Have mercy on me when Thou comest at the last day.

V. My soul is deeply troubled, do Thou, O Lord, afford it comfort.

R. Have mercy on me when Thou comest at the last day

Lectio VI. Job xiv.

 uis mihi hoc tribuat, ut in inferno protegas me; et abscondas me, donec pertranseat furor tuus, et constituas mihi tempus, in quo recorderis mei? Putasne mortuus homo rursum vivat? Cunctis diebus, quibus nunc milito, expecto donec veniat immutatio mea. Vocabis me, et ego respondebo tibi in operi manuum tuarum porriges dexteram, Tu quidem gressus meus dinumerasti; sed parce peccatis meis.

R. Ne recorderis peccata mea, Domine: * Dum veneris judicare saeculum per ignem.
V. Dirige Domine Deus meus in conspectu tuo vitam meam.
R. Dum veneris judicare saeculum per ignem.
Requiem aeternam dona eis Domine: et lux perpetua luceat eis.
R. Dum veneris judicare saeculum per ignem.

IN III NOCTURNO
[Feria iv. et Sabbato.]

Ant. Complaceat.

Psalmus xxxix.

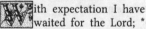 xpectans expectavi Dominum, * et intendit

The Sixth Lesson. Job xiv.

Who will grant me this, that Thou mayest protect me in hell, and hide me till Thy wrath pass, and appoint me a time when Thou wilt remember me? Dost Thou think that a dead man shall live again? I shall therefore patiently wait all the days in which I am now in warfare, till my change come. Thou wilt call me, and I shall answer Thee: Thou wilt stretch forth Thy right hand to the work of Thy hands. Thou indeed hast numbered my steps, but spare my sins.

R. Remember not my sins, O Lord, * when Thou shalt come to judge the world by fire.
V. Guide my steps, O Lord, my God, to walk in Thy presence.
R. When Thou shalt come to judge the world by fire.
Eternal rest grant to them, O Lord, and let perpetual light shine upon them.
R. When Thou shalt come to judge the world by fire.

THIRD NOCTURN
[For Wednesday and Saturday.]

Ant. Be pleased.

Psalm xxxix.

With expectation I have waited for the Lord; *

mihi.

Et exaudivit preces meas: * et eduxit me de lacu miseriae, et de luto faecis.

Et statuit super petram pedes meos; * et direxit gressus meos.

Et immisit in os meum canticum novum * carmen Deo nostro.

Videbunt multi, et timebunt: * et sperabunt in Domino.

Beatus vir, cujus est nomen Domini spes ejus: * et non respexit in vanitates et insanias falsas.

Multa fecisti tu, Domine, Deus meus, mirabilia tua: * et cogitationibus tuis non est, qui similis sit tibi.

Annuntiavi et locutus sum: * multiplicati sunt super numerum.

Sacrificium et oblationem noluisti: * aures autem perfecisti mihi.

Holocaustum et pro peccato non postulasti; * tunc dixi: Ecce venio.

In capite libri scriptum est de me, ut facerem voluntatem tuam: * Deus meus, volui, et legem tuam in medio cordis mei.

Annuntiavi justitiam tuam in ecclesia magna, * ecce labia mea non prohibebo, Domine, tu scisti.

Justitiam tuam non abscondi in

and He was attentive to me.

And He heard my prayers: * and brought me out of the pit of misery and the mire of dregs.

And He set my feet upon a rock: * and guided my steps.

And He put a new canticle into my mouth, * a song of jubilee to our God.

Many shall see, and shall fear; * and they shall hope in the Lord.

Blessed is the man whose trust is in the Name of the Lord: * and who hath not had regard to vanities and lying follies.

Thou hast multiplied Thy wonderful works, O Lord my God; * and in Thy thoughts there is none like to Thee.

I have declared and I have spoken: * they are multiplied above number.

Sacrifice and oblation Thou didst not desire; * but Thou hast pierced ears for me.

Burnt-offering and sin-offering Thou didst not require; * then said I, Behold, I come.

In the head of the book it is written of me that I should do Thy will; * I have desired it, O my God, and Thy law in the midst of my heart.

I have declared Thy justice in a great church; * lo, I will not restrain my lips: O Lord, Thou knowest it.

I have not hid Thy

corde meo: * veritatem tuam et salutare tuum dixi.

Non abscondi misericordiam tuam, et veritatem tuam * a concilio multo.

Tu autem, Domine, ne longe facias miserationes tuas a me: * misericordia tua et veritas tua semper susceperunt me. *

Quoniam circumdederunt me mala quorum non est numerus:* comprehenderunt me iniquitates meae, et non potui ut viderem.

Multiplicatae sunt super capillos capitis mei: * et cor meum dereliquit me.

Complaceat tibi, Domine, ut eruas me: * Domine, ad adjuvandum me respice.

Confundantur et revereantur simul, qui quaerunt animam meam, * ut auferant eam.

Convertantur retrorsum, et revereantur, * qui volunt mihi mala.

Ferant confestim confusionem suam, * qui dicunt mihi: Euge, euge.

Exultent et laetentur super te omnes quaerentes te: * et dicant semper: Magnificetur Dominus, qui diligunt salutare tuum.

Ego autem mendicus sum et pauper: * Dominus sollicitus est mei.

righteousness within my heart: * I have declared Thy truth and Thy salvation.

I have not concealed Thy mercy nor Thy truth * from a great council.

Withhold not, O Lord, Thy tender mercies from me; * Thy mercy and Thy truth have always upheld me.

For evils without number have surrounded me; * my iniquities have overtaken me, and I was not able to see.

They are multiplied above the hairs of my head: * and my heart hath forsaken me.

Be pleased, O Lord, to deliver me; * look down, O Lord, to help me.

Let them be confounded and ashamed together, * who seek my soul to take it away.

Let them be turned backward and be ashamed, * who desire evils to me.

Let them immediately bear their confusion, * that say to me, 'Tis well, 'tis well.

Let all who seek Thee rejoice and be glad in Thee; * and let those who love Thy salvation, say always: May the Lord be glorified.

For though I am a beggar and poor: * the Lord taketh care of me.

Adjutor meus, et protector, tu es: * Deus meus ne tardaveris.

Requiem aeternam, etc.

Ant. Complaceat tibi, Domine, ut eripias me: Domine, ad adjuvandum me respice.

Ant. Sana, Domine.

Psalmus xl.

Beatus qui intelligit super egenum et pauperem: * in die mala liberabit eum Dominus.

Dominus conservet eum, et vivificet eum, et beatum faciat eum in terra: * et non tradat eum in animam inimicorum ejus.

Dominus opem ferat illi super lectum doloris ejus: * universum stratum ejus versasti in infirmitate ejus.

Ego dixi: Domine, miserere mei: * sana animam meam, quia peccavi tibi.

Inimici mei dixerunt mala mihi: * Quando morietur, et peribit nomen ejus?

Et si ingrediabatur ut videret, vana loquebatur, * cor ejus congregavit iniquitatem sibi.

Egrediebatur foras, * et loquebatur in idipsum.

Adversum me susurrabant omnes inimici mei: * adversum

Thou art my helper and my protector, * O my God, be not slack.

Eternal rest, etc.

Ant. Be pleased, O Lord, to deliver me; Lord, look down to help me.

Ant. Heal my soul, O Lord.

Psalm xl.

Blessed is he who understandeth concerning the needy and the poor; * the Lord will deliver him in the evil day.

The Lord preserve him, and give him life, and make him blessed on earth: * and deliver him not up to the will of his enemies,

The Lord help him on his bed of sorrow: * Thou hast turned all his couch in his sickness.

I said, O Lord, be Thou merciful to me: * heal my soul, for I have sinned against Thee.

Mine enemies have spoken evils against me: * when shall he die and his name perish?

And if he came in to see me, he spoke vain things: * his heart gathered together iniquity to itself.

He went out, * and spoke to the same purpose.

All mine enemies whispered together against me; * they

me cogitabant mala mihi.

Verbum iniquum constituerunt adversum me: * Numquid qui dormit non adjiciet ut resurgat?

Etenim homo pacis meae, in quo speravi: * qui edebat panes meos, magnificavit super me supplantationem.

Tu autem, Domine, miserere mei, et resuscita me: * et retribuam eis.

In hoc cognovi, quoniam voluisti me * quoniam non gaudebit inimicus meus super me.

Me autem propter innocentiam suscepisti: * et confirmasti me in conspectu tuo in aeternum.

Benedictus Dominus Deus Israel a saeculo, et usque in saeculum: * fiat, fiat.

Requiem aeternam, etc.

Ant. Sana, Domine, animam meam, quia peccavi tibi.

Ant. Sitivit.

Psalmus xli.

uemadmodum desiderat cervus ad fontes aquarum: * ita desiderat anima mea ad te, Deus.

Sitivit anima mea ad Deum fortem, vivum; * quando veniam, et apparebo ante faciem Dei?

Fuerunt mihi lacrimae meae panes die ac nocte: * dum

devised evils against me.

An unjust word they formed against me: * shall he who sleeps rise again no more?

For even the man of my peace, in whom I trusted, * who ate my bread, hath greatly supplanted me.

But Thou, O Lord, take pity on me, and resuscitate me, * and I will requite them.

By this I know, that Thou hast had a good will for me; * because my enemy shall not rejoice over me.

But Thou hast upheld me on account of my innocence; * and hast established me in Thy sight for ever.

Blessed be the Lord God of Israel from eternity to eternity; * so be it, so be it.

Eternal rest, etc.

Ant. Heal my soul, O Lord, for I have sinned against Thee.

Ant. My soul hath thirsted.

Psalm xli.

s the hart panteth after the fountains of water; * so my soul panteth after Thee, O God.

My soul hath thirsted after the strong and living God: * when shall I come and appear before the face of God?

My tears have been my bread day and night: * whilst it is said

dicitur mihi quotidie: Ubi est Deus tuus?

Haec recordatus sum, et effudi in me animam meam: * quoniam transibo in locum tabernaculi admirabilis, usque ad domum Dei.

In voce exultationis, et confessionis, * sonus epulantis.

Quare tristis es anima mea? * et quare conturbas me?

Spera in Deo, quoniam adhuc confitebor illi: * salutare vultus mei, et Deus meus.

Ad meipsum anima mea conturbata est: * propterea memor ero tui de terra Jordanis, et Hermoniim a monte modico.

Abyssus abyssum invocat, * in voce cataractarum tuarum.

Omnia excelsa tua, et fluctus tui * super me transierunt.

In die mandavit Dominus misericordiam suam: * et nocte canticum ejus.

Apud me oratio Deo vitae meae, * dicam Deo: Susceptor meus es.

Quare oblitus es mei? * et quare contristatus incedo dum affligit me inimicus?

Dum confringuntur ossa mea, * exprobraverunt mihi, qui tribulant me inimici mei.

Dum dicunt mihi, per singulos

to me daily, Where is thy God?

These things I remembered, and poured out my soul in me: * for I shall go over into the place of the wonderful tabernacle, even to the house of God:

With the voice of joy and praise; * the noise of one feasting.

Why art thou sad, O my soul? * and why dost thou trouble me?

Hope in God, for I will give praise to Him; * the salvation of my countenance, and my God.

My soul is troubled within myself; * therefore will I remember Thee from the land of Jordan and Hermoniim, from the little hill.

Deep calleth on deep, * at the noise of Thy flood-gates.

All thy heights and thy billows * have passed over me.

In the day time the Lord hath commanded His mercy; * and a canticle to Him in the night.

With me is prayer to the God of my life, * I will say to God: Thou art my support.

Why hast Thou forgotten me? * and why go I mourning, while my enemy afflicteth me?

While my bones are broken, * mine enemies who trouble me have reproached me.

Whilst every day they say to me: Where is thy God? * why

dies: Ubi est Deus tuus? * quare tristis es anima mea? et quare conturbas me?

Spera in Deo, quoniam adhuc confitebor illi: * salutare vultus mei, et Deus meus.

Requiem aeternam, etc.

Ant. Sitivit anima mea ad Deum fortem vivum; quando veniam, et apparebo ante faciem Domini.

V. Ne trades bestiis animas confitentes tibi.

R. Et animas pauperum tuorum ne obliviscaris in finem.

Pater noster, etc., totum secreto.

Lectio VII. Job xvii.

piritus meus attenuabitur, dies mei breviabuntur, et solum mihi superest sepulchrum. Non peccavi, et in amaritudinibus moratur oculus meus. Libera me Domine, et pone me juxta te, et cujusvis manus pugnet contra me. Dies mei transierunt, cogitationes meae dissipatae sunt, torquentes cor meum. Noctem verterunt in diem, et rursum post tenebras spero lucem. Si sustinuero, infernus domus mea est, et in tenebris stravi lectulum meum. Putredini dixi: Pater meus es, mater mea, et soror mea, vermibus. Ubi est ego nunc praestolatio mea, et patientiam

art thou cast down, O my soul? and why dost thou disquiet me? Hope in God, for I will still give praise to Him; * the salvation of my countenance, and my God.

Eternal rest, etc.

Ant. My soul hath thirsted after the strong and living God: when shall I come and appear before the face of God?

V. Deliver not to beasts the souls of them who praise Thee.

R. And continue not to reject the souls of Thy poor.

Our Father, etc., all in silence.

The Seventh Lesson. Job xviii.

y spirit shall be wasted, my days shall be shortened, and only the grave remaineth for me; I have not sinned, and my eye abideth in bitterness. Deliver me, O Lord, and set me beside Thee, and let any man's hand fight against me. My days have passed away, my thoughts are dissipated, tormenting my heart. They have turned night into day, and after darkness I hope for light again. If I wait, hell is in my house, and I have made my bed in darkness. I have said to rottenness, thou art my father; to worms, [you are] my mother and my sister. Where is now my hope, and who hath regard

meam quis considerat?

R. Peccantem me quotidie, et non me poenitentem, timor mortis conturbat me: * Quia in inferno nulla est redemptio, miserere mei Deus, et salva me.

V. Deus in nomine tuo salvum me fac, et in virtute tua libera me.
R. Quia in inferno nulla est redemptio, miserere mei Deus, et salva me.

Lectio VIII. Job xix.

elli meae, consumptis carnibus, adhaesit os meum, et derelicta sunt tantummodo labia circa dentes meos. Miseremini mei, miseremini mei, saltem vos amici mei, quia manus Domini tetigit me. Quare persequimini me sicut Deus, et carnibus meis saturamini? Quis mihi tribuat, ut scribantur sermones mei? quis mihi det, ut exarentur in libro stylo ferreo, et plumbi lamina, vel celte sculpantur in silice? Scio enim quod Redemptor meus vivit, et in novissimo die de terra surrecturus sum: Et rursum circumdabor pelle mea, et in carne mea videbo Deum meum. Quem visurus sum ego ipse, et oculi mei conspecturi sunt, et

to my patience?

R. Whilst I am sinning daily, and not repenting, the fear of death disturbs me greatly: * [O God] since out of hell there is no redemption, have mercy on me, and save me.
V. Save me, O God, through Thy sacred Name, and rescue me by Thy power.
R. O God, since out of hell there is no redemption, have mercy on me, and save me.

The Eighth Lesson. Job xix.

he flesh being consumed, my bone hath cleaved to my skin, and nothing but lips are left about my teeth. Take pity on me, take pity on me, at least you my friends, because the hand of the Lord has touched me. Why do you persecute me as God, and glut yourselves with my flesh? Who will grant me that my words may be written? Who will grant me that they may be marked down in a book with an iron pen and in a plate of lead, or else be graven with an instrument of flint-stone? For I know that my Redeemer liveth, and on the last day I shall rise again from the earth. And I shall be clothed again with my skin, and in my flesh I shall see

non alius: reposita est haec spes mea in sinu meo.

my God: whom I myself shall see, and my eyes shall behold. This my hope is laid up in my bosom.

R. Domine secundum actum meum noli me judicare: nihil dignum in conspectu tuo egi: ideo deprecor majestatem tuam, * Ut tu Deus deleas iniquitatem meam.

R. Do not judge me, O Lord, according to my deeds, for I have done nothing to merit Thine approbation; therefore I humbly entreat Thy Divine Majesty, * that Thou, O God, wilt forgive me all my iniquity.

V. Amplius lava me, Domine, ab injustitia mea, et a delicto meo munda me.
R. Ut tu Deus deleas iniquitatem meam.

V. Wash me, O Lord, still more from my guilt, and cleanse me from the stains of sin.
R. That thou, O God, wilt forgive me all mine iniquity.

Lectio IX. Job x.

Quare de vulva eduxisti me? qui utinam consumptus essem, ne oculus me videret. Fuissem quasi non essem, de utero translatus ad tumulum. Numquid non paucitas dierum meorum finietur brevi? Dimitte ergo me, ut plangam paululum dolorem meum antequam vadam: et non revertar ad terram tenebrosam, et opertam mortis caligine: terram miseriae et tenebrarum, ubi umbra mortis, et nullus ordo, sed sempiternus horror inhabitat.

The Ninth Lesson. Job x.

Why didst Thou bring me forth out of the womb? O that I had been consumed that eye might not see me. I should have been as if I had not been, carried from the womb to the grave. Shall not the fewness of my days be shortly ended? Suffer me, therefore, that I may lament my sorrow a little before I go, and return no more, to a land that is dark and covered with the mist of death: a land of misery and darkness, where the shadow of death, and no order, but everlasting horror dwelleth.

R. Libera me Domine de morte aeterna, in die illa tremenda: * Quando coeli movendi sunt et terra: * Dum veneris judicare saeculum per ignem.

V. Tremens factus sum ego, et timeo, dum discussio venerit, atque ventura ira.

R. Quando coeli movendi sunt et terra.

V. Dies illa, dies irae, calamitatis et miseriae; dies magna et amara valde.

R. Dum veneris judicare saeculum per ignem.

V. Requiem aeternam dona eis, Domine: et lux perpetua luceat eis.

R. Libera me Domine de morte aeterna, in die illa tremenda: Quando coeli movendi sunt et terra: Dum veneris judicare saeculum per ignem.

R. Deliver me, O Lord, from eternal death on that dreadful day: * when the heavens and earth shall be moved: * whilst Thou wilt come to judge the world by fire.

V. I am seized with trembling and dread, while I reflect on the rigorous examination and vengeful wrath of the day.

R. When the heavens and earth shall be moved.

V. That day shall be a day of wrath, calamity, and misery; the great day of extreme bitterness and terror.

R. Whilst Thou wilt come to judge the world by fire.

V. Eternal rest grant to them, O Lord, and let perpetual light shine upon them.

R. Deliver me, O Lord, from eternal death on that dreadful day, when the heavens and earth shall be moved, whilst Thou wilt come to judge the world by fire.

[*The above Responsory is always said when the office is of a double rite; but when the Office is simple, that is, when only one Nocturn is said at Matins, the following is substituted:*]

Aliud Resp.

R. Libera me Domine, de viis inferni, qui portas aereas confregisti, et visitasti

R. Deliver me, O Lord, from the evil ways which lead to hell, Thou who didst break down its

infernum, et dedisti eis lumen, ut viderent te: * Qui erant in poenis tenebrarum.

V. Clamantes et dicentes: Advenisti Redemptor noster.
R. Qui erant in poenis tenebrarum.
V. Requiem aeternam dona eis, Domine, et lux perpetua luceat eis.
R. Qui erant in poenis tenebrarum.

AD LAUDES
Ant. Exultabunt.
Psalmus l.

Miserere mei Deus, * secundum magnam misericordiam tuam.
Et secundum multitudinem miserationum tuarum, * dele iniquitatem meam.
Amplius lava me ab iniquitate mea: * et a peccato meo munda me.
Quoniam iniquitatem meam ego cognosco: * et peccatum meum contra me est semper.
Tibi soli peccavi, et malum coram te feci: * ut justificeris in sermonibus tuis, et vincas cum judicaris.

Ecce enim iniquitatibus

brazen gates, who didst descend into Limbo to visit the faithful souls there, and didst give light to behold Thee to those: * Who were detained in darkness.
V. They cried out with joy, saying, Thou art at length come, O Thou, our Redeemer.
R. Who were detained in darkness.
V. Eternal rest grant to them, O Lord, and let perpetual light shine upon them.
R. Who were detained in darkness.

LAUDS
Ant. The bones.
Psalm l.

Have mercy on me, O God, * according to Thy great mercy.
And according to the multitude of Thy tender mercies, * blot out my iniquity.
Wash me yet more from my iniquity: * and cleanse me from my sin.
For I know my iniquity; * and my sin is always before me.

To Thee only have I sinned, and have done evil before Thee: * I acknowledge it, that Thou mayest be justified in Thy words, and mayest prevail when Thou art judged.
For behold I was conceived in

conceptus sum * et in peccatis concepit me mater mea.

iniquities: * and in sins did my mother conceive me.

Ecce enim veritatem dilexisti: * incerta et occulta sapientiae tuae manifestasti mihi.

For Thou hast loved truth: * the uncertain and hidden things of Thy wisdom Thou hast made manifest to me.

Asperges me hyssopo, et mundabor; * lavabis me, et super nivem dealbabor.

Thou shalt sprinkle me with hyssop, and I shall be cleansed; * Thou shalt wash me, and I shall be made whiter than snow.

Auditui meo dabis gaudium et laetitiam: * et exultabunt ossa humiliata.

To my hearing Thou shalt give joy and gladness; * and the bones that have been humbled shall rejoice.

Averte faciem tuam a peccatis meis: * et omnes iniquitates meas dele.

Turn away Thy face from my sins; * and blot out all my iniquities.

Cor mundum crea in me, Deus: * et spiritum rectum innova in visceribus meis.

Create a clean heart in me, O God, * and renew a right spirit within my bowels.

Ne projicias me a facie tua; * et Spiritum sanctum tuum ne auferas a me.

Cast me not away from Thy face; * and take not Thy Holy Spirit from me.

Redde mihi laetitiam salutaris tui, * et spiritu principali confirma me.

Restore unto me the joy of Thy salvation; * and strengthen me with a perfect spirit.

Docebo iniquos vias tuas: * et impii ad te convertentur.

I will teach the unjust Thy ways; * and the wicked shall be converted to Thee.

Libera me de sanguinibus, Deus, Deus salutis meae: * et exultabit lingua mea justitiam tuam.

Deliver me from blood, O God, Thou God of my salvation; * and my tongue shall extol Thy justice.

Domine, labia mea aperies: * et os meum annuntiabit laudem tuam.

O Lord, Thou wilt open my lips, * and my mouth shall declare Thy praise.

Quoniam si voluisses

For if Thou hadst desired

sacrificium dedissem utique: * holocaustis non delectaberis.

sacrifice, I would indeed have given it: * with burnt- offerings Thou wilt not be delighted.

Sacrificium Deo spiritus contribulatus: * cor contritum et humiliatum, Deus, non despicies.

A sacrifice to God is an afflicted spirit * a contrite and humbled heart, O God, Thou wilt not despise.

Benigne fac, Domine, in bona voluntate tua Sion: * ut aedificentur muri Jerusalem.

Deal favourably, O Lord, in Thy good-will with Sion: * that the walls of Jerusalem may be built up.

Tunc acceptabis sacrificium justitiae, oblationes, et holocausta: * tunc imponent super altare tuum vitulos.

Then shalt Thou accept the sacrifice of justice, oblations and whole-burnt offerings; then shall they lay calves upon Thy altar.

Requiem aeternam * dona eis, Domine.

Eternal rest * grant to them, O Lord.

Et lux perpetua * luceat eis.

And let perpetual light shine upon them.

Ant. Exultabunt Domino ossa humiliata.

Ant. The bones that have been humbled shall rejoice in the Lord.

Ant. Exaudi, Domine.
Psalmus lxiv.

Ant. O Lord, hear my prayer.
Psalm lxiv.

e decet hymnus, Deus, in Sion: * et tibi reddetur votum in Jerusalem.

hymn, O God, becometh Thee in Sion: * and a vow shall be paid to Thee in Jerusalem.

Exaudi orationem meam: * ad te omnis caro veniet.

Hear my prayer: * all flesh shall come to Thee.

Verba iniquorum praevaluerunt super nos: * et impietatibus nostris tu propitiaberis.

The words of the wicked have prevailed over us: * and Thou wilt pardon our trangressions.

Beatus, quem elegisti, et assumpsisti:* inhabitabit in atriis tuis.

Blessed is he whom Thou hast chosen, and taken to Thee; * he shall dwell in Thy courts.

Replebimur in bonis domus tuae: * sanctum est templum tuum, mirabile in aequitate.

Exaudi nos, Deus, salutaris noster, * spes omnium finium terrae, et in mari longe.

Praeparans montes in virtute tua, accinctus potentia: * qui conturbas profundum maris sonum fluctuum ejus.

Turbabuntur gentes, et timebunt, qui habitant terminos, a signis tuis: * exitus matutini et vespere delectabis.

Visitasti terram, et inebriasti eam: * multiplicasti locupletare eam.

Flumen Dei repletum est aquis, parasti cibum illorum: * quoniam ita est praeparatio ejus.

Rivos ejus inebria, multiplica genimina ejus: * in stillicidiis ejus laetabitur germinans.

Benedices coronae anni benignitatis tuae * et campi tui replebuntur ubertate.

Pinguescent speciosa deserti: *

We shall be filled with the good things of Thy house: * holy is Thy temple, wonderful in justice.

Hear us, O God, our Saviour, * who art the hope of all the ends of the earth, and in the sea afar off.

Thou who preparest the mountains by Thy strength, being girded with power: * who troublest the depth of the sea, the noise of its waves.

The Gentiles shall be troubled, and they that dwell in the uttermost borders, shall be afraid at Thy signs: * Thou shalt make the outgoings of the morning and the evening to be joyful.

Thou hast visited the earth, and hast plentifully watered it: * Thou hast many ways enriched it.

The river of God is filled with water, Thou hast prepared their food: * for thus is its preparation.

Fill up plentifully the streams thereof, multiply its fruits: * it shall spring up and rejoice in its showers.

Thou shalt bless the crown of the year of Thy goodness: and Thy fields shall be filled with plenty.

The beautiful places of the wilderness shall grow fat: * and et exultatione colles accigentur.

the hills shall be girded about with joy.

Induti sunt arietes ovium, et valles abundabunt frumento: * clamabunt, etenim hymnum dicent.

The rams of the flock are clothed, and the vales shall abound with corn: * they shall shout, yea, they shall sing a hymn.

Requiem aeternam, etc.

Eternal rest, etc.

Ant. Exaudi, Domine, orationem meam: ad te omnis caro veniet.

Ant. O Lord, hear my prayer: all flesh shall come to Thee.

Ant. Me suscepit.
Psalmus lxii

Ant. Thy right hand.
Psalm lxii

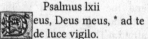eus, Deus meus, * ad te de luce vigilo.
Sitivit in te anima mea, * quam multipliciter tibi caro mea.

God, my God, * to Thee do I watch at break of day.
For Thee My soul hath thirsted; * for Thee my flesh, O how many ways!

In terra deserta, et invia, et inaquosa: * sic in sancto apparui tibi, ut viderem virtutem tuam, et gloriam tuam.

In a desert land, and where there is no way, and no water: * so in the sanctuary have I come before Thee, to see Thy power and Thy glory.

Quoniam melior est misericordia tua super vitas: * labia mea laudabunt te.

For Thy mercy is better than lives: * Thee my lips shall praise.

Sic benedicam te in vita mea: * et in nomine tuo levabo manus meas.

Thus will I bless Thee all my life: * and in Thy Name I will lift up my hands.

Sicut adipe et pinguedine repleatur anima mea: * et labiis exultationis laudabit os meum.

Let my soul be filled as with marrow and fatness: * and my mouth shall praise Thee with joyful lips.

Si memor fui tui super stratum meum, in matutinis meditabor

If I have remembered Thee upon my bed, I will meditate on

in te: * quia fuisti adjutor meus.

Et in velamento alarum tuarum exsultabo; adhaesit anima mea post te: * me suscepit dextera tua.

Ipsi vero in vanum quaesierunt animam meam, introibunt in inferiora terrae, * tradentur in manus gladii, partes vulpium erunt.

Rex vero laetabitur in Deo, laudabuntur omnes qui jurant in eo: * quia obstructum est os loquentium iniqua.

Thee in the morning: * because Thou hast been my helper.

I will rejoice under the covert of Thy wings; my soul hath stuck close to Thee: * Thy right hand hath received me.

But they have sought my soul in vain; they shall descend into the lower parts of the earth: * they shall be delivered into the hands of the sword, and shall be a prey to foxes.

But the king shall rejoice in God; all shall be praised who swear by Him: * because the mouth is stopped of those who speak evil things.

[*The Versicle*, Eternal Rest, etc., *is not said here.*]

Psalmus lxvi.

Deus misereatur nostri, et benedicat nobis: * illuminet vultum suum super nos, et misereatur nostri.

Ut cognoscamus in terra viam tuam; * in omnibus Gentibus salutare tuum.

Confiteantur tibi populi Deus: * confiteantur tibi populi omnes.

Laetentur et exultent gentes: * quoniam judicas populos in aequitate, et Gentes in terra dirigis.

Confiteantur tibi populi, Deus: * confiteantur tibi populi

Psalm, lxvi.

May God have mercy on us and bless us: * may He cause the light of His countenance to shine upon us, and may He have mercy on us.

That we may know Thy way on earth: * Thy salvation in all nations.

Let peoples confess to Thee, O God: * let all peoples give praise to Thee.

Let the nations be glad and rejoice: * for Thou judge the people with equity, and rulest the nations of the earth.

Let peoples, O God, confess to Thee: let all peoples give their omnes: * terra dedit fructum suum.

Benedicat nos, Deus, Deus noster, benedicat nos Deus: * et metuant eum omnes fines terrae.

Requiem aeternam, etc.

Ant. Me suscepit dextera tua, Domine.

Ant. A porta inferi.

Canticum Ezechiæ. Isa. xxxviii.

go dixi: In dimidio dierum meorum: * vadam ad portas inferi.

Quaesivi residuum annorum meorum: * dixi: Non videbo Dominum Deum in terra viventium.

Non aspiciam hominem ultra, * et habitatorem quietis.

Generatio mea ablata est, et convoluta est a me, * quasi tabernaculum pastorum.

Praecisa est velut a texente vita mea: dum adhuc ordirer, succidit me: * de mane usque ad vesperam finies me.

Sperabam usque ad mane, * quasi leo sic contrivit omnia ossa mea.

De mane usque ad vesperam finies me:* sicut pullus hirundinis sic clamabo, meditabor ut columba.

Attenuati sunt oculi mei, * suspicientes in excelsum:

praises to Thee: * the earth hath yielded her fruit.

May God, our God, bless us; may God bless us: * and all the ends of the earth fear Him.

Eternal rest, etc.

Ant. Thy right hand, O Lord, hath received me.

Ant. From the gate of hell.

Canticle of Ezechias. Is. xxxviii.

said: In the midst of my days * I shall go down to the gates of hell.

I sought for the residue of my years: * I said: I shall not see the Lord God in the land of the living.

I shall behold man no more, * nor the inhabitant of rest.

My generation is at an end, and it is rolled away from me, * like the tents of shepherds.

My life is cut off, as by a weaver whilst I was yet but beginning He cut me off: * from morning even to night Thou wilt make an end of me.

I hoped till morning: * as a lion so hath He broken all my bones.

From morning even to night Thou wilt make an end of me; * I will cry like a young swallow, I will meditate like a dove.

My eyes are become weak * looking upward.

Domine, vim patior, responde pro me. * Quid dicam, aut quid respondebit mihi, cum ipse fecerit?

Recogitabo tibi omnes annos meos, * in amaritudine animae meae.
Domine, si sic vivitur, et in talibus vita spiritus mei, corripies me, et vivificabis me. * Ecce in pace amaritudo mea amarissima:

Tu autem eruisti animam meam ut non periret, * projecisti post tergum tuum omnia peccata mea.
Quia non infernus confitebitur tibi, neque mors laudabit te: * non expectabunt qui descendunt in lacum, veritatem tuam.
Vivens vivens ipse confitebitur tibi, sicut et ego hodie: * pater filiis notam faciet veritatem tuam.
Domine, salvum me fac, * et psalmos nostros cantabimus cunctis diebus vitae nostrae in domo Domini.
Requiem aeternam, etc.
Ant. A porta inferi, erue Domine animam meam.

Ant. Omnis spiritus.
    Psalmus cxlviii.
audate Dominum de

Lord, I suffer violence, answer Thou for me. * What shall I say? or what will He reply to me, whereas He Himself hath done it?
I will recount to Thee all my years, * in the bitterness of my soul.
O Lord, if such be the life of man, and the life of my spirit be in such things as these, Thou shalt correct me, and make me to live: * behold, in peace is my bitterness most bitter.

But Thou hast delivered my soul that it should not perish: * Thou hast cast all my sins behind Thy back.
For hell shall not confess to Thee, neither shall death praise Thee: * nor shall they that go down into the pit, look for Thy truth.
The living, the living, he shall give praise to Thee, as I do this day: * the father shall make Thy truth known to the children.
O Lord, save me, * and we will sing psalms to Thee all the days of our lives in the house of the Lord.
Eternal rest, etc.
Ant. From the gate of hell, deliver my soul, O Lord.

Ant. Let every spirit.
    Psalm cxlviii.
raise ye the Lord from

coelis: * laudate eum in excelsis.
Laudate eum, omnes angeli ejus: * laudate eum, omnes virtutes ejus.
Laudate eum, sol et luna: * laudate eum, omnes stellae et lumen.
Laudate eum, coeli coelorum: * et aquae omnes, quae super coelos sunt, laudent nomen Domini.
Quia ipse dixit, et facta sunt: * ipse mandavit, et creata sunt.

Statuit ea in aeternum, et in saeculum saeculi: * praeceptum posuit, et non praeteribit.

Laudate Dominum de terra, * dracones, et omnes abyssi.
Ignis, grando, nix, glacies, spiritus procellarum: * quae faciunt verbum ejus.
Montes, et omnes colles: * ligna fructifera, et omnes cedri.

Bestiae, et universa pecora: * serpentes, et volucres pennatae.
Reges terrae, et omnes populi: * principes, et omnes judices terrae.
Juvenes et virgines: * senes cum junioribus laudent nomen Domini: * quia exaltatum est nomen ejus solius.
Confessio ejus super coelum et terram; * et exaltavit cornu populi sui.

the heavens: * praise Him in the high places.
Praise ye Him, all His Angels: * praise ye Him, all His hosts.

Praise ye Him, O sun and moon: * praise Him, all ye stars and light.
Praise Him, ye heavens of heavens! * and let all the waters that are above the heavens praise the Name of the Lord.
For He spoke, and they were made: * He commanded, and they were created.
He hath established them for ever, and for ages and ages: * He hath made a decree, and it shall not pass away.
Praise the Lord from the earth, * ye dragons and all ye deeps.
Fire, hail, snow, ice, stormy winds: * which fulfil His word.

Mountains, and all hills: * fruitbearing trees, and all cedars.
Beasts, and all cattle: * serpents, and feathered fowls.
Kings of the earth, and all people: * princes and all judges of the earth.
Young men and maidens; let the old with the younger, praise the Name of the Lord: * for His Name alone is exalted.
His praise is above heaven and

Hymnus omnibus sanctis ejus: * filiis Israel, populo appropinquanti sibi.

Psalmus cxlix.

Cantate Domino canticum novum: * laus ejus in ecclesia sanctorum.

Laetetur Israel in eo, qui fecit eum; * et filii Sion exultent in rege suo.

Laudent nomen ejus in choro: * in tympano et psalterio psallant ei:

Quia beneplacitum est Domino in populo suo: * et exaltabit mansuetos in salutem.

Exultabunt sancti in gloria: * laetabuntur in cubilibus suis.

Exaltationes Dei in gutture eorum: * et gladii ancipites in manibus eorum.

Ad faciendam vindictam in nationibus, * increpationes in populis.

Ad alligandos reges eorum in compedibus: * et nobiles eorum in manicis ferreis.

Ut faciant in eis judicium conscriptum: * gloria haec est omnibus sanctis ejus.

earth,* and He hath exalted the horn of His people.

A hymn to all His saints: * to the children of Israel, a people approaching to Him.

[*The Versicle,* Eternal rest, *is not said here.*]

Psalm cxlix.

Sing ye to the Lord a new canticle: * let His praise be in the Church of the saints.

Let Israel rejoice in Him who made him; * and let the children of Sion be joyful in their king.

Let them praise His Name in choir: * let them sing to Him with the timbrel and the psaltery.

For the Lord is well pleased with His people: * and He will exalt the meek unto salvation.

The saints shall rejoice in glory: * they shall be joyful in their beds.

The high praises of God shall be in their mouths: * and two-edged swords in their hands.

To execute vengeance upon the nations, * chastisements among the people.

To bind their kings with fetters, * and their nobles with manacles of iron.

To execute upon them the judgment that is written: * this glory is to all His saints.

[*The Versicle,* Eternal rest, *is not said here.*]

Psalmus cl.

Laudate Dominum in sanctis ejus: * laudate eum in firmamento virtutis ejus.

Laudate eum in virtutibus ejus: * laudate eum secundum multitudinem magnitudinis ejus.

Laudate eum in sono tubae: * laudate eum in psalterio et cithara.

Laudate eum in tympano et choro: * laudate eum in chordis et organo.

Laudate eum in cymbalis benesonantibus: laudate eum in cymbalis jubilationis: * omnis spiritus laudet Dominum.

Requiem aeternam, etc.

Ant. Omnis spiritus laudet Dominum.

V. Audivi vocem de coelo dicentem mihi.

R. Beati mortui, qui in Domino moriuntur.

Ant. Ego sum.

Canticum Zachariæ. Luc i.

Benedictus Dominus Deus Israel, * quia visitavit, et fecit redemptionem plebis suae:

Et erexit cornu salutis nobis: * in domo David, pueri sui.

Psalm cl.

Praise ye the Lord in His holy places:* praise Him in the firmament of His power.

Praise ye Him for His mighty acts: * praise ye Him according to the multitude of His greatness.

Praise Him with sound of trumpet: * praise Him with psaltery and harp.

Praise Him with timbrel and choir:

praise Him with strings and organs.

Praise Him on the high-sounding cymbals: praise Him on cymbals of joy: * let every spirit praise the Lord.

Eternal rest, etc.

Ant. Let every spirit praise the Lord.

V. I have heard a voice from Heaven say to me.

R. Blessed are the dead, that die in the Lord.

Ant. I am.

Benedictus. Luke i.

Blessed be the Lord God of Israel: * because He hath visited and wrought the redemption of His people.

And hath raised up a horn of salvation to us: * in the house of David His servant.

Sicut locutus est per os sanctorum, * qui a saeculo sunt, prophetarum ejus.

Salutem ex inimicis nostris, * et de manu omnium, qui oderunt nos.

Ad faciendam misericordiam cum patribus nostris: * et memorari testamenti sui sancti.

Jusjurandum, quod juravit ad Abraham patrem nostrum, * daturum se nobis.

Ut sine timore, de manu inimicorum nostrorum liberati, * serviamus illi.

In sanctitate et justitia coram ipso, * omnibus diebus nostris.

Et tu puer, propheta Altissimi vocaberis: * praeibis enim ante faciem Domini, parare vias ejus:

Ad dandam scientiam salutis plebi ejus: * in remissionem peccatorum eorum:

Per viscera misericordiae Dei nostri: * in quibus visitavit nos, oriens ex alto:

Illuminare his, qui in tenebris, et in umbra mortis sedent: * ad dirigendos pedes nostros in viam pacis.

Requiem aeternam, etc.

Ant. Ego sum resurrectio, et vita: qui credit in me, etiam si mortuus fuerit, vivet: et omnis qui vivit, et credit in me, non morietur in aeternum.

As He spoke by the mouth of His holy prophets, * who are from the beginning.

Salvation from our enemies, * and from the hand of all who hate us.

To perform mercy to our fathers; * and to remember His holy testament.

The oath, which He swore to Abraham our father, * that He would grant us.

That being delivered from the hand of our enemies, we may serve Him * without fear.

In holiness and justice before Him, all our days.

And thou, child, shalt be called the prophet of the Highest; * for thou shalt go before the face of the Lord, to prepare His ways:

To give knowledge of salvation to His people, * unto the remission of their sins.

Through the bowels of the mercy of our God: * in which the Orient from on high hath visited us:

To enlighten them that sit in darkness and in the shadow of death; * to direct our feet into the way of peace.

Eternal rest, etc.

Ant. I am the resurrection and the life; he who believeth in Me, although he be dead, shall live, and everyone who liveth and believeth in Me, shall not meet with eternal death.

[*After the Anthem of the Canticle, the following Prayers, Psalms, and Versicles are always recited except on All Souls' Day, and on the day of Deposition.*]

Pater noster, *secreto.*

Our Father, in silence.

V. Et ne nos inducas in tentationem.

V. And lead us not into temptation.

R. Sed libera nos a malo.

R. But deliver us from evil.

Ps. De Profundis, ut supra, p. 265.

Psalm: Out of the depth, as above, p. 265.

[At the end of Vespers instead of the Psalm, *De profundis*, is said the following:]

[In Vesperis decitur Ps. seq.]

Psalm cxlv.

auda anima mea Dominum, laudabo Dominum in vita mea: * psallam Deo meo quamdiu fuero.

Psalm cxlv.

raise the Lord, O my soul, in my life I will praise the Lord: * I will sing to my God as long as I shall be.

Nolite confidere in principibus: * in filiis hominum, in quibus non est salus.

Put not your trust in princes: * [nor] in the children of men, in whom there is no salvation.

Exibit spiritus ejus, et revertetur in terram suam: * in illa die peribunt omnes cogitationes eorum.

His spirit shall go forth, and he shall return into his earth: * in that day all their thoughts shall perish.

Beatus, cujus Deus Jacob adjutor ejus, spes ejus in Domino Deo ipsius: * qui fecit coelum et terram, mare et omnia quae in eis sunt:

Blessed is he, who hath the God of Jacob for his helper, whose hope is in the Lord his God: * who made heaven and earth, the sea, and all things that are in them.

Qui custodit veritatem in saeculum, fecit judicium

Who keepeth truth for ever: who executeth judgment to

injuriam patientibus: * dat escam esurientibus.

Dominus solvit compeditos; * Dominus illuminat caecos.

Dominus erigit elisos: * Dominus diligit justos.

Dominus custodit advenas, pupillum et viduam suscipiet; * et vias peccatorum disperdet.

Regnabit Dominus in saecula, Deus tuus, Sion, * in generationem et generationem.
Requiem aeternam, etc.
V. A porta inferi.
R. Erue, Domine, animas eorum.
V. Requiescant in pace.
R. Amen.
V. Domine, exaudi orationem meam.
R. Et clamor meus ad te veniat.

V. Dominus vobiscum.
R. Et cum spiritu tuo.

Oremus.

Deus qui inter Apostolicos sacerdotes famulos tuos pontificali seu sacerdotali, fecisti dignitate vigere; praesta quaesumus, ut eorum quoque perpetuo aggregentur consortio.

those who suffer wrong: * who giveth food to the hungry.

The Lord looseth them that are fettered: * the Lord enlighteneth the blind.

The Lord lifteth up those who are cast down: * the Lord loveth the just.

The Lord keepeth the strangers: He will protect the orphan and the widow; * and the ways of sinners He will destroy.

The Lord shall reign for ever: He is thy God, O Sion, * unto generation and generation.
Eternal rest, etc.
V. From the gates of hell.
R. Deliver their souls, O Lord.
V. May they rest in peace.
R. Amen.
V. O Lord, hear my prayer.

R. And let my cry come unto Thee.
V. The Lord be with you.
R. And with thy spirit.

Let us pray.

God, by whose favour Thy servants were raised to the dignity of bishops and priests; grant, we beseech Thee, that they may be admitted into the eternal society of Thy Apostles in Heaven.

Deus veniae largitor, et humanae salutis amator, quaesumus clementiam tuam, ut nostrae congregationis fratres propinquos et benefactores, qui ex hoc saeculo transierunt, beata Maria semper Virgine intercedente, eum omnibus sanctis tuis, ac perpetuae beatudinis consortium pervenire concedas.

God, bounteous in mercy, and lover of the salvation of mankind, we humbly beseech Thy divine clemency in behalf of the brethren of our holy society, our relations and benefactors, who are departed from this life, through the intercession of the ever blessed Virgin Mary, and of all the saints, that Thou wouldst receive them into their company in the fruition of eternal bliss. Through our Lord Jesus Christ, etc.

Fidelium, Deus, omnium conditor, et redemptor, animabus famulorum famularumque tuarum remissionem cunctorum tribue peccatorum: ut indulgentiam, quam semper optaverunt, piis supplicationibus consequantur. Qui vivis et regnas in saecula saeculorum. Amen.

God, the Creator and Redeemer of all the faithful, give to the souls of Thy servants departed the full remission of all their sins: that, through the help of pious supplications, they may obtain the pardon they have always desired: Who livest and reignest, world without end. Amen.

In Die Depositionis.

Absolve, quaesumus Domine, animam famuli tui N. ut defunctus (famulae tuæ N. defuncta) saeculo, tibi vivat: et quae per fragilitatem carnis humana conversatione commisit, tu venia misericordissimae pietatis

Prayer on the day of Decease or Burial.

Absolve, we beseech Thee, O Lord, the soul of Thy servant N., that being dead to this world, he (she) may live to Thee, and that he (she) may obtain from Thy great mercy the plenary remission of his (her) sins, committed by

absterge. Per Dominum nostrum Jesum Christum Filium tuum, qui tecum vivit et regnat in unitate Spiritus sancti, Deus, per omnia saecula saeculorum. R. Amen .

Alia Oratio.

Deus, cui proprium est misereri semper et parcere, te supplices exoramus pro anima famuli tui N. (famulae tuae N.) quam hodie de hoc saeculo migrare jussisti, ut non tradas eam in manus inimici, neque obliviscaris in finem; sed jubeas eam a sanctis Angelis suscipi, et ad patriam paradisi perduci; ut, quia in te speravit et credidit, non poenas inferni sustineat, sed gaudia aeterna possideat. Per Dominum nostrum Jesum Christum, etc. Amen.

Oratio in die 3, 7, 30.

Quaesumus Domine, ut animae famuli tui N. (famulae tuae N.) cujus despositionis diem tertium (septimum, vel trigesimum), commemoramus, Sanctorum atque Electorum tuorum largiri

human frailty while on earth. Through our Lord Jesus Christ, Thy Son, who liveth and reigneth with Thee and the Holy Ghost, one God, world without end. R. Amen.

Another Prayer on the day of Decease or Burial.

God, whose attribute it is always to have mercy and to spare, we humbly present our prayers to Thee for the soul of Thy servant N., which Thou hast this day called out of this world, beseeching Thee not to deliver it into the hands of the enemy, nor to forget it for ever, but to command Thy holy Angels to receive it, and to bear it into Paradise: that as it has believed and hoped in Thee, it may be delivered from the pains of hell, and inherit eternal life. Through our Lord Jesus Christ, etc.

Prayer on the third, seventh, or thirtieth day after death.

Admit, we beseech thee, O Lord, the soul of thy servant N. on this the third (seventh, or thirtieth) day of decease, which we commemorate, into the society of Thy saints, and refresh it

digneris consortium; et rorem misericordiae tuse perennem infundas. Per Dominum nostrum Jesum Christum, etc. Amen.

with the perpetual dew of Thy mercy. Through our Lord Jesus Christ, etc.

In Anniversario.

Deus indulgentiarum Domine: da animae famuli tui N. (famulae tuae N.) [animabus famulorum, famularumque tuarum] cujus (quorum) anniversarium depositionis diem commemoramus, refrigerii sedem, quietis beatitudinem, et luminis claritatem. Per Dominum nostrum Jesum Christum, etc. Amen.

Prayer on the anniversary day of decease.

God, the Lord of mercy, grant to the soul of Thy servant N., whose anniversary day of decease we commemorate, a place of comfort, a happy rest, and the light of glory. Through our Lord Jesus Christ, etc.

Pro Summo Pontifice.

Deus, qui inter summos Sacerdotes famulum tuum N. ineffabili tua dispositione connumerari voluisti: praesta, quaesumus; ut qui unigeniti Filii tui vices in terris gerebat, sanctorum tuorum Pontificum consortio perpetuo aggregetur. Per eumdem Dominum nostrum Jesum Christum, etc. Amen.

Prayer for the Sovereign Pontiff deceased.

God, who wast pleased in Thy divine providence to have Thy servant N. numbered among the chief pastors of Thy Church; grant, we beseech Thee, that he who represented the person of Thy only begotten Son on earth, may be admitted into the company of Thy holy prelates in Heaven. Through the same Lord Jesus Christ, etc.

Pro Episcopo vel Sacerdote.

Deus, qui inter apostolicos Sacerdotes famulum tuum N. pontificali sacerdotali fecisti dignitate vigere: praesta, quaesumus; ut eorum quoque perpetuo aggregetur consortio. Per Dominum nostrum Jesum Christum, etc. Amen.

Alia Oratio pro Episcopo.

Da nobis, Domine, ut animam famuli tui N. episcopi, quam de hujus saeculi eduxisti laborioso certamine, sanctorum tuorum tribuas esse consortem. Per Dominum nostrum Jesum Christum, etc. Amen.

Alia Oratio pro Sacerdote.

Praesta, quaesumus Domine ut anima famuli tui N. sacerdotis, quem in hoc saeculo commorantem, sacris muneribus decorasti, in coelesti sede gloriosa semper exsultet. Per Dominum nostrum Jesum Christum, etc. Amen.

Prayer for a deceased Bishop or Priest.

God, by whose favour Thy servant N. was raised to the dignity of a bishop (priest) and honoured with the apostolical functions; grant, we beseech Thee, that he may be admitted into the eternal society of Thy Apostles in Heaven. Through our Lord Jesus Christ, etc.

Another Prayer for a deceased Bishop.

Hear our prayer, O Lord, and grant that the soul of Thy servant and bishop N., whom Thou hast rescued from the painful conflicts of this world, may partake of the bliss of Thy saints. Through our Lord Jesus Christ, etc.

Another Prayer for a deceased Priest.

Grant, we beseech Thee, O Lord, that the soul of Thy servant N., whom Thou hast adorned with the sacred character of priesthood whilst on earth, may ever rejoice in celestial bliss. Through our Lord Jesus Christ, etc.

Pro Patre vel Matre.

Deus, qui nos patrem et matrem honorare praecepisti, miserere dementur animae patris mei (matris meae) ejusque peccata dimitte: meque eum (eam) in aeternae claritatis gaudio fac videre. Per Dominum nostrum Jesum Christum, etc. Amen.

Pro Uno defuncto.

Inclina, Domine, aurem tuam ad preces nostras, quibus misericordiam tuam supplices deprecamur: ut animam famuli tui N., quam de hoc saeculo migrare jussisti, in pacis ac lucis regione constituas, et Sanctorum tuorum jubeas esse consortem. Per Dominum nostrum Jesum Christum, etc. Amen.

Pro Una defuncta.

Quaesumus, Domine, pro tua pietate miserere animae famulae tuae N., et a contagiis mortalitatis exutam in aeternae salvationis partem restitue. Per Dominum nostrum Jesum Christum, etc. Amen.

Prayer for a deceased Father or Mother.

O God, who hast commanded us to honour our father and mother, mercifully show pity to the soul of my father (of my mother), forgive him his faults (her faults), and grant that I may see him (her) hereafter in the joys of Thy eternal glory. Through our Lord Jesus Christ, etc.

Prayer for a Man deceased.

Graciously hear, O Lord, the prayers we address to Thee, by which we humbly entreat Thy mercy to receive into the kingdom of peace and light the soul of Thy servant N., whom Thou hast called out of this world, and to reckon him among Thy blessed. Through our Lord Jesus Christ, etc.

Prayer for a Woman deceased.

We beseech Thee, O Lord, to show Thy bountiful mercy to the soul of Thy servant N., and being now freed from the corruption of this mortal life, grant to her the portion of Thy eternal inheritance of bliss. Through our Lord Jesus Christ, etc. Amen.

V. Requiem aeternam dona eis, Domine.

R. Et lux perpetua luceat eis.

V. Requiescant in pace.

R. Amen.

Finis Officii Defunctorum

V. Eternal rest grant to them, O Lord.

R. And let perpetual light shine upon them.

V. May they rest in peace.

R. Amen.

End of the Office of the Dead

MISSA PRO DEFUNCTIS
Ad Tumbam.

At the Catafalque or Bier.

The Bier or Catafalque is placed in the middle of the Church with lighted candles around it. The body of a layman is placed with his feet to the Altar, the body of a Priest with his head to the Altar. The officiating Priest stands at the feet, and the crossbearer and acolytes at the head of the corpse. Then are said or sung the following prayers; but the first prayer 'Enter not' is only said when the body is present.

When the Office for the Dead is said solemnly in Choir, as is done in many Churches on All Souls' Day or on the day of Burial, the body being present in the Church, it is usually followed by the Mass for the Dead, given as above, pp. 54-80. Then follow the prayers:

Non intres in judicium cum servo tuo, Domine, quia nullus apud te justificabitur homo, nisi per te omnium peccatorum ei tribuatur remissio. Non ergo eum, quaesumus, tua judicialis sententia premat, quem tibi vera supplicatio fidei Christianae commendat: sed gratia tua illa succurrente mereatur evadere judicium ultionis, qui, dum viveret insignitus est signaculo sanctae Trinitatis: qui vivis et regnas in

Enter not into judgment, O Lord, with Thy servant, for in Thy sight shall no man be justified, unless by Thee is granted to him the remission of all his sins. Let not then, we beseech Thee, the sentence of Thy judgment fall heavy upon him whom the true supplication of Christian Faith recommends to Thee; but by the assistance of Thy grace may he be worthy to escape the judgment of Thy vengeance, who whilst he lived was sealed

saecula saeculorum.

R. Amen.

RESPONSORIUM.

Libera me, Domine, de morte aeterna, in die illa tremenda: * Quando coeli movendi sunt, et terra: * Dum veneris judicare saeculum per ignem.

V. Tremens factus sum ego, et timeo dum discussio venerit, atque ventura ira.

R. Quando coeli movendi sunt et terra.

V. Dies illa, dies irae, calamitatis et miseriae: dies magna, et amara valde.

R. Dum veneris judicare saeculum per ignem,

V. Requiem aeternam dona eis, Domine, et lux perpetua luceat eis.

R. Libera me, Domine, de morte aeterna, in die illa tremenda, quando coeli movendi sunt et terra. Dum veneris judicare saeculum per ignem.

Kyrie eleison.
Christe eleison.
Kyrie eleison.
Pater noster, *secreto.*
Here the Priest sprinkles the Bier or Catafalque with holy water

with the seal of the Holy Trinity: Who livest and reignest for ever and ever.

R. Amen.

RESPONSORY.

Deliver me, O Lord, from everlasting death in that dreadful day: * When the heavens and the earth shall be moved: * When Thou shalt come to judge the world by fire.

V. I tremble and quake for fear, when I think of the searching and the wrath to come.

R. When the heavens and earth shall be moved.

V. O that day! that day of wrath, of wretchedness and woe! that day so great and very bitter!

R. When Thou shalt come to judge the world by fire.

V. Eternal rest give unto them, O Lord, and let perpetual light shine upon them.

R. Deliver me, O Lord, from eternal death on that dreadful day, when the heavens and earth shall be moved, when Thou wilt come to judge the world by fire.

Lord have mercy on us.
Christ have mercy on us.
Lord have mercy on us.
Our Father, *in silence.*

and incenses it.
V. Et ne nos inducas in tentationem.
R. Sed libera nos a malo.
V. A porta inferi.
R. Erue Domine animam ejus (animas eorum).
V. Requiescat (requiescant) in pace.
R. Amen.
V. Domine exaudi orationem meam.
R. Et clamor meus ad te veniat.

V. Dominus vobiscum.
R. Et cum spiritu tuo.

[Oratio, ut supra, p. 307, seq.]
Antiphon sung when the body is carried out of the Church.

In paradisum deducant te angeli: in tuo adventu suscipiant te martyres, et perducant te in civitatem sanctam Jerusalem. Chorus Angelorum te suscipiat, cum Lazaro quondam paupere, aeternam habeas requiem.

V. And lead us not into temptation.
R. But deliver us from evil.
V. From the gates of hell.
R. Deliver his (her) soul (their souls), O Lord.
V. May he (she, they) rest in peace.
R. Amen.
V. O Lord, hear my prayer.

R. And let my cry come unto Thee.
V. The Lord be with you.
R. And with thy spirit.

Let us pray.
[*The proper prayer for one or more deceased, is one of the Prayers at the end of Lauds, p. 307 and foll., but with the short conclusion,* Through Christ our Lord. *R.* Amen.]
May the angels lead thee into Paradise! may the martyrs receive thee at thy coming, and bring thee into the holy city Jerusalem. May the Choir of Angels receive thee, and with Lazarus, who once was poor, mayest thou have eternal rest.

SEPULTURAE ORDO

THE ORDER OF THE BURIAL OF THE DEAD
At the Reception of the Body

The Priest, vested in surplice, black stole, and black cope, with clerks bearing Cross, candles, and holy water, meets the body either at the house of the deceased, or at the entrance of the Church, or at the Cemetery gates, according to circumstances of time and place. Wherever he goes to meet it, he stands at the feet of the body, sprinkles it with holy water, and then says the following prayers:—

Ant. Si iniquitates observaveris, Domine, Domine, quis sustinebit?

Psalmus cxxix *De Profundis.*

De profundis clamavi ad te, Domine: Domine exaudi vocem meam.

Fiant aures tuae intendentes in vocem deprecationis meae.

Si iniquitates observaveris, Domine: Domine, quis sustinebit?

Quia apud te propitiatio est: et propter legem tuam sustinui te, Domine.

Sustinuit anima mea in verbo ejus: speravit anima mea in Domino.

A custodia matutina usque ad noctem: speret Israel in Domino.

Quia apud Dominum misericordia: et copiosa apud

Ant. If Thou, O Lord, wilt observe iniquities; Lord, who shall endure it?

Psalm cxxix *Out of the depths.*

Out of the depths I have cried to thee, O Lord: Lord, hear my voice.

Let thy ears be attentive to the voice of my supplication.

If thou, O Lord, wilt observe iniquities, Lord, who shall endure it?

For with thee there is merciful forgiveness: and by reason of thy law I have waited for thee, O Lord.

My soul hath relied on his word: my soul hath hoped in the Lord.

From the morning watch even until night: let Israel hope in the Lord.

Because with the Lord there is

eum redemptio.
Et ipse redimet Israel ex omnibus iniquitatibus ejus.
Requiem aeternam dona ei, Domine.
Et lux perpetua luceat ei.
Ant. Si iniquitates observaveris, Domine, Domine, quis sustinebit?

Ant. Exultabunt Domino ossa humiliata.
When the Body is carried to the Church or to the grave.
Psalmus l, *Miserere* (see p. 294).

Ant. Exultabunt.

When the Body enters the Church.
Subvenite, Sancti Dei, occurrite Angeli Domini, suscipientes animam ejus, offerentes eam in conspectu Altissimi.

V. Suscipiat te Christus qui vocavit te et in sinum Abrahae Angeli deducant te.

R. Suscipientes animam ejus.
Requiem aeternam dona ei, Domine, et lux perpetua luceat ei.

Offerentes eam in conspectu Altissimi.

mercy: and with him plentiful redemption.
And he shall redeem Israel from all his iniquities.
Eternal rest give unto him, O Lord.
And let perpetual light shine upon him.
Ant. If thou, O Lord, wilt observe iniquities, Lord, who shall endure it?

Ant. The bones that have been humbled shall rejoice in the Lord.

Psalm l. *Have mercy on me* (p. 294).
Ant. The bones.

Or at the grave (when not said in Church).
Come to his assistance, ye Saints of God meet him, ye Angels of the Lord, receiving his soul, offering it in the sight of the Most High.
V. May Christ receive thee, who has called thee; and may the Angels conduct thee to Abraham's bosom.
R. Receiving his soul.
Eternal rest give unto him, O Lord, and let perpetual light shine upon him.

Offering it in the sight of the Most High.

When Mass and the office are, of necessity, omitted the "Non intres" and following prayers are said at the grave, p. 313.

After the "In Paradisum" the grave is blessed (where the cemetery is not consecrated. The body being deposited in the middle of the Church, the Office of the Dead may be chanted, followed by Mass and the other prayers as given above, pp. 350—447.

When Mass cannot be celebrated, the prayers p. 443 are here said. Blessing of the Grave).

Oremus.

Deus, cujus miseratione animae fidelium requiescunt, hunc tumulum bene ✠ dicere dignare, eique Angelum tuum sanctum deputa custodem: et quorum quarumque corpora hic sepeliuntur, animas eorum ab omnibus absolve vinculis delictorum, ut in te semper cum sanctis tuis sine fine laetentur. Per Christum Dominum nostrum.

R. Amen.

(The Priest sprinkles the Body and the Grave with holy water, and incenses them. Then the following Antiphon and Canticle are said or sung.)

Ant. Ego sum resurrectio et

Let us pray.

O God, by whose mercy the souls of the faithful find rest, vouchsafe to bless ✠ this grave, and depute Thy holy Angel to guard it: and absolve from every bond of sin the souls of those whose bodies are herein interred, that in Thee they may for ever rejoice with Thy Saints. Through Christ our Lord.

R. Amen.

(In private funerals, necessarily performed in the house, whilst the canticle Benedictus is sung, blessed earth is put into the coffin.)

Ant. I am the resurrection and

vita: qui credit in me, etiam si mortuus fuerit, vivet: et omnis qui vivit, et credit in me, non morietur in aeternum.

Benedictus Dominus Deus Israel: quia visitavit, et fecit redemptionem plebis suae:

Et erexit cornu salutis nobis: in domo David pueri sui.
Sicut locutus est per os sanctorum, qui a saeculo sunt prophetarum ejus:
Salutem ex inimicis nostris, et de manu omnium qui oderunt nos.

Ad faciendam misericordiam cum patribus nostris: et memorari testamenti sui sancti.
Jusjurandum, quod juravit ad Abraham patrem nostrum, daturum se nobis.
Ut sine timore, de manu inimicorum nostrorum liberati, serviamus illi:
In sanctitate et justitia coram ipso, omnibus diebus nostris.
Et tu puer, propheta Altissimi vocaberis: praeibis enim ante faciem Domini parare vias ejus:

Ad dandam scientiam salutis plebi ejus, in remissionem peccatorum eorum:

the life: He that believeth in Me, although he be dead, shall live, and every one that liveth and believeth in Me, shall not die for ever.

Blessed be the Lord God of Israel, because he hath visited and wrought the redemption of his people.
And hath raised up a horn of salvation to us: in the house of David his servant.
As he spoke by the mouth of his holy prophets, who are from the beginning:
Salvation from our enemies, and from the hand of all that hate us.
To perform mercy to our fathers: and to remember his holy covenant.
The oath which he swore to Abraham our father, that he would grant to us.
That being delivered from the hand of our enemies, we may serve him without fear:
In holiness and justice before him, all our days.
And thou, child, shalt be called the prophet of the most High: for thou shalt go before the face of the Lord to prepare his ways:
To give knowledge of salvation to his people, unto the remission of their sins:
Through the bowels of the

Per viscera misericordiae Dei nostri: in quibus visitavit nos Oriens ex alto:

Illuminare his qui in tenebris et in umbra mortis sedent: ad dirigendos pedes nostros in viam pacis.

Requiem aeternam dona ei, Domine, et lux perpetua luceat ei.

Ant. Ego sum.

Then the Priest shall say.
Kyrie eleison.
Christe eleison.
Kyrie eleison.
Pater noster.
Meanwhile he sprinkles the Body.
V. Et ne nos inducas in tentationem.
R. Sed libera nos a malo.
V. A porta inferi.
R. Erue, Domine, animam ejus.
V. Requiescat in pace.
R. Amen.
V. Domine exaudi orationem meam.
R. Et clamor meus ad te veniat.
V. Dominus vobiscum.
R. Et cum spiritu tuo.
Oremus.
Fac, quaesumus, Domine, hanc cum servo tuo defuncto (vel famula tua defuncta) misericordiam, ut factorum suorum, in poenis non recipiat

mercy of our God: in which the Orient from on high hath visited us:
To enlighten them that sit in darkness, and in the shadow of death: to direct our feet in the way of peace.
Eternal rest give unto him, O Lord. And let perpetual light shine upon him.

Ant. I am.

Lord have mercy.
Christ have mercy.
Lord have mercy.
Our Father.

V. And lead us not into temptation.
R. But deliver us from evil.
V. From the gate of hell.
R. Deliver his soul, O Lord.
V. May he rest in peace.
R. Amen.
V. O Lord, hear my prayer.
R. And let my cry come unto Thee.
V. The Lord be with you.
R. And with thy spirit.
Let us pray.
Grant this mercy, O Lord, we beseech Thee, to Thy servant (or handmaid) departed, that he may not receive in punishment the requital of his deeds, who in

vicem, qui tuam in votis tenuit
voluntatem: ut sicut hic eum
vera fides junxit fidelium
turmis, ita illic eum tua
miseratio societ angelicis
choris. Per Christum Dominum
nostrum.
R. Amen.

V. Requiem aeternam dona ei,
Domine.
R. Et lux perpetua luceat ei.

V. Requiescat in pace.
R. Amen.
V. Anima ejus, et animae
omnium fidelium defunctorum
per misericordiam Dei
requiescant in pace.
R. Amen.

desire did keep Thy will: and as
the true faith here united him
to the company of the faithful,
so may Thy mercy unite him
above to the choirs of Angels.
Through Christ our Lord.
R. Amen.

V. Eternal rest give unto him,
O Lord
R. And let perpetual light
shine upon him.
V. May he rest in peace.
R. Amen.
V. May his soul, and the souls
of all the faithful departed,
through the mercy of God, rest
in peace.
R. Amen.
Then for the living there may
be added.

Let us pray.
Grant, O Lord, we beseech
Thee, that whilst we lament the
departure of Thy servant, we
may always remember that we
are most certainly to follow
him. Give us grace to prepare
for that last hour by a good and
holy life, that we may not be
taken unprepared by sudden
death; but may be ever on the
watch, that, when Thou shalt
call, we may go forth to meet
the Bridegroom, and enter with
him into glory everlasting.

Through Jesus Christ our Lord. Amen.

On returning from the grave to the Church or Sacristy is recited:
Ant. Si iniquitates observaveris, Domine, Domine, quis sustinebit?

Psalmus cxxix.

e profundis clamavi ad te, Domine: * Domine, exaudi vocem meam.

Fiant aures tuæ intendentes, * in vocem deprecationis meæ.

Si iniquitates observaveris, Domine, * Domine, quis sustinebit?

Quia apud te propitiatio est: * et propter legem tuam sustinui te, Domine.

Sustinuit anima mea in verbo ejus: * speravit anima mea in Domino.

A custodia matutina usque ad noctem, * speret Israel in Domino.

Quia apud Dominum misericordia: * et copiosa apud eum redemptio.

Et ipse redimet Israel, * ex omnibus iniquitatibus ejus.

Requiem aeternam, etc.

Ant. Si iniquitates observaveris, Domine, Domine, quis sustinebit?

On returning from the grave to the Church or Sacristy is recited:
Ant. If Thou, O Lord, wilt observe iniquities, Lord, who shall endure it?

Psalm cxxix.

ut of the depths I have cried to Thee, O Lord: * Lord, hear my voice.

Let thine ears be attentive * to the voice of my supplication.

If thou, O Lord, wilt mark iniquities; * Lord, who shall stand it?

For with Thee there is merciful forgiveness: * and by reason of Thy law I have waited for Thee, O Lord.

My soul hath relied on His word: * my soul hath hoped in the Lord.

From the morning watch even until night * let Israel hope in the Lord.

Because with the Lord there is mercy: * and with Him plentiful redemption.

And He shall redeem Israel * from all his iniquities.

Eternal rest, etc.

Ant. If Thou wilt mark our iniquities, O Lord, Lord, who shall stand it?

ur duties to our departed relatives and friends do not close when we have consigned their bodies to the grave. It is one of the greatest duties of Christian Charity to pray for the repose of the souls of the faithful departed. They ever cry out to us from the cleansing flames of purgatory, in the words of holy Job: *"Have pity on me, have pity on me, at least you my friends, for the Hand of the Lord is heavy upon me."* Offer up for them your prayers, communions, indulgences, and procure, according as you are able, the Holy Sacrifice to be offered for them. This should be an especial duty on the recurrence of the anniversaries of your friends and relations. Enrol yourself in a Purgatorial Society, and fulfil carefully all its obligations.

ORDO SEPELIENDI PARVULOS

THE ORDER OF THE BURIAL OF INFANTS

When an infant, a baptized child, shall have departed this life before coming to the use of reason, it shall be dressed as befits its age, and a crown, or garland of flowers, or of aromatic, or savoury herbs, in token of its bodily purity and virginity, shall be laid upon it. The Priest, vested in white cope or surplice, and white stole, with others of the clergy if they be at hand, preceded by the Cross, which is borne without its staff, shall go to the house of the deceased, or to the gate of the Church, or Cemetery, with a Cleric bearing the Holy Water Stoup. The Priest shall sprinkle the body and say:

Ant. Sit nomen Domini benedictum ex hoc nunc et usque in saeculum.

Psalmus cxii.

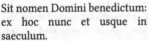audate, pueri, Dominum: laudate nomen Domini.

Sit nomen Domini benedictum: ex hoc nunc et usque in saeculum.

A solis ortu usque ad occasum: laudabile nomen Domini.

Excelsus super omnes gentes Dominus: et super coelos gloria ejus.

Quis sicut Dominus Deus noster, qui in altis habitat: et

Ant. Blessed be the name of the Lord from this time forth for evermore.

Psalm cxii.

Praise the Lord, ye children: praise ye the name of the Lord.

Blessed be the name of the Lord: from this time forth for evermore.

From the rising up of the sun unto the going down of the same: the name of the Lord is worthy to be praised.

The Lord is high above all nations: and his glory above the heavens.

Who is like unto the Lord our God, who dwelleth on high: and regardeth the things that are

humilia respicit in coelo et in terra?

Suscitans a terra inopem: et de stercore erigens pauperem:

Ut collocet eum cum principibus: cum principibus populi sui.

Qui habitare facit sterilem in domo: matrem filiorum laetantem.

Gloria Patri, &c.

Ant. Sit nomen Domini benedictum et hoc nunc et usque in saeculum.

When the Church is reached is said:

Ant. Hic accipiet benedictionem a Domino, et misericordiam a Deo, salutari suo, quia haec est generatio quaerentium Dominum.

Psalmus xxiii.

Domini est terra, et plenitudo ejus: orbis terrarum, et universi qui habitant in eo.

Quia ipse super maria fundavit eum: et super flumina praeparavit eum.

Quis ascendet in montem Domini? aut quis stabit in loco sancto ejus?

Innocens manibus et mundo corde, qui non accepit in vano animam suam, nec juravit in dolo proximo suo.

lowly in heaven and in earth?

Who raiseth up the needy from the earth: and lifteth the poor from off the dunghill:

That He may set him with the princes: even with the princes of His people.

Who maketh the barren woman to dwell in her house: the joyful mother of children.

Glory be to the Father, &c.

Ant. Blessed be the name of the Lord from this time forth for evermore.

At the grave (*when not said in Church*).

Ant. He shall receive a blessing from the Lord, and mercy from God, his Saviour, for this is the generation of them that seek the Lord.

Psalm xxiii.

The earth is the Lord's, and the fulness thereof: the world, and all they that dwell therein.

For he hath founded it upon the seas: and hath prepared it upon the rivers.

Who shall ascend into the mountain of the Lord: or who shall stand in his holy place?

The innocent in hands and clean of heart, who hath not taken his soul in vain, nor sworn deceitfully to his neighbour.

Hic accipiet benedictionem a Domino: et misericordiam a Deo salutari suo.

Haec est generatio quaerentium eum quaerentium faciem Dei Jacob.

Attollite portas principes vestras, et elevamini portae aeternales: et introibit Rex gloriae.

Quis est iste Rex gloriae? Dominus fortis et potens, Dominus potens in praelio.

Attollite portas principes vestras, et elevamini portae aeternales: et introibit Rex gloriae.

Quis est iste Rex gloriae? Dominus virtutum, ipse est Rex gloriae.

Gloria Patria, etc.

Ant. Hic accipiet benedictionem a Domino, et misericordiam a Deo, salutari suo, quia haec est generatio quaerentium Dominum.

Kyrie eleison.
Christe eleison.
Kyrie eleison.
Pater noster, etc., *secreto.*
Meanwhile he sprinkles the body.

V. Et ne nos inducas in tentationem.
R. Sed libera nos a malo.
V. Me autem propter innocentiam suscepisti.

He shall receive a blessing from the Lord: and mercy from God his Saviour.

This is the generation of them that seek him: of them that seek the face of the God of Jacob.

Lift up your gates, O ye princes, and be ye lifted up, O eternal gates: and the King of glory shall enter in.

Who is this King of glory? the Lord, strong and mighty: the Lord, mighty in battle.

Lift up your gates, O ye princes, and be ye lifted up, O eternal gates: and the King of glory shall enter in.

Who is this King of glory? the Lord of hosts, he is the King of glory.

Glory be to the Father, etc.

Ant. He shall receive a blessing from the Lord, and mercy from God, his Saviour, for this is the generation of them that seek the Lord.

Lord have mercy.
Christ have mercy.
Lord have mercy.
Our Father, etc., *secretly.*

V. And lead us not into temptation.
R. But deliver us from evil.
V. But me hast Thou received, because of mine innocence.

R. Et confirmasti me in conspectu tuo in aeternum.

V. Dominus vobiscum.

R. Et cum spiritu tuo.

Oremus.

Omnipotens et mitissime Deus, qui omnibus parvulis renatis fonte baptismatis, dum migrant a saeculo, sine ullis eorum meritis, vitam illico largiris aeternam, sicut animae hujus parvuli hodie credimus te fecisse: fac nos quaesumus Domine, per intercessionem beatae Mariae, semper virginis, et omnium Sanctorum tuorum, hic purificatis tibi mentibus famulari, et in Paradiso cum beatis parvulis perenniter sociari. Per Christum Dominum nostrum.

R. Amen.

Whilst the body is being borne to the grave, and
even if it be not then buried, shall be said:

Ant. Juvenes et virgines, senes cum junioribus laudent nomen Domini.

Psalmus cxlviii.

Laudate Dominum de coelis: laudate eum in excelsis.

Laudate eum omnes Angeli ejus: laudate eum omnes

R. And hast confirmed me in Thy sight for ever.

V. The Lord be with you.

R. And with thy spirit.

Let us pray.

Almighty and most merciful God, who unto all little children born again in the fountain of baptism, dost immediately, without any merits of theirs, give eternal life when they depart out of this world, even as we believe Thou hast done to the soul of this little child this day; grant unto us, we beseech Thee, O Lord, through the intercession of the blessed Mary ever Virgin and all Thy Saints, that we may serve Thee here with pure minds, and be companions of the blessed little ones in Paradise for ever. Through Christ our Lord.

R. Amen.

Ant. Young men and maidens, let the old with the younger praise the name of the Lord.

Psalm cxlviii.

Praise ye the Lord from the heavens: praise ye him in the high places.

Praise ye him all his Angels: praise ye him all his hosts.

virtutes ejus.
Laudate eum sol et luna: laudate eum omnes stellae et lumen.
Laudate eum coeli coelorum: et aquae omnes quae super coelos sunt, laudent nomen Domini.

Quia ipse dixit, et facta sunt: ipse mandavit, et creata sunt.

Statuit ea in aeternum, et in saeculum saeculi: praeceptum posuit, et non praeteribit.

Laudate Dominum de terra: dracones, et omnes abyssi.
Ignis, grando, nix, glacies, spiritus procellarum: quae faciunt verbum ejus.
Montes et omnes colles: ligna fructifera et omnes cedri.
Bestiae et universa pecora: serpentes et volucres pennatae.
Reges terrae et omnes populi: principes et omnes judices terrae.
Juvenes et virgines: senes cum junioribus laudent nomen Domini: quia exaltatum est nomen ejus solius.
Confessio ejus super coelum et terram: et exaltavit cornu populi sui.
Hymnus omnibus sanctis ejus: filiis Israel populo appropinquanti sibi.
Gloria Patri, etc.

Praise ye him, O sun and moon: praise him all ye stars and light.

Praise him ye heavens of heavens: and let all the waters that are above the heavens praise the name of the Lord.
For he spoke, and they were made: he commanded and they were created.
He hath established them for ever, and for ages of ages: he hath made a decree, and it shall not pass away.
Praise the Lord from the earth: ye dragons, and all ye deeps.
Fire, hail, snow, ice, stormy winds: which fulfil his word.

Mountains and all hills: fruitful trees and all cedars.
Beasts and all cattle: serpents and feathered fowls.
Kings of the earth and all people: princes and all judges of the earth.
Old men and maidens: let the old with the young praise the name of the Lord, for his name alone is exalted.
The praise of him is above heaven and earth: and he hath exalted the horn of his people.
A hymn to all his saints: to the children of Israel, a people approaching to him.
Glory be to the Father, etc.

Ant. Juvenes et virgines, senes cum junioribus laudent nomen Domini.

Kyrie eleison.
Christe eleison.
Kyrie eleison.
Pater noster, secreto.
V. Et ne nos inducas in tentationem.
R. Sed libera nos a malo.
V. Sinite parvulos venire ad me.

R. Talium est enim regnum caelorum.
V. Dominus vobiscum.
R. Et cum spiritu tuo.
　　　Oremus.

Omnipotens, sempiterne Deus, sanctae puritatis amator, qui animam hujus parvuli ad coelorum regnum hodie misericorditer vocare dignatus es: digneris etiam, Domine, ita nobiscum misericorditer agere ut meritis tuae sanctissimae Passionis et intercessione beatae Mariae, semper Virginis, et omnium Sanctorum tuorum, in eodem regno nos cum omnibus Sanctis et electis tuis semper facias congaudere. Qui vivis et regnas, cum Deo Patre, in unitate Spiritus Sancti Deus, per omnia saecula saeculorum.
R. Amen.

Ant. Old men and maidens, let the old with the younger praise the name of the Lord.

Lord have mercy.
Christ have mercy.
Lord have mercy.
Our Father, secretly.
V. And lead us not into temptation.
R. But deliver us from evil.
V. Suffer little children to come unto me.

R. For of such is the kingdom of heaven.
V. The Lord be with you.
R. And with thy spirit.
　　　Let us pray.

Almighty, everlasting God, lover of holy purity, who hast this day mercifully vouchsafed to call the soul of this little one unto the kingdom of heaven, vouchsafe also, O Lord, to deal so mercifully with us, that, by the merits of Thy most holy Passion, and by the intercession of blessed Mary ever Virgin and all thy Saints, we also may evermore rejoice in the same kingdom with all Thy Saints and Elect. Who livest and reignest with God the Father, in the unity of the Holy Ghost, God for ever and ever.
R. Amen.

Blessing of the Grave.
(Where the Cemetery is not consecrated.)

Oremus.

Deus, cujus miseratione animae fidelium requiescunt, hunc tumulum bene ✠ dicere dignare, eique Angelum tuum sanctum deputa custodem: et quorum quarumque corpora hic sepeliuntur, animas eorum ab omnibus absolve vinculis delictorum, ut in te semper cum sanctis tuis sine fine laetentur. Per Christum Dominum nostrum.

R. Amen.

The Priest sprinkles and incenses the body and the grave; the body is then buried. On returning to the Church, is said:

Ant. Benedicite.

Benedicite omnia opera Domini Domino: laudate et superexaltate eum in saecula.

Benedicite angeli Domini Domino: benedicite coeli Domino.

Benedicite aquae omnes, quae super coelos sunt Domino: benedicite omnes virtutes Domini Domino.

Benedicite sol et luna Domino, benedicite stellae coeli Domino.

Benedicite omnis imber et ros

Let us pray.

O God, by whose mercy the souls of the faithful find rest, vouchsafe to bless ✠ this grave, and depute Thy holy Angel to guard it: and absolve from every bond of sin the souls of those whose bodies are herein interred, that in Thee they may for ever rejoice with Thy Saints. Through Christ our Lord.

R. Amen.

Ant. Bless.

All ye works of the Lord, bless the Lord: praise and exalt him above for ever.

O all ye angels of the Lord, bless the Lord: O ye heavens, bless the Lord.

O all ye waters that are above the heavens, bless the Lord: O all ye powers of the Lord, bless the Lord.

O ye sun and moon, bless the Lord: O ye stars of heaven, bless the Lord.

O every shower and dew, bless ye the Lord: O all ye spirits of

Domino: benedicite omnes spiritus Dei Domino.

Benedicite ignis et aestus Domino: benedicite frigus et aestus Domino.

Benedicite rores et pruina Domino: benedicite gelu et frigus Domino.

Benedicite glacies et nives Domino: benedicite noctes et dies Domino.

Benedicite lux et tenebrae Domino: benedicite fulgura et nubes Domino.

Benedicat terra Dominum: laudet et superexaltet eum in saecula.

Benedicite montes et colles Domino: benedicite universa germinantia in terra Domino.

Benedicite fontes Domino * benedicite maria et flumina Domino.

Benedicite cete et omnia quae moventur in aquis Domino: benedicite omnes volucres coeli Domino.

Benedicite, omnes bestiae et pecora Domino: benedicite filii hominum Domino.

Benedicat Israel Dominum: laudet et superexaltet eum in saecula.

Benedicite sacerdotes Domini Domino: benedicite servi Domini Domino.

Benedicite spiritus et animae

God, bless the Lord.

O ye fire and heat, bless the Lord: O ye cold and heat, bless the Lord.

O ye dews and hoar frost, bless the Lord: O ye frost and cold, bless the Lord.

O ye ice and snow, bless the Lord: O ye nights and days, bless the Lord.

O ye light and darkness, bless the Lord: O ye lightnings and clouds, bless the Lord.

O let the earth bless the Lord: let it praise and exalt him above all for ever.

O ye mountains and hills, bless the Lord: O all ye things that spring up in the earth, bless the Lord.

O ye fountains, bless the Lord: O ye seas and rivers, bless the Lord.

O ye whales, and all that move in the waters, bless the Lord: O all ye fowls of the air, bless the Lord.

O all ye beasts and cattle, bless the Lord: O ye sons of men, bless the Lord.

O let Israel bless the Lord: let them praise and exalt him above all for ever.

O ye priests of the Lord, bless the Lord: O ye servants of the Lord, bless the Lord.

O ye spirits and souls of the just, bless the Lord: O ye holy

justorum Domino: benedicite sancti et humiles corde Domino.
Benedicite Anania, Azaria, Misael Domino: laudate et superexaltate eum in saecula.
Benedicamus Patrem et Filium cum Sancto Spiritu: laudemus et superexaltemus eum in saecula.
Benedictus es Domine, in firmamento coeli: et laudabilis et gloriosus et superexaltatus in saecula.

Ant. Benedicite Dominum omnes electi ejus: agite dies laetitiae et confitemini illi.
Then before the altar the Priest says:
V Dominus vobiscum.
R. Et cum spiritu tuo.
    Oremus.
eus, qui miro ordine Angelorum ministeria hominumque dispensas: concede propitius: ut a quibus tibi ministrantibus in coelo semper assistitur, ab his in terra vita nostra muniatur. Per Christum Dominum nostrum.
R. Amen.

and humble of heart, bless the Lord.
O Ananias, Azarias, and Misael, bless ye the Lord: praise and exalt him above all for ever.
Let us bless the Father, and the Son, with the Holy Spirit: let us praise and exalt him above all for ever.
Thou, O Lord, art blessed in the firmament of heaven: and worthy to be praised and glorious and exalted above all for ever.

Ant. Bless the Lord, ail ye his elect: keep days of gladness, and give praise to him.

V. The Lord be with you.
R. And with thy spirit.
    Let us pray.
God, who in wonderful order disposest the services of men and Angels: mercifully grant that those who always attend and serve thee in heaven, may also guard our lives here on earth. Through Christ our Lord.
R. Amen.

9 781953 746054